DEVELOPMENT, ADMINISTRATION AND AID IN THE MIDDLE EAST

Development, Administration and Aid in the Middle East

GERD NONNEMAN

ROUTLEDGE
London and New York

First published 1988
by Routledge
11 New Fetter Lane, London EC4P 4EE
29 West 35th Street, New York, NY 10001

Printed and bound in Great Britain by
Biddles Ltd, Guildford and King's Lynn

British Library Cataloguing in Publication Data

Nonneman, Gerd
    Development, administration and aid in
    the Middle East.
    1. Middle East. Economic conditions
    I. Title
    330.956'052

    ISBN 0-415-00104-8

Library of Congress Cataloging Publication Data
    ISBN 0-415-00104-8

CONTENTS

FIGURES & TABLES

Figures

Tables

For A A J Van Bilsen,
mentor and source of inspiration

PREFACE

The present study started as the Middle Eastern part of a larger research project on the administration of development and aid, inspired and led by Prof. em. A.A.J. Van Bilsen, and based at Gent University (Belgium). Much of the research for this book was made possible by the sponsorship of the VLIR (Board of Flemish Universities). The aim was to present an up–to–date comparative overview of the subject, providing both data for reference, and analysis. This has been carried on in the present volume, which covers the Middle East and North Africa, including Ethiopia, but excluding Iran, Turkey, Lebanon and Palestine. Due to material constraints, Libya, Tunisia and Morocco could be covered only peripherally. In the course of our research, fieldwork was carried out between November 1985 and April 1986 in Egypt, Sudan, Ethiopia, Djibouti, the Yemen Arab Republic (Yemen AR), Saudi Arabia, Oman, the United Arab Emirates (UAE), Kuwait, Jordan and Syria. In addition we could draw on previous personal experience in the area, particularly Iraq.

The helping hands along the way were too many to list here – my thanks to them are no less fulsome for it. Specific mention must be made, however, of Prof. Van Bilsen's untiring support and initiative; the contributions on Algeria by Gent University's Dirk Beke; and the assistance received from the Belgian diplomatic community in the Middle East. Regular contacts with Geert Laporte and Jean Bossuyt, at Gent University, kept the project going and morale high. The Abdalla and Gillespie families in Khartoum, Tsega Mintesnot in Addis Ababa, Tim Mackintosh–Smith in Sanaa, Johann Rattenstetter in Riyadh, Duncan and Christalla Kirby in Oman, Janet Seng in Abu Dhabi, and Jan and Mike James in Damascus all helped make my trip particularly enjoyable and affordable. Special thanks must also go to Mr. Ishaq Rashid, single–handedly running AFESD's Coordination Secretariat, for repeatedly providing me with comprehensive and up–to–date figures on the Arab development funds. Last but not least, the extensive and constructive criticism of Nazih Ayubi and Tim Niblock of Exeter University, has been invaluable. Un-

1

fortunately, I alone have to bear responsibility for any deficiencies which still remain.

Development administration and the administration of aid, as well as the antecedents, present state and future potential of the economy of countries studied, are, for all practical purposes, partly overlapping constituents of a complex whole that also encompasses politics in the broadest sense of the word. Each of these elements, therefore, will have to figure in the present study, although the focus will remain on the administration of development and aid. The framework might be called a political economy one, though without the ideological connotations which that term has carried.

In this work, 'the Middle East' will be taken to mean the Arab world (with the exception of Palestine, and of Mauritania and Somalia) plus Ethiopia. The justification for the latter's inclusion is its geographical location and the interesting point of reference it provides as one of the only two Marxist states in the region. When the term 'Western Asia' or 'ECWA (Economic Commission for W.A.) region' is used, this covers the Arab countries except the Maghreb, Libya, Mauritania, Somalia, Sudan and Djibouti.

'Development' will be taken to mean any evolution in the social and economic fields, be this the result of market forces or of conscious policies. It includes any improvements in the general well–being of the people. 'Development administration', as distinct from 'public administration', has been defined in many ways, usually referring to organised efforts or a bureaucratic process to achieve socio–economic progress (e.g. Garcia–Zamor, 1973: 422; Riggs, 1971: 73). As Quah [1979] has pointed out, however, such definitions are biased towards the positive achievement function, and implicitly discount the possibility of failure. Following Quah,

> development administration refers to the administration of developmental programmes designed to promote nation–building and socio–economic development and the concomitant development of administrative practices and institutions necessary for the implementation of such programmes [1979: 32].

The above definition is workable, with the proviso that the term 'nation–building' should also refer to considerations of legitimacy and regime survival: with that modification it will be adopted hereunder.

'Aid' will be defined for the purposes of this study as all non–military financial, technical and commodity assistance of a concessionary nature. This definition will be amended when appropriate or necessary, e.g. when no break–down is available. Since massive 'political' or military infusions of funds usually have economic implications, they also have to be covered. 'ODA' stands for 'official development asistance', as defined by the OECD's Development Assistance Committee (DAC).

The main question motivating and underlying studies such as the present one is always 'why is it so difficult for the Third World — *in casu* the Middle East — to achieve development?' In order to have any hope of finding an answer, one needs to enquire how that development has been tackled in those countries in the past and how it is today. Two major facets of this are, domestically, development administration, and, internationally, development aid. The aim of this study will therefore be to consider the past and present problems affecting those two. We will, thus, need to discuss (1) past and present trends and problems in the socio–economic development of the region; (2) development administration, looking both at purely 'administrative' problems and at those with deeper roots; and (3) development aid and its administration.

In the majority of countries in this region the State has grown ever more powerful and important; State and Bureaucracy have come to play a large role in all aspects of development. For the administration of development and aid to be investigated fruitfully, therefore, it is necessary to examine more closely the role of the State and the function of the Bureaucracy (as 'embodiment' of the State) in a wider political economy framework. There is indeed little point in studying problems of a purely 'administrative' or 'technical' nature without placing them in the wider, national and international, politico–economic context that may be the main determinant.

This study will, then, be organised as follows:
  I. Historical, Political and Economic Setting of Middle Eastern Development
 II. State, Bureaucracy and Development in the Middle East
      A. Role of the State and functions of the Bureaucracy
      B. 'Development–mindedness'

Where specifically matters of administration are concerned, the present study will focus in particular on the aid–recipient countries of the Middle East. The Arab donor countries will mainly be looked at *qua* donors, under Chapter 6. However, these 'rich' countries do form part of the picture of Middle Eastern development administration, and, more importantly, are a determining factor in the economic structure of the whole Middle East. Chapters 1 — 5 look at them in that light, but this research project has not covered the specific structures of their domestic development administrations.

A crucial part of this work are the charts, or 'figures', depicting the administrative structures of the development administrations and aid administrations of the various countries. Mainly based on the author's fieldwork, they greatly reduce the needed volume of text. The same is true for the 42 tables dispersed throughout the text.

For the transliteration of Arabic in the course of the text (mainly names) a simple system without diacritical marks, 'ain or hamza has been adopted. This avoids unnecessary confusion for non–Arabic readers, while leaving no room for misinterpretation by those with knowledge of Arabic. Arabic names and titles in the bibliography have been rendered in a similarly simple form, reflecting the pronounciation, but without indicating long vowels (exception: *'aamm*). In these names and titles, Hamza (') is only transcribed where it occurs in the middle of a word; 'ain (') always is.

Day–month–year references to newspapers and periodicals will be rendered in figures, in that order, following the British system.

Middle Eastern history offers several significant factors and distinguishing features which help to understand the later development of the countries of the region. The discussion, interesting though it may be, about the influence of Islam as a factor in the non–achievement of industrial development in the Middle East, will not be expanded on here. Suffice it to say, to avoid misunderstandings, that the argument attributing this failure to the religion of Islam, has been shown wrong [Rodinson, 1966 ; Turner, 1974], although a role was undoubtedly played by the social and political make–up of the pre–colonial state under Islam,with its combination of patrimonialism and prebendalism [Turner, 1974; 1984].

Many of the present Middle Eastern states were colonised or otherwise occupied: the whole of North Africa, Sudan, Djibouti, Aden; Syria and Iraq as well as Ethiopia were more briefly under respectively French, British and Italian control, whereas the small Gulf states, though under British 'protection', had a fair degree of internal sovereignty; Saudi Arabia was never colonised nor occupied — at least not since its integration as a nation–state by King Abdul–Aziz — and Jordan was in fact created by the British, but then left to get on with its own internal affairs, albeit with generous British advice and assistance.

For reasons of natural resources, trade routes or strategic location, several countries in the region acquired an increasing importance for the West. With colonisation or occupation they were gradually integrated into the emerging world economy. After the Second World War, force came to fulfil an ever smaller role in the completion of this integration also outside the framework of colonialism. Political development in the Arab world went in diverse directions. In some cases — mainly the non–colonised countries — traditional political structures lived on or were reinforced and 'frozen'; in others, liberation struggles led to either 'radical' or quasi–liberal regimes; in still others independence was granted to similarly liberal–minded governments which usually proved ineffective and collapsed in the face of military intervention. In Egypt, Nasir took over and led a populist, increasingly socialist regime; in Syria, a sequence of civilian and traditional military regimes was eventually broken off by a coalition of radical Arab Nationalists (the Baath party) and the army. Generally, excepting the traditional monarchies, there was a shift in power from the 'feudal' and/or upper 'class' to the bourgeoisie, followed in some cases by a further shift to the petty bourgeoisie, or arguably what Halpern [1963] called the 'new middle class' of modern–educated lower and middle bourgeoisie, including a new type of officer from those ranks.

On the level of the Arab World as a whole (*i.e.* excluding Ethiopia), an important phenomenon was the growth of Arab Nationalism: the initially romantic, German–influenced idea of one nation for the Arab people. This evolution began under the last Ottoman Sultans, focussing only on the Mashreq, and acquired political impetus with the World War I alliance between the Arab Legion and the Allied Forces, to be further strengthened in the bitter wake of broken promises after the war. Having emerged from Ottoman and Colonial rule, disintegrated and without any appropriate models readily available (domestic politics had either been 'unnecessary' or suppressed), the resulting territorial units all had to start searching for a fitting political system. As they were separate, and subject to different influences, they went about it in different ways. The concept of pan–Arabism itself was therefore approached in different ways and became an instrument whereby regimes sought to legitimise themselves, claiming to represent the only 'true' form of Arab Nationalist ideology [Owen, 1983: 20–21]. It became, in fact, a reason for *not* joining others. The idea of political integration retained its salience, not only as a legitimising factor, but also in reaction to perceived threats from the outside world. It was in the non–political realm, however, that the unity of the Arab World became to some extent a reality, though not as ideologues would have foreseen. After all, as Amin [1978] cogently argues, the classical empire of Islam, too, was to a large extent based on economic realities.

By the 1960s the dominant politico–economic voice in the Middle East had become that of 'independent' Arab Socialism, or Nasirism; the downward class–shift as described above had resulted in populist/socialist policies (although popular participation remained a mirage) in the republics, the centre of gravity among which was Egypt. The importance of the economic and political shift which took place from the early 1970s onwards cannot be overstated. The Egyptian defeat in the 1967 war, together with the emerging weaknesses of Nasir's economic policies, provided fertile ground for the changes wrought by the quadrupling of oil–prices in the wake of the 1973 war, and subsequent rises. The centre of gravity shifted to the Gulf, where Saudi Arabia and its neighbours were amassing prestige and unprecedented wealth. The tone of politics and economic policies became 'moderate', more in tune with the oil–monarchies' preferences, and hence with those of the West. Another, crucial, result was the effective integration of the labour market throughout the Arab world, new employment being created in the oil countries which could not themselves provide the necessary labour force. The rise in revenues of the oil exporters is indicated in Table 1.1. An indication of their dependence on oil exports is given in Table 1.2. Even when applying the 'OPEC Import Price Index' [Alnasrawi, 1984: 28], real revenues almost quadrupled from 1970 to 1980, declining again thereafter. The importance of inter–Arab migration is clear from Tables 1.3 – 1.4: by 1975 there were at least 1.7 million migrant Arab workers in the Arab world, a figure which rises to c. 3.5 million when their dependents are added. In the early 1980s the estimated number of inter–Arab migrant workers (including the scantily documented migration to Iraq) rose to c. 4 million, with some sources putting the figure even higher [Birks & Sinclair, 1980b: 25 – 35; 128 – 166; Nijim, 1985: 42–43; Halliday, 1984: 4]. A consequence of the inflow of oil money was a huge rise in imports for the new rich and the consolidation of the link with and dependence on the market economies of the West. Finally, there was a vast increase in inter–Arab financial assistance, mainly from the Arab Gulf countries to the poorer Arab states.

The present picture is therefore characterised by a number of features. *First*, the region can be divided into an oil–rich group, including Saudi Arabia, Kuwait, the UAE, Qatar, Iraq, and Libya; and an oil–poor group including all the others, apart from Algeria, Oman and Bahrain, who hover in between the two. It is striking that very few of the region's countries can be classified as LLDCs on the basis of their GNP/capita figures (see Table 2.1): only Djibouti, Ethiopia, Sudan and the two Yemens can in fact be labelled thus. In the case of North Yemen, moreover, that label is not really justified when taking into account the remittances (official and non–official) of Yemenis working abroad. From 1988, moreover,

Table 1.1
Arab OPEC Oil Revenues, 1970 – 1985, in million US $

	Algeria	Iraq	Kuwait	Libya	Qatar	Saudi	UAE
1970	272	598	820	1,351	122	1,214	212
1971	324	986	995	1,674	198	1,945	410
1972	613	699	1,425	1,563	255	2,795	551
1973	988	1,843	1,780	2,223	400	4,340	900
1974	3,299	5,700	6,545	6,000	1,600	22,574	5,536
1975	3,262	7,500	6,420	5,100	1,700	25,676	6,000
1976	3,699	8,500	8,500	7,500	2,020	33,500	7,000
1977	4,255	9,631	8,900	8,850	1,994	42,384	9,030
1978	5,000	9,800	9,200	8,600	2,000	36,538	8,000
1979	7,200	20,300	16,000	14,000	3,100	55,500	12,400
1980	11,700	26,500	18,300	23,200	5,200	104,200	19,200
1981	10,800	10,400	14,900	15,600	5,300	113,200	18,700
1982	8,500	9,500	10,000	14,000	4,200	76,000	16,000
1983	9,000	8,400	9,900	11,200	3,000	46,100	12,800
1984	9,000	10,400	10,800	10,400	4,400	43,700	13,000
1985	8,000	12,000	9,000	10,000	3,000	28,000	12,000

Source: Petroleum Economist, various issues.

Table 1.2
Oil Exports as percentage of
Total Exports of Arab OPEC Members

Country	1970	1974	1978	1980
Algeria	67.5	91.0	91.7	91.7
Iraq	94.2	98.6	98.6	99.2
Kuwait	93.8	94.3	90.5	98.8
Libya	100.0	99.9	99.9	99.9
Qatar	96.4	98.2	98.4	95.0
Saudi Arabia	99.5	99.7	99.7	99.9
UAE	96.3	98.7	94.9	93.8

Source: IMF, *International Financial Statistics*, various issues.

Table 1.3.
Migrant Workers in the Arab Labour–importing Countries by Country of Origin (thousands)[a]

Country of Origin	1975		1985[b]	
	Number	%	Number	%
Egypt	353.7	22.0	616.9	18.2
Iran	70.0	4.3	98.1	2.9
Iraq	18.7	1.2	11.6	0.3
Jordan	139.0	8.6	267.0	7.9
Lebanon	28.5	1.8	71.7	2.1
Morocco	2.2	0.1	9.8	0.3
Oman	30.8	1.9	44.6	1.3
Sudan	26.0	1.6	80.0	2.4
Syria	38.1	2.4	91.8	2.7
Tunisia	29.8	1.8	62.2	1.8
Yemen AR	328.5	20.4	381.0	11.2
PDRY	45.8	2.8	80.9	2.4
India	141.9	8.8	291.2	8.6
Pakistan	205.7	12.8	446.0	13.1
East Asia	20.5	1.3	369.9	10.9
Other	130.8	8.2	472.8	13.9
Total	1,601.0	100.0	3,395.5	100.0

Notes:

a. Labour–importing countries are Algeria, Bahrain, Iraq, Kuwait, Libya, Oman, Qatar, Saudi Arabia and the UAE.

b. 1985 figures are projections. At least in the case of Egypt the real 1985 figure is much higher, as it includes over one million workers in Iraq.

Source: Serageldin, Socknat *et al.*,1983: 46.

the country will become an oil exporter after the commercialisation of large recently discovered reserves [*FT*, 19–3–87]. Even the People's Democratic Republic of Yemen (PDRY) is poised to join the ranks of the minor oil producers from 1988 [*De Standaard*, 16–4–87].

Second, almost parallel with the above dichotomy (Iraq excepted), there is that between thinly populated countries and those which are more heavily populated: compare for instance the UAE and Egypt.

Third, the oil countries today can be described as *rent-economies*: their economies are largely dependent on the 'rent' derived from the extraction of oil and gas. Even the non–oil components of GDP are to a considerable degree dependent on that

Table 1.4
Migrant workers' remittances in $ millions and
as percentage of merchandise exports, 1975 – 1981

Countries	1975		1980		1981	
	$ millions	%	$ millions	%	$ millions	%
Morocco	533.0	35	1,054.2	44	1,012.9	44
Algeria	412.8	..	406.1	..	..	..
Tunisia	144.5	18	303.3	17	357.3	17
Egypt	365.5	23	2,695.5	70	2,181.4	54
Yemen AR	309.7	2180	1,255.5	9960	926.5	9000
PDRY	61.9	320	352.1	590	..	..
Jordan	166.7	110	792.4	140	1,047.3	140
Sudan	6.1	..	256.0	..	366.4	..
Syria	52.2	..	773.1	..	581.3	..

Note: these figures include only official bank transfers.
Source: Halliday, 1984: tables 6 – 7

rent. It can indeed be argued that they do not produce wealth, but simply preside over a shift in their wealth, from a finite natural resource to a substitute in the form of funds.

Fourth, this prevalence of rent–economy and oil–dependence has to a large extent spread to the non–oil countries. They have become dependent on the direct inflow of funds either as assistance or as investments, and on the labour markets of, and flow of remittances from, the wealthier states. The extent of this dependence is already indicated by the high percentages which remittances represent in proportion to merchandise exports, as given in Table 1.4. It is confirmed by the proportion of particularly the Jordanian, Omani and Yemeni labour forces that was working abroad in 1975: respectively 28, 28 and 20 per cent [Birks & Sinclair, 1980b: 136]. Whatever advantages those remittances may have had, dependence certainly has had detrimental effects on the oil–poor economies. Both oil–prices and the resulting need for labour in the Gulf and Libya have been unpredictable, which has meant that most labour–exporting countries have come to live in an atmosphere of uncertainty or false certainty. It became risky to make any prognoses about their own economies. Altough the need was often felt to install some system to mobilise as many resources as possible into productive development efforts, they usually had to relax controls over foreign currency exchanges in order to tempt migrant workers to bring their earnings back officially. It appeared that they had little choice but to open up their economies. This combination of uncertainty, loosening controls, and dependence, led in varying degrees to these states' losing control of their own economies.

This evolution, needless to say, went hand in hand with the further integration of Middle Eastern economies into the world economic system as indicated earlier. In addition to the above factors, however, there were two other elements that explain the tendency observable throughout much of the region towards an economic 'open door policy' or *infitah* as it was first called in Egypt. One, already hinted at above, was the perceived failure of the radical era to fulfill its promise, politically as well as economically. Egypt's populist policies had used up available resources by the end of the 1960s and its regime had just lost a war. A similar combination of factors led to Syria's gradual adoption of a form of *infitah* under Asad. The other element is to be found in the needs of political elites: the commercial bourgeoisie in several countries provided an important potential ally for a leader such as Saddam Hussein of Iraq [Khafaji, 1984; Springborg, 1985], and an adversary to be pacified for a minoritarian regime such as Syria's.

The marxist PDRY does not escape these national, regional and international pressures of economic and political realities. The clearest example of this is its dependence on remittances of workers in the Gulf states, and aid from those states and the Arab world as a whole. Ethiopia, however, falls largely outside the picture drawn above although it, too, depends on external aid for the realisation of its development programmes.

2

STATE, BUREAUCRACY AND DEVELOPMENT IN THE MIDDLE EAST
The backdrop to development administration

This is not the place to expand too far on the subject of and theories about the role of the state and the shape and size of bureaucracies. It seems necessary, however, to offer some general considerations and briefly frame the question in its politico–economic setting. With reference to the Middle East, the reader may find it particularly useful to consult Ayubi [1985; 1986a], Gellner [1981] and Turner [1974].

In all Middle Eastern countries the state has come to play a very important role. Its functions and powers have expanded greatly, whether in avowedly socialist countries or staunchly anti–socialist ones (like Saudi Arabia). It is not only the official ideology which varies. The historical background, too, differs quite strikingly from country to country. Apart from the distinction between traditional nomadic societies on the one hand, and those with an established central rule (Ottoman) on the other, there is the colonial element. In Egypt there was a distinct, millenia–old tradition of central rule which was built upon in colonial times, and was used to produce the heaviest, most extensive bureaucracy in the Middle East. In the cases of Sudan, Djibouti, Syria, Iraq and the PDRY, the state was shaped by the respective colonial powers — although in the latter case the link with the present form has become faint. Jordan was created as a nation–state by the British, but not colonised, and local political traditions and aspirations were the building stones. The non–colonised countries (Saudi Arabia, Kuwait, the UAE, Bahrain, Qatar and the Sultanate of Oman) can be considered to have state forms which evolved from their indigenous traditions. It will be noticed that all of the latter category (including Jordan — at least untill the influx of Palestinians) are 'desert kingdoms', with a powerful monarch but a form of traditional participation. In each of these cases, however, it is clear that they were either perpetuated and reinforced, or installed (Jordan) by external powers. Even the Saudi state in the first half of the century had to rely very much on companies' and governments' loans and cash grants [Holden & Johns, 1982: 38–158]. North Yemen stands apart in that a republican system replaced the traditional rule of the Imam in a country where Western imperial power did not hold sway.

These divergent backgrounds notwithstanding, in all of those countries the state acquired similar functions, and underwent similar expansions in its power and its executive apparatus — the bureaucracy. Clearly, this overwhelming role of the state must therefore have other causes than colonisation. Nor is an explanation in terms of Wittfogel's 'oriental despotism' [1957], deriving from a 'hydraulic society' based upon the management of extensive irrigation works such as in Egypt, sufficient.

The 'hydraulic' argument does indeed have some salience. Certainly established tradition was an important conditioning factor in the shaping of the modern Egyptian state and in allowing it to become such an overwhelming presence. As for the oil monarchies of the Gulf, the state became far stronger than ever before thanks to the intervention of foreign powers and to the advent of the oil age. As oil prices went up and government income rose, no other social group could compete with a state that acquired such resources. Four other, more general considerations may be offered to complete the explanation as to the state's power and the similarities in the functions and shapes of its bureaucracies.

The *imitation factor* has been very important. Certainly in the Middle East there was rarely an indigenous political and administrative model available for the new realities of the 20th century international economic system. In fact, imitation in bureaucratic organisation started already in pre–colonial times when the Ottoman rulers, as well as Muhammad Ali in Egypt and later Mustafa Kemal in Turkey, tried to recreate some of the power they had been rapidly losing to the Europeans, by emulating the latter's apparently successful ways in administrative organisation, among other things. This West–East flow of influences was maintained — strengthened often by the role of Western advisers — in conjunction with an East–East flow. Throughout the post–World War I period, Egyptian influence in shaping bureaucratic systems throughout the Arab Middle East has been very important, both directly via Egyptians in other Arab bureaucracies, and indirectly via the introduction of Egyptian bureaucratic values by the many Egyptian teachers in other Arab countries [cf. Nurallah, 1978: 108–109].

In the above, a second possible way of looking at the phenomenon is already implicit, *viz.* the perspective of the world economic system and the Third World's integration into it. This perspective has recently been refined by Mathias & Salama [1983]. They argue that the function of the state in the Third World is to act as a bridge for and an agent of the laws of the centre–dominated 'compound world economy'. In that sense it should not be surprising that the Third World state has to adopt certain functions and instruments to cope with that role. Also, the integration into the compound world economy and the implied specialisation within the international division of labour make it necessary to develop infrastructure as well as the forces of production accordingly (because of the great gap with the developed economies); it follows, therefore, that state intervention in the under–developed countries must be far more important than in the developed economies. This argument provides one explanation for the overwhelming presence of the state. A final point they make is about the nature of 'state violence' in the Third World. In the developed countries, the basis of legitimacy, they argue, is the fetichizing effect of the generalisation of merchandisation. The state is necessary to counter its defetichizing effects; legitimisation comes first, and only where it fails repression (violence) is necessary. But in the under–developed countries there is a different basis. The installation of the exogenous mercantile relations and capitalist relations of production, in an environment that is not by itself going to do so, necessitates violence. Thus violence, here, comes before legitimisation. In some cases violence may even be legitimising, when ritualised. Indeed,they go on to argue, the regime of a new state will have to use, for a large part, the traditional forms of legitimisation — destroying their bases in the process — since there is no sufficient basis for a 'capitalist legitimacy'. In turn, this inadequate legitimacy calls for other ways of remaining on top: hence more violence, corruption, etc. This could be used to explain the nature of Middle Eastern bureaucracies as instruments of control/violence. The interesting elements provided by this theoretical framework notwithstanding, some of its weaknesses need to be pointed out: the case of the Gulf states, where the crucial element is the availability of funds, shows the theory to be at least partially deficient. Because of the capacity to co–opt, the legitimisation–violence sequence is that of the developed countries, rather than the other way round; and because of the ability to subsidise industry, the integration of the economy into the compound world economy does not necessarily mean the exacerbation of class differences via state intervention as Mathias & Salama see it. Also, if 'state ' is to be explained by reference to the centre and the compound world economy, that totally over-looks the fact that there was, in the Islamic empire up to and including the Ottomans, a powerful, relatively autonomous state, before any significant European intervention took place. The general critique one could formulate, is that the model, by attempting to be all–encompassing, is both too vague and too rigid, though it provides valuable insights.

Leaving such neo–Marxian approaches aside, it is clear that once a Third World society (or elite) has adopted the value system of 'modern development', only the state is in a position to oversee all the components of the process supposedly leading towards that goal. At least initially only the state can acquire/ accumulate the resources to go into it. A clear example of this is constituted by the oil countries, for which the term 'hydrocarbon societies' has been suggested in partial parallel with the 'hydraulic society' model. The large role of the state is often accepted as necessary in the first stages of the developmental process. In the Middle East this is accentuated by the spreading of the rentier–economy.

The inadequate legitimacy referred to by Mathias & Salama can also be accommodated in a less controversial framework, that of political underdevelopment. As described earlier, the Middle East's political underdevelopment can be seen as the result of the colonial and pre–colonial situation. In looking for ideolog-ical frameworks, the newly independent countries had to start almost 'from scratch'. The resultant lack of legitimacy helps ex-plain why regimes have had to rely on force and control to remain in power and why widespread participation has not become the norm. There is no doubt that the control function of the state bureaucracies in the Middle East is very important, and that this function has been and remains a major determinant in shaping those bureaucracies [Ayubi, 1985: 22–23]. Direct, physical con-trol is only one of several ways of remaining in power: it is ideally complemented by popular acquiescence, which will result from (a) the creation of popular dependence on the regime; (b) pacification and co-optation (e.g. 'buying off'); and (c) genuinely legitimising acts and ideology. Finally, there is the important consideration of external support for such regimes — a consideration which will again to an extent determine shape, functions and acts of the state bureaucracy.

The question of 'development–mindedness'

The developmental aspect can clearly fit into the political frameworks just discussed. This raises the question of the role of genuine development–mindedness: is it justifiable to describe Middle
Eastern regimes (and others, for that matter) as really only interested in power, paying homage to development only in as far
as it accommodates that craving ? It is not. There is certainly
a difference between regimes as to their commitment to the development of their societies. But it is objectively impossible to
answer the question as to how genuine that commitment is. One
can only state that considerations of both power and development
are always present side by side. However, because survival is necessary to implement any development policy, it will *in extremis*
always remain the crucial consideration for any regime (compare
Wriggins, 1969). In Figure 2.1, the above elements in addition
to a few others are brought together to indicate how this author
perceives the ways in which a regime's resource allocation policies
relate to the consideration of survival.

Even if it appears impossible to objectively answer the question whether regimes pursue development for its own sake, one can
still assess the weight of developmental considerations in overall
policies. There are cases where, for example, the interests of a
certain social group have priority (say, the business community in
Jordan), although such priorities can in fact go hand in hand with
development objectives — witness the attention for the rural areas
in Syria. The most important measuring stick of development–
mindedness, at least where a somewhat longer–term perspective
is available, remains the results of policies, as measured by a whole
range of socio–economic indicators. GNP has become somewhat
discredited as such an indicator, mainly because it sometimes has
very little to do with actual development (e.g. the oil states), because in some cases GDP is more appropriate (but only in some),
and because it does not tell us anything about the evolution in
the situation of the people who are supposed to be development's
aim and instrument. The discussion about the adequacy of development indicators has been going on for years (see for example
Baster, 1972; Taylor, 1980) and is far from reaching its conclusion. We will not try to offer anything more conclusive in these
pages, nor could we. The reference to some obviously important
indicators may suffice: such as vital statistics, literacy, indication
of income distribution over the deciles of the population, and land
reform. Income distribution data for the Middle East are rarely

Figure 2.1 Resource Allocation and Regime Survival

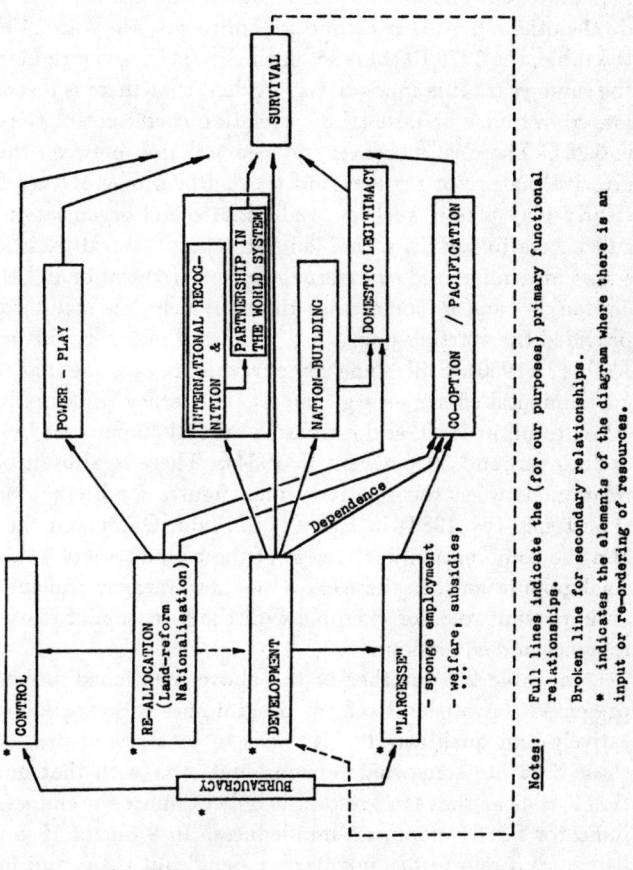

Notes: Full lines indicate the (for our purposes) primary functional relationships.

Broken line for secondary relationships.

* indicates the elements of the diagram where there is an input or re-ordering of resources.

available. The other indicators for the area have been brought
together in Tables 2.1 – 2.2. Table 2.1 presents general economic
indicators as well as vital statistics and literacy rates. It also
lists the 'Physical Quality of Life Index' (PQLI) as developed by
the Overseas Development Council in Washington in 1977, and
which is based on (a) infant mortality, (b) life expectancy at age
1, and (c) literacy at 15 years of age and over [Nijim, 1985: 44–47;
Morris, 1979] It needs to be stressed that this PQLI is a macro–
indicator, and tells us nothing about social justice; nor, indeed,
do the others [for other composite indicators, see Ward, 1980]. In
the table, the 1979 PQLI is set against the GNP/capita figures for
the same year. It is immediately evident that there is a strikingly
low co–variance at best (the correlation coefficient of the values
is 0.28). There is, moreover, no clear relation between the 'progressive' nature of regimes and the better scores. Other factors
clearly play a role, such as traditional social organisation, difficult access to certain areas, long–standing cultural traditions —
sometimes influenced by external elements (education in Lebanon,
Jordan) — and in some cases the extremely low standards that
provided the starting point (e.g. a literacy of 5 per cent in Saudi
Arabia in 1960). Still, some comparisons are possible that refer to
governmental efforts — e.g. the rise in literacy rates in Ethiopia
(close to nil in 1960, and estimated around 35 per cent by 1983),
or Iraq (around 50 per cent in 1984). There is also an obvious
relation between the relatively high figures for literacy and life
expectancy (by 1984) in Kuwait, Bahrain, Qatar and the UAE,
and the combination in the case of these countries of wealth and
small populations. In these cases too, however, government played
an important role, for example with the provision of free or even
remunerated education.

In Table 2.2, another of the above–mentioned indicators is
presented. Arab land reform programmes are assessed quantitatively and qualitatively. It needs to be stressed that some of
these data are somewhat tenuous, but even with that qualifica-
tion it is clear that land reform is only of limited usefulness as an
indicator for development–mindedness. In 9 out of 19 countries
listed, land reform has not been a significant issue, and in those
where it has, the impact on equality is nowhere more than moderate, nor has it been quantitatively very important (except in
Iraq). Iraq, Tunisia, Algeria and Syria emerge as the best cases;
lowest come Yemen, Jordan and Morocco. One can detect an ideological dividing line here, though that is blurred by Tunisia —

certainly less than 'radical' — and the low scores of Egypt where land reform under Nasir had been one of the great legitimacy-generating programmes. Egypt is indeed an interesting example, since its land reform programme, though undoubtedly having a developmental content, equally stemmed from a strong political motivation. Rather than raising up the poorest landless, the programme created a new influential farmer middle class ('kulak') , while largely eliminating the big landholders as a political upper class [see Waterbury, 1984: 263–282; Richards, 1982: 176–179].

Assessment of the national economies' structural development, judged by their absorption capacity and viability, can again provide a major indicator of effectiveness of development policies. As stressed by Osama [1987: 17–19], development can only be judged genuine if advances are made towards a "continually productive base": *growth* and *welfare* are not enough. It is beyond the scope of this study to attempt a full assessment of this kind — the reader is referred to sources such as the *Middle East Economic Digest (MEED)'s* annual reviews, the yearly ECWA surveys, the issues of *The Middle East and North Africa*, and the country reports of the World Bank. But some general remarks can be offered. First, oil remains the mainstay of the Middle Eastern economy. The dependence of the non–oil states on their richer brothers has been explained above and will be further illustrated under the chapter on aid. The oil states themselves remain overly dependent on their one 'crop'— even Algeria which is not commonly seen as purely an oil state, obtains c. 98 per cent of its export earnings from hydrocarbons [*MEED*, 21-12-85]. Kuwait has followed a sound foreign investment policy — income from which now provides about half of the state's annual income — and Saudi Arabia is following that lead. But their productive base outside and independent of the oil sector has not been significantly expanded, at least not in a viable way. This, of course, has more to do with the lack of resources (money excepted) than with governmental failure, although during the 1970s white elephants and duplication figured quite prominently in investment. Agriculture has declined in proportion to other sectors, although with massive infusions of subsidies and water it is now being encouraged again. Given domestic potential, government economic development policies in the Gulf today are no worse than those in many other developing countries. The success of such policies, however, depends on the emerging tendency toward economic integration being reinforced and carried through. Economically, the

Table 2.1 General Economic and Development Indicators for the Middle East

COUNTRIES	Area sq.km	Popul. 1983 ('000)	Density 1983	Average % incr. '80-83	Life Expectancy '60	'70	'75-'80	'84	Child Mortality (1-4 yr, 0/000) '60	'70	'83	Literacy (% over 15yr) '60	'70	'83	PQLI 1979	GNP/cap 1979	GNP 1983 £ mn	GNP/cap 1983
Algeria	2,381,741	20,500	8.6	3.3	...	...	55.3	...	...	...	13[a]	...	26[c]	...	41	1,110	49,450	2,400
Bahrain	622	400[a]	643	5.0[a]	...	...	66.1	68	...	...	1[b]	...	40[c]	...	61	3,790	4,120	10,360
Djibouti	22,000	330	15	2.1	...	...	...	...	...	...	...	...	...	...	...	...	180[a]	480
Egypt	1,001,449	45,915	46	2.9	46	49	54.7	57	23	20	14	26	40	44	44	310	31,880	700
Ethiopia	1,221,900	42,169[a]	35	2.7	43	47	40.9	47*	42	33	30	...	13[a]	35	...	...	4,860[b]	140
Iraq	434,924	14,110[b]	32	3.2[b]	...	...	59.0	59	...	2	...	...	...	...	45	1,530	39,500[b]	3,020
Jordan	97,740	3,247	33	3.6	46	54	60.1	64	26	12	5	32	62	70	47	710	4,400[c]	1,710
Kuwait	17,818	1,695[c]	95	4.5[c]	...	...	69.2	71	...	...	1	...	60[e]	...	75	12,700	30,290	18,180
Lebanon	10,400	2,635	253	-0.4	...	...	65.0	...	...	10[c]	...	...	...	...	79	1,070	3,290[d]	1,070
Libya	1,759,540	3,469	2	4.5	...	...	55.4	...	...	...	...	...	39[d]	...	43	6,680	25,100	7,500
Mauretania	1,030,700	1,779	1.7	2.9	...	...	42.0	...	...	...	...	...	...	...	18	270	720	440
Morocco	446,550	20,420[b]	46	3.3	46	50	55.4	52*	36	26	12	14	21	28	40	570	15,620	750
Oman	212,457	1,131	5.3	5.0	...	...	47.3	50	...	...	...	...	...	...	31	...	7,070	6,240
Qatar	11,000	281[b]	26	4.5	...	...	69.1	71	...	...	...	...	...	...	...	11,670	5,960	21,170
Saudi Arabia	2,149,690	10,421	4.8	4.1	43	48	53.0	56	47	30	13	5	15	25	29	4,980	127,080	12,180
Somalia	637,657	5,269	8.3	4.5	...	...	40.9	...	...	...	...	...	...	...	19	110	1,140	250
Sudan	2,505,813	20,564	8.2	2.2	38	41	45.1	47*	40	32	19	13	15	32	34	300	8,420	400
Syria	185,180	9,611	52	3.4	...	...	64.4	67*	...	3.5.	...	...	40[e]	...	52	900	16,510	1,680
Tunisia	163,610	6,886	42	1.9	48	54	58.1	61*	36	20	8	16	24	37	46	860	8,860	1,290
UAE	83,600	1,206	14	5.9	...	...	69.1	71	...	...	...	...	55[e]	...	34	14,420	25,770	21,340
Yemen AR	195,000	6,232	32	2.3	36	...	41.3	44	60	...	...	...	...	9[b]	27	390	3,930	510
PDRY	332,968	2,158	6.5	3.1	36	...	44.0	46	59	...	27	...	27[ef]	...	32	320	1,020	510

Notes and Sources: see next page.

Notes to Table 2.1

Exceptions to table headings

			% INCREASE	
POPULATION :	a.	1984	a.	1971–1981
	b.	Autumn 1982	b.	1979–1982
	c.	April 1985	c.	1980–1985

LIFE EXPECTANCY: * 1983

CHILD MORTALITY:	a.	1982
	b.	1981
	c.	1973
	Iraq and Syria: 1977	

LITERACY RATES:	a.	1974	b. 1980
	c.	1971	d. 1973
	e.	1975	f. for age 10 and over

GNP 1983:	a.	1981, est. on 1979–1981 base period
	b.	provisional 1980, est. on 1978–1980 base
	c.	East Bank only
	d.	1974, est. on 1974–1976 base period

Sources for Table 2.1

1) For PQLI & GNP 1979: Nijim, 1985: 44–47

2) UN, *Population and Vital Statistics Reports*
   UN, *Demographic Yearbook 1983*
   UN, *Statistical Yearbook 1982*
   UN, *World Population Prospects: Estimates and Projections as Assessed in 1982.*
   (= *Population Studies*, no. 86)(New York, 1983)
   UNESCO, *Statistical Yearbook*, 1982
   The World Bank Atlas 1985
   OECD, 1985: 270
   ECWA,*Survey...1985* (Country Tables)
   World Bank, 1983

Table 2.2 Assessment of Arab Land Reform Programmes, 1952-1978

Country	Year Begun	Redistributed Land up to 1978				Beneficiaries as % of Total Agricultural Households	Effectiveness of Reform in Reaching Institutional Goals	Impact on Equality in Agriculture
		Hectares (1,000s)	Beneficiaries (1,000s)	Average Hectares per Beneficiary	As a % of Total Arable Land			
Oil-Rich								
Bahrain*	-	-	-	-	-	-	-	-
Iraq	1958	1,152	223	5.2	15.5	41.3	Moderate	Moderate
Kuwait*	-	-	-	-	-	-	-	-
Libya	1970	71	5	14.2	2.9	3.4	High	Negligible
Oman*	-	-	-	-	-	-	-	-
Saudi Arabia*	-	-	-	-	-	-	-	-
UAE*	-	-	-	-	-	-	-	-
Oil-Poor								
Algeria	1972	1,538	130	11.8	22.3	18.3	High	Moderate
Egypt	1958	1,048	342	3.1	36.1	10.7	Moderate	Small
Jordan⌐	-	-	-	-	-	-	-	-
Lebanon*	-	-	-	-	-	-	-	-
Mauritania*	-	-	-	-	-	-	-	-

						Low	Negligible
Morocco	1957	335	24	13.9	4.5	1.0	Low	Negligible
Somalia*	-	-	-	-	-	-	-	-
Sudan*	-	-	-	-	-	-	-	-
Syria	1958	1,150	54	13.0	12.7	18.0	Moderate	Moderate
Tunisia	1971	558	75	7.4	18.6	23.0	High	Moderate
Yemen AR†	-	-	-	-	-	-	-	-
Yemen PDR	1968	126	31	4.1	54.8	11.2	High	Small

As compiled by SHAW, 1984: Table IV.

* Not a significant issue

† No reform

only long–term chance the Gulf countries have is on an integrated *Gulf Cooperation Council* level. Even then, however, better links to the rest of the Arab economies will be necessary. [cf. Kubursi, 1984].

Iraq, with a better provision of human and natural resources — including extensive agricultural land — presents a different case. Iraqi government policies have laid great stress on industrialisation, in some cases with remarkable success, and the country's economic potential at the eve of the Gulf war was one of, if not the most, impressive in the Middle East. Here too, though, agriculture had suffered, both from lack of attention and from the style of government intervention. Socialised agriculture proved no more of a success here than anywhere else.

This decline of agriculture has occurred throughout the Arab Middle East, both because of similar governmental priorities in some countries (Algeria), and because of shifts caused by the wider structural changes in the Arab economy due to the growing importance of oil and labour migration. Both direct oil wealth and migrant workers' earnings tend to stimulate different tastes and thus a different consumption pattern, demanding imported foodstuffs, while at the same time emigration of agricultural workers has an immediate effect on agriculture. Arab countries have become increasingly dependent on food imports. From the beginning to the end of the 1970s, Arab food imports went up from \$ 2 billion to \$ 20 billion, whereas the ratio of agricultural exports to agricultural imports declined from 83 per cent to only 17 per cent [AFESD, 1982: 153–157].

Recently, a shift in government attention in favour of agriculture has been noticeable in most countries of the region. Saudi Arabia, Oman, Jordan, Iraq, Egypt and Algeria are prime examples, and results are beginning to emerge. Others, like Syria and Ethiopia, never lost sight of the agricultural sector in favour of industrialisation (although they still aimed for the development of mainly small–scale industry). In the Sudan, agriculture and agro–industries were and remain the main focus for development. The 'breadbasket strategy', aspiring to make Sudan the breadbasket of the Arab World, has proved a failure so far, due to misguided big–scheme development, bad planning and management, and corruption, as well as the wider economic shifts referred to above [cf. Awad, 1983; Niblock, 1985]. The idea, however, should not be considered dead and buried yet, although post–Nimeiri Sudan now finds itself with a legacy of overwhelming debts, severely affecting its ability to tackle its development needs.

Iraq (because of the war), Egypt and Yemen AR also face extremely serious debt problems [ECWA, 1985]. In other cases indebtedness is offset by the international financial and business community's perception of the economy as basically sound and creditworthy, as is true for Jordan. Indeed, except for the GCC countries, all countries in the ECWA region have been able to sustain steady (albeit very moderate) growth rates throughout the first half of the 1980s [ibid.].

Particularly since 1980, the development plans of the ECWA member countries have given increasing priority to the manufacturing sector. 'Investment in industry, including manufacturing, has increased consistently in both absolute terms and as a percentage of total investment in most member countries'[ibid.: 159]. But, the 1984 ECWA Survey notes,

> the growth performance of the manufacturing sector in Western Asia in the early 1980s was well below the rate achieved during the 1970s. This poor performance is mainly due to the fall in oil production and revenues ... The share of mining and quarrying in GDP decreased from 55.1 per cent to 36.6 per cent and to 30.5 per cent in 1980, 1983 and 1984 respectively. The decrease in contribution of mining and quarrying to GDP was not, however, compensated by a better performance in the manufacturing sector [ibid.: 158].

Moreover, over half of the region's value added in manufacturing is by now concentrated in the GCC countries, where it is to a large extent accounted for by hydrocarbon–related industries.

Much, in short, remains to be achieved, and many basic weaknesses do not look set to disappear before the next century. One of the few countries which appeared to have great potential and relatively successful government policies to achieve viable long term economic development, Iraq, has now seen all that go for nought. This leads us back to politics. The country's full–scale war with Iran was the result of a political decision by a narrow ruling group. Politics, too, were a factor in Sudan's economic problems (and vice versa). Many characteristics of bureaucracies and resource allocation in the Middle East can be traced back to past and present politics, one element amongst which is the authoritarian nature of the state and bureacracy. Political participation, and political rights in general, are sometimes considered goals to be reached by socio–economic development — they may equally be seen as another indicator of such development. It can also be argued, however, that a good degree of popular participation in the decision–making process will lead to (a) political stability in the longer term, which is good both in itself and for economic development; and (b) better policy choices, since the mental reservoir from which one draws is much larger, and because decisions will be closer to popular aspirations — which may again be seen as a goal in itself and as making for more effectiveness in the management of the society. However, this argument is not always applicable in its entirety. Existing regimes do to a certain extent have to take account of popular aspirations to generate or maintain sufficient legitimacy, both when these aspirations demand developmentally 'wrong' policies and in the opposite case. Taking the Gulf states as an example: the largesse of the regimes, in providing free services, salaried education, privileged jobs, beautified cities, etc., is very much in tune with a local 'ethos', formed by the contrast of the harsh past and sudden wealth. In that sense, regimes in the Gulf are indeed close to popular aspirations in that 'the people', if given the power, would almost certainly make very similar resource allocative decisions (although a difference would conceivably be made in foreign policy). Another example is the populism of regimes such as Nasir's. Their policies helped to create a popular constituency, but proved not sustainable in the long run: only the Gulf states had enough funds at their disposal to carry them through — for now.

The concept of charity economies

Although the number of LLDCs, ('poorest countries') in the region is far less than in the case of Africa, their presence still warrants, at the end of this chapter, a brief discussion of the phenomenon and implications of 'charity economies'— a term coined by Abu–Lughod [1984] and given further relevance by Calhoun *et al.* [1986]. The latter define it as those economies which combine a high level of external financial dependence with a very low level of domestic economic production. Thus for example the Sudan, where

> foreign aid and related activities account for the absolute majority of economic activity; without it, we might reasonably say, there would be no national level economy but only local subsistence economies. [Calhoun *et al.*,1986: 5]

This means that such economies, the way we find them today, have in fact been created by the international aid effort in its widest sense. The bureaucracies have been shaped accordingly, aimed towards the outside world and donors in particular, rather than being organically linked to, and oriented towards, the indigenous aspects of development. This, of course, is an ideal–type situation. Bureaucracies are unlikely to be totally determined in this way. But the cases of the Sudan, the Yemens, and Djibouti would seem to come rather close to it. Moreover, the same factor is also discernible in many of the other countries, although diminishing in importance in line with lower dependence and a larger domestic economic production.

DEVELOPMENT ADMINISTRATION IN THE MIDDLE EAST: SPECIFICALLY DETERMINING ELEMENTS & RESULTANT CHARACTERISTICS AND PROBLEMS

The present chapter aims to discuss the specific characteristics and problems of Middle Eastern development administration, as well as providing an overview of administrative structures in the 11 countries central to this study, *viz.* Algeria, Egypt, Sudan, Ethiopia, Djibouti, Syria, Jordan, Iraq, Oman, the Yemen Arab Republic and the PDRY. Before doing so, however, it seems useful to present a brief review of the elements which have acted as determinants.

A Brief Review of Specifically Determining Elements

In the previous chapter the background of State and Bureaucracy in the Middle East was examined, and it was found that elements from that background have helped determine the specific shape and functions that the bureaucracies (or public administration) have adopted. Those elements could be grouped around three main points:

(1) the integration of the Middle Eastern economies into the international economic system;

(2) the central place of the State;

(3) the 'charity economy' phenomenon, particularly for highly dependent LLDCs.

It can be argued that those three points are closely interrelated.

One specifically determining feature that emerged, was the control function of the bureaucracy, which becomes clear when studying all governmental administrations in the area. Ayubi states:

> Part of the reason why central, monocratic types of administration are favoured and sustained in the Arab world is the useful "control" functions that this type of bureaucracy can serve. This is the reason why other types of organisation and administration are not tried, and why, when they are adopted within various programmes

of "administrative reform", they are used only as techniques that are void of any power–sharing devices. [1985: 22–23].

Another function was termed 'largesse' in Figure 2.1, which includes the function of 'sponge employment'. Those so employed are made dependent on the system. This function, therefore, dictates a size of bureaucracy larger than would be necessary on grounds of work load or efficiency. The prime example is Egypt [Ayubi, 1980; 1985]; but the same phenomenon is found all over the region. In Kuwait, the Amir himself stated in 1979 that c. 64,000 civil servants were redundant, but that for social reasons it was not feasible to dismiss them. Ironically, there is often a shortage of professional staff in the departments concerned with development administration (except in Egypt), due to a lack of suitably qualified people.

Some other determining elements, however, lie outside the framework of the previous chapter, although there are often links. The general under–development of the area (at least with reference to the standards the countries have set for themselves, and which are a reflection of Western ways) is a major factor. The available physical, social, economic and human resources infrastructure within which an administration for the administration of development must emerge, is often not up to that achievement.

Aspects of Arab culture are also of importance. A tradition of strong paternalistic authority in families and tribes makes its influence felt in wider society. Education in the Arab world, moreover, has traditionally (after the great flowering of the classical era) been based on memorising rather than personal thinking. This characteristic is still present in today's education, even at university level, and will often have a negative impact on the intellectual abilities or predilections of the bureaucrats thus formed. Finally, bringing us back to politics, there is the still salient tribal tradition and tribal organisation of a large part of Arab society: central government can never ignore that.

There remain two groups of fundamentally political elements: the first group concerns the structure of power; the second the limits on elites' choices. The patrimonial tradition and system of leadership continues to influence administrative behaviour in many parts of the Middle East. In the Gulf this has a direct reflection in present government structures. Coupled to this is the importance of personal ties and contact. Both combine to explain the importance of access to the top of the pyramid, in the bureaucratic system. Simply put, the bureaucrat who has personal access to the top, will be listened to; personal power is a function of access. The traditional preponderance of kinship and personal ties over other considerations lives on throughout bureaucratic organisation. Due to both inadequate political development (as discussed earlier) and fossilised traditional influences, the usual situation in today's Middle East is that of relatively small groups ruling the remainder of the population. Partly to remind the lower–placed of the ruling group's power, there is often a large turn–over in the government administration below the top–level. This naturally leads to (a) civil servants' fearing they may lose their jobs; (b) sudden changes in policy; and (c) the passing–on of decisions to the top, which usually means to non–experts. This is another factor militating towards personal and group interests, rather than developmentally sound criteria, determining policy choices. As Weinbaum [1982: 102] puts it:

> Administrative structures ... come to represent largely disparate economic interests, institution– alized at the national level but also manifested through clientele re- lationships that reach down to the lower rungs of the bureaucracy.

It has been indicated earlier in this study that the room for manoeuvre which regimes have, if they want to stay in power, is limited. Middle Eastern regimes have often resorted to what could be termed (when stretching the term somewhat) 'populism'. What was and is at stake, at any rate, is the creation of a power base within a 'classless', 'unified' nation, the acquisition and main- tenance of a degree of legitimacy, and generally pacifying and if possible co–opting large enough (or important enough) sections of the population. What this has in fact led to, with the possible ex- ceptions of Ethiopia and the PDRY, is policy choices which lack consistency. Economic policy turns out to be neither genuinely capitalist, nor genuinely socialist. It is claimed that the solution had to be a 'third way', be it called 'Arab Socialism' or otherwise; Nasir gave moving speeches to that effect. The principle of reject- ing uncritical application of foreign models is in itself commend- able — if a well thought–out, consistent, appropriate synthesis is arrived at instead. But, due partly to deficient understand- ing, partly to the political need to co–opt this group, pacify that, and generally to 'do things immediately', Middle Eastern policy- makers have rather 'picked piecemeal from or oscillated between largely contradictory or incompatible approaches' [ibid.: 111]. As

Jacquemot [1984: 253–257] has rightly pointed out: one of the main factors militating against successful planning in the Third World, is the fact that elites find it next to impossible to commit themselves explicitly to a long–term choice for one particular societal model. This holds true for the Middle East, including the still largely tribal society of the PDRY, although possibly Ethiopia may be excepted. Political realities may change relatively quickly, and pragmatic adaptation to those will often ignore previously adopted 'long–term' plans.

Middle Eastern Development Administration: Characteristics and Problems

From the background as described in the previous section, the characteristics and problems of Middle Eastern development adminstration (including the implementation aspect) can be derived. They are of four kinds: (1) those related to the international environment; (2) those stemming from domestic politics; (3) those caused by the general underdevelopment; and (4) those related to cultural/behavioural causes. There is no sharp distinction between these four ; they overlap and interrelate. As presented here, the division is one of convenience.

1.

Within the international economic system, Middle Eastern countries are dependent on unreliable and unpredictable factors such as the state of the oil market, the markets for some other raw materials, and foreign assistance. This dependence will often, as it has done in the past, make Middle Eastern countries' efforts at long–term planning, or even in budget projections on a shorter time–scale, a difficult if not futile excercise. This is true both for the oil producers and for the non–oil producing states. The slide in oil income since 1982 eventually led Saudi Arabia twice to postpone publication of any 1986/1987 budget, for a total of 10 months [*FT*, 11–3–86; *The Middle East*, January 1987: 29]. Assistance to poor Arab countries dropped. The labour market in the oil states shrank — thus affecting remittances from migrant workers. The drop in phosphate prices has caused balance of payments problems for Morocco. One of the main factors limiting Ethiopian development efforts (apart from the civil war) has been the extremely low level of foreign assistance (excluding relief aid). Foreign investment has often proved a similarly elusive source of development input, both because of political unrest frightening away investors, and because it often has not gone into development–oriented projects: witness, for instance, the case of Egypt [Ayubi, 1982b]. All this has in effect resulted, to various degrees, in governments' losing control over their countries' economies. Niblock [1985: 15], for instance, in an article on Sudan, talks about the country's 'economic disintegration'. Of course, the effects of this dependent situation were intensified by the performance — or lack thereof – of the individual development administrations. The domestic explanations for this are grouped under sub–sections 2 — 4 below. But the aid–factor itself, via the charity economy phenomenon, also played a role, albeit more so in some countries than in others.

It is clear that in some of the poorer countries of the region — and also, though to a lesser extent, in others — the present structure of the economy and the bureaucracy to administer it have been created with a view to external inputs. It is not surprising that such bureaucracies, not tuned to indigenous economic realities, lack effectiveness in managing the latter. The problem of this inherent disconnection is often sharpened by some aspects of today's international assistance campaign. So much time and effort on the part of national administrations is spent on liaising with the donor community, that there is often little left for domestic concerns. Some of the blame for this must go to the lack of coordinated procedures among donors. Referring to their experience in working with and within the Sudanese administration, Calhoun *et al.* [1986: 5] write:

> The various external actors ... who may call for effective central government nonetheless help in many ways to undermine it. Their agents demand constant attention from senior government oficials, distracting the latter from their domestic duties.

2.

Middle Eastern bureaucracies are generally characterised by rigidity, a monolithic structure and concentration of decision–making at the top. A different form of organisation might prove more effective, but, as pointed out in the previous chapter, the regimes, though sometimes realising the disadvantages of their bureaucracies for developmental purposes, value them as an instrument of control. The results include slowness, and fear to take decisions on the part of employees.

The passing–on of decisions to the top, usually means that even quite technical decisions will be taken by the non–experts that usually compose the political top. Bad management will thus result — both because decisions are made by unqualified people, and because the power thus left in the hands of those top few opens the door to personal preferences, interests and corruption by both domestic and foreign groups. Sudan under Nimeiri is a good example of this. Incompetence and corruption explain to a large extent the 'policy' choices of the 1970s and early 1980s (see for instance Niblock, 1985: 16–17). Egypt, at least prior to the Mubarak era, provides more examples of the importance of personal gain on the part of ministers and high officials in development–related decisions; and a picturesque description of a decision–making process with a particularly high role of personal preferences and gain for the elite, is given by the previous economic adviser to the Sultan of Oman in his book on the situation in that country up to the mid–1970s [Townsend, 1977].

Earlier, it has been explained how political realities will often lead to the withdrawal of political support for a technically elaborated long–term development policy. The structure of power, moreover, was shown to lead to frequent changes in staffing and, concomitant with this, in administrative structures. The frequent reorganisation and creation of new departments have other grounds too. Sometimes they can be justified on grounds of better efficiency. More often, they are no more than formal but empty responses to a perceived problem: 'set up a new department and the problem will go away'. New departments may be created as a favour to people who have enough power to extract such a favour, or when the regime feels it to be politically expedient. Favours may take the form of a directorship or even a ministerial post (a practice not entirely alien to Western developed countries either).

The results of this are often (a) inexperience in people supposed to deal with a certain job, and (b) discontinuity in policies. Work or research carried out by predecessors will often be disregarded and, for the sake of creating an impression, newly appointed high–level officials tend to come forward with 'new policies', each time disrupting what went before. A case in point is Egypt, with frequent reorganisations, new appointments and shifts in policy. The economic retrenchment mood of the early 1980s ran into political dificulties, and in September 1982 the Minister of Economy and Foreign Trade was replaced by Dr Mustafa al–Said. Six other ministers who had advocated cuts in subsidies were also dismissed. Dr al–Said announced a major economic reform programme, but little came of this. In 1983 and 1984 he tried to bring foreign exchange and banking activities under some control, but opposition from banking circles, business interests and political rivals eventually forced him to resign in the aftermath of a banking scandal — amid accusations of personal irregularities. His successor, Sultan Abu Ali, immediately reversed most of his policies [MENA 1986: 352,359]. In Syria, the large turnover in the State Planning Council is deemed by the international assistance community to constitute a key factor reducing work efficiency. In Jordan similar sources complain about frequent 'changes of mind'. The author's contacts and experiences with the Iraqi administration from 1982–1984 suggest that this holds true for Iraq also. It must be stressed that changes may, of course, be for the better. The all–encompassing reorganisation in Ethiopia leading to the establishment of the National Council for Central Planning which is powerful and directly involved in all sectors of the economy, was, within a central planning framework, positive — although significant results still have to be awaited. The upgrading of Jordan's Development Council to a Ministry in late 1984, was a necessary step, but did not go far enough. Yet even if reforms are well meant, the pitfalls remain.

In several countries intra–bureaucratic conflicts are prominent. The potential for these has, in fact, often been deliberately built in to administrative structures, by creating parallel responsibilities over different departments, and keeping delineations of responsibilities vague. The aim is evidently to reinforce the power position of the leadership. Examples of such intra–bureaucratic conflict or overlapping responsibilities can be found in most Middle Eastern countries, except perhaps — but it is still early to judge — in Ethiopia. Inevitably, this leads to reduced efficiency, contradictory measures etc. A recent example in Egypt was when the Central Bank Governor stated that the Supply and Home Trade Ministry's 1986 decision to allow private–sector food importers to use the free market exchange rates, had been announced without consulting the Central Bank. In his view , expressed at a MEED conference, it was not a good decision and would result in problems [*MEED*, 29-3-86: 12]. There is in Egypt a persisting vagueness (though not in official explanations) about the respective roles in the development planning process, of (1) the Ministry of Planning and International Co–operation, (2) the Central Agency for Public Mobilisation and Statistics(CAPMAS), and (3) the Ministry of Finance. In fact, it appears that the actual status of the Planning Ministry depends (and has done so since Nasir) on the personal prestige and power of the Minister heading it, and on the other personalities in the Cabinet at the time. It would appear that at the time of writing it is again at, or near, the top of a wave.

In Sudan, 'some ministries took the initiative of starting projects, financed by external loans which they negotiated themselves, without obtaining the prior approval of the central planning agency' [Niblock, 1985: 16–17]. Responsibility for administering grants and loans is spread over four departments (see figure 3.2): the Central Budget Administration, the Foreign Aid Administration, the General Directorate for Foreign Financing, and the General Directorate for Commodity Aid. In Syria, it is unclear what the delineation of responsibilities is between the State Planning Council and the Governorate Planning Directorates. In Jordan, development efforts on the local government level are the vaguely defined responsibilities of (a) local government, (b) the Regional Planning Department in the Ministry of Planning, and (c) the Directorate for Regional Planning, which comes under the competency of the Ministry of Municipal and Rural Affairs and Environment. As for the administration of aid, in principle the Economic and Technical Co–operation Directorate of the Planning Ministry is responsible for specific development ODA, whereas other ODA and financing falls under the Ministry of Finance. But the actual distinction is vague; in addition, some line ministries play a (vaguely defined) role.

In some countries, the development administration is formally well organised and may even, considered by itself, work well. In Oman, for example, the Development Council Technical Seretariat (DCTS) functions well on the basis of a relatively small but hard–working and able staff. The influence of that administration's work on the actual allocation of resources, however, has still been relatively small. In this case the cause lies both in political tradition and expediency, and in the sudden influx of money after oil price rises. As Townsend [1984: 46] puts it:

> When everything can be bought at once, what is the relevance of deciding priorities? Why should a government style that is traditionally paternalistic let itself be encumbered with impersonal rules which could act to impede the desire of the government to reward a tribal leader by building a road through his tribal territory, for example? Why should a ruler whose government and leadership style combines a mixture of generosity

and impulse agree to consult the plan document before awarding a contract to a favoured friend who is to be rewarded ? And why, in a country where defence and security reasons are, rightly or wrongly, used to justify a large range of government decisions made on an essentially pragmatic basis, should a five–year plan be allowed to get in the way of such decisions ?

These considerations apply in non–oil states as well as in oil states, even though the former do not enjoy a similar access to funds (except in so far as the latter factor is replaced by ODA). In fact, the quote admirably sums up the essence of the political factor in development planning in the Middle East, as exposed in this and previous chapters. In fairness to Oman, one has to observe that the country's development, particularly in the early 1980s, was kept relatively well in hand. By comparison with most other oil states, the economy was then more carefully managed; Oman remains thoroughly creditworthy in commercial bankers' eyes. During the 1970s, however, and again after 1983 (until the collapse of oil prices in 1986), the main general policy thrust emerging from the DCTS was one of fast expansion and expenditure, which appears to have been the result of the DCTS Director's personal predilections: having the ear and confidence of the Sultan, his opinions have carried disproportionate weight. Quite apart from DCTS advice, the Omani government indulged in a spending spree on the eve of the collapse of the oil market, in order to beautify the capital for the 1985 GCC summit, running seriously into deficit in the process. These expenses were not foreseen in plan documents. The experience shows how real the limits to planning still are.

One last further aspect of political realities (already touched upon in the above quote) which requires a mention is tribalism. In most Middle Eastern countries this remains a significant force, even if it does not constitute the main structure of society. In countries such as the Yemens and Djibouti, central government can not simply impose its will on the tribal groups. Some form of explicit or implicit mutual understanding needs to be achieved or maintained. In order to have an impact and not see its chances for survival destroyed, the central government must on the one hand respect the tribal balance of power, and on the other try to use that balance for its own purposes. This has implications for development policy as well as for the characteristics of the administration. In the allocation of resources (projects), no important tribal group should feel discriminated against. Such considerations are also of prime importance in the presumably 'scientifically planned' development of the PDRY, particularly in the Hadramaut. In the Yemen AR, to conclude with a last example, the political leadership (which, under Col. Ali Abdullah Saleh, has shown itself to be skilled at understanding and managing the tribal balance of power) appointed a member of one of the smaller tribes as head of the Central Planning Organisation. Someone from a major tribe could have used the position, with his tribal power base, to acquire a stronger position than was desirable. He would be able to divert resources to the benefit of his tribe, and in so doing (or in being suspected of so doing) would upset the other major tribes. A planning minister from a small tribe does not pose such a problem: his power base in no way threatens the big tribes, which makes him acceptable to them all (for an illustration of tribal/traditional realities to be reckoned with in Yemeni public administration, see Koenig & Bolay, 1982: 227–229).

3.

The general underdevelopment of most countries in the region (that is, underdevelopment with reference to the standards they set themselves) has four main consequences with a direct impact on development administration. First, due to the underdevelopment of the human resource base, there is a lack of qualified people to man the administration. Egypt is excepted: it has an over-supply of graduates, although in fact even their education often does not prepare them for the jobs in hand. In the Yemen AR, the whole concept of planning — and of the required education — is so new, that little of the necessary knowledge and experience are available domestically. This gap can only partly be filled by foreign expertise. In Ethiopia, where serious efforts to develop the human resources base date only from 1974, the lack of graduates in public administration, economics, agriculture and other technical subjects, is felt acutely (see the number of professionals, indicated in Figure 3.5, in departments such as Macro-planning (10 people), or the Foreign Economic Relations Department). Some personnel in Ethiopia are sent abroad for further study even while employed; and at present (1986) the time of the few professionals concerned with the administration of foreign aid is partly taken up with learning how to use the newly acquired computers. Under-staffing may also be caused by the lack of funds. This is probably true for Syria (Figure 3.8), where, for instance, the Directorate for Overall Planning is manned by only four professionals.

Second, lack of resources means that high wages cannot be afforded. Underpaid bureaucrats tend to look for other jobs on the side, and neglect their first. This is true for nearly all Middle Eastern countries apart from the Gulf states, Ethiopia and the PDRY — in the latter two because of control, in the former because of wealth. In Iraq many government employees work as taxi drivers outside and sometimes even during working hours. In Egypt absenteeism is recognised as a plague, and even when present, many unmotivated personnel, there and elsewhere, tend to spend rather less energy on the job than required. Low pay of course also makes employees all the more amenable to corruption. In a sense, corruption has the positive role of at least getting something done, but it is never conducive to a concerted development effort.

Third, the lack of reliable information due to defective data gathering and unfamiliarity with (or unavailability of) computers, can cripple the planning effort from the start. This poses a dilemma: bad planning, planning based on defective data, can indeed be worse than no planning at all. Such an outcome, however, is not inevitable: it does not seem to have happened in the Yemen AR, although the latter is a typical example of a country where the newness of planning efforts mean that data on crucial sectors of the economy and population are often non–existent.

Finally, the lack of resources and funds, as well as of experience in managing 'modern' development efforts, reinforces dependence on donors. The states concerned have often proved unable, due to lack of funds and/or knowledge, to challenge the resource allocation priorities imposed on them by foreign advisers and investors. It is hardly necessary to argue this extensively; mentioning the cases of Egypt and Sudan should suffice. In Egypt, although priorities are officially determined by the Plan, it is clear that in fact American aid has been conditional on acceptance of certain policy choices and particular projects [Handoussa, 1984]. In Sudan, the Kenana sugar project is only one of many examples. The main contractor (Lonhro of the UK) was also the initial consultant, and apart from the role of corruption, neither the Sudanese government nor the Arab investors appeared able to see through Lonhro's feasibility study of the project. It has since become clear that this study was unreliable and in fact 'rigged' so as to gain the contract for Lonhro. As a result, Sudan ended up with a giant project that affected agricultural social relations and, heavily, the country's reserves [Wohlmuth, 1983].

4.

A final category of problematic characteristics is related to socio–
cultural background. The danger here is to overstate the case
by attributing proportionately too great a share in the blame
for administrative failure to Arab culture. One does not wish
to end up in the fortunately old–fashioned school blaming the
non–achievement of industrialisation on Islam. From the previous sections and chapters it should be clear that other elements
have played a major role. That being said, however, it cannot be
denied that some elements of the dominant culture in the Middle East have had a negative impact on the kind of development
administration one has tried to develop. This often happened in
conjunction with, or because of, the factors mentioned under the
previous sections.

   One such element is the nature of education in most of the
Middle East, which has been and still is to too large an extent
based on memorising rather than independent thinking. This contributes to the lack of initiative of most government employees in
the Middle East. Family traditions may also exert an influence:
it is conceivable that the strongly paternalistic ways — the father
being the near–absolute authority, and respect for his decisions
being the cardinal duty — inhibit enthusiasm for independent decisions [Palmer & Nakib, 1981: 74]. Osama [1987: 88] scathingly
describes how the products of this non– critical/authoritarian up-
bringing at home and at school, subsequently 'join the government
agencies where they continue not to think'. But the explanation
can not be complete without (1) the above–mentioned fear, originating in political realities, of loss of job; and (2) the simple lack
of interest in the content and meaning of the job. That lack of
interest is again partly explained by low wages (see above) and
by the fact that the idea of a Weberian administration was introduced from abroad and had little connection with local traditions,
customs and values. It is this gap which, in this author's view,
is largely responsible for most of the 'behavioural' problems with
which Middle Eastern administrations are beset.

   The fact itself that the system of organisation and decision–
making was foreign already reduced its effectiveness in the society
in which it was supposed to work. And it was almost inevitable
that the people who came in contact with it, both inside it and
outside, would apply their own standards and values in interpreting it. The form could be assimilated, but it was perceived differently, and attributed different functions. In that sense it is not

so surprising that one finds, as Palmer & Nakib [1981: 70] put it, an absence of any notion of professional conscience among most government employees. That attitude, moreover, is reinforced by the often negative way in which many people in the Middle East, including civil servants, see their administrations: not performing too well, and mainly instruments of control. Traditional values come first: the personal has priority over the impersonal, both in the kind of way people prefer the administration to work, and in the priorities of the employees as to whom or what to attend to first. 'Personal priorities' mean (a) the employee himself, rather than the bureaucracy or 'society at large' (several surveys have established that most government employees in the Middle East consider the bureaucracy firstly as a vehicle for personal advancement); (b) attention to the employee's kin, friends and those who have done a favour, and for their needs, rather than to other jobs on hand — and certainly rather than looking for new non-personal problems. Although these factors are not totally absent from administration in the developed world, their prevalence and salience in the Middle East have made them far more detrimental for bureaucracies in the area than for their developed counterparts. The situation is made still worse, however, by recruitment and personnel–evaluation policies, which are, as a result of the non–adapted value system, usually based on criteria such as sect, personal acquaintance, family etc., rather than on the universal one of merit.

— — —

The result of all the above is that, as was stated before, the basic framework for successful planning and for an effective 'modern' development administration, is absent. Development plans therefore often come to serve essentially as window–dressing exercises, for the benefit both of potential donors, and of the domestic audience as a way to generate legitimacy. One need only look at the planning efforts in Sudan under Nimeiri to find resounding evidence of this.

— — —

Administrative Structures

The reader is referred to Figures 3.1 — 3.16 for organisational and planning charts of 11 countries in the region: Egypt, Sudan, Ethiopia, Djibouti, Syria, Jordan, Iraq, Oman, Yemen AR, the PDRY and Algeria. Apart from the chart on Algeria, for which thanks go to Dirk Beke of Gent University, the others are based on official information and the author's own research. Since general characteristics have been expanded upon earlier, the following section will be limited to a brief overview of (1) the position of the bodies concerned with planning, in the overall structure of the administration, and (2) the position of the aid administration.

1. Development Administration

Apart from being great top–down pyramids, the structure of the different administrations varies considerably. In some countries the planning organisation or ministry is formally on the same level or even lower than the line ministries; in others, it is situated higher, for instance directly under the PM. Even in some of the latter cases, however, the long–run impact of planning on policies may still not be significant since real decision–making happens elsewhere and/or is influenced by unforeseen events.

In **Egypt**, the Planning Ministry is on the same level as other ministries, but headed by a Deputy Premier who is also responsible for CAPMAS and Finance. Theoretically he has the power to enforce plan policies, but over the last decades much has depended on who was heading the Ministry and who else was influential. The real decision–making power lies with what the Egyptians call 'the Economic Group' within the Cabinet, which brings together the ministers and officials most influential at that moment and includes the specifically economy–oriented ministers. Egypt stands out by the sheer size of the administration: the Ministry of Planning and International Co–operation employs, all–in, some 2500 people. The investment budget is drawn up by the Ministry of Finance, and actual investment on the basis of domestic resources has since July 1980, at least officially, been the responsibility of the National Investment Bank.

In **Sudan**, (Figure 3.2) planning is the responsibility of the Planning Wing of the Ministry of Finance, Economy and Planning. The central directorate is that of General Planning, which employs some 50 professionals. The Ministry is on a par with other ministries, and in effect has had little power to force plan policies on other ministries with powerful incumbent heads. In fact, this and other international and domestic factors referred to earlier have resulted in there being precious little planned development, although over 500 people in the Ministry are supposed to be working on it.

In **Ethiopia** (Figures 3.3 — 3.6), the Office of the National Committee for Central Planning (ONCCP) is placed directly under the Head of State. It encompasses, in its present reorganised form (which still has to prove its worth), all sectors of development, down to the local level (Figure 3.5) and has enforcing power over line ministries and commissions. In fact during the planning process achievement of consensus is always attempted. But once agreed the plan gains the stamp of approval of the highest leadership and is binding — unless amended in the wake of periodical evaluations. Its professional staff exceeds 350. Power lies with the 'Provisional Military Administrative Council', which is in the process of being absorbed/transformed into the top of the newly created 'Workers' Party of Ethiopia'. The present ONCCP organisation was preceded by the establishment in 1979 of a 'Central Planning Supreme Council' with similar but less wide and penetrating power. The first reorganisation of the development administration inherited from the pre–revolutionary era [Mulat, 1985:97], came only in 1977.

Djibouti (Figure 3.7) has no Planning Ministry. Instead there is a 'Planning Bureau' in the Ministry of Finance and National Economy. In fact, resource allocation is decided via consensus at the Cabinet level, with an important input from French advisers and other donors. A single line ministry cannot on its own authority start a big project. The management of development so far — there being so much need and the choices being fairly obvious — has proved comparatively effective. Djibouti is a special case: its economy rests on its development as a service centre and transit point for trade, and on foreign assistance and the presence of the French.

In **Syria** (Figure 3.8), the 'State Planning Council' (SPC) is positioned higher than the line ministries, under a Minister of State for Planning Affairs. During plan formulation supreme authority for resource allocation lies with the 'Supreme Planning Commission'. This is headed by the Prime Minister, and consists of the Planning Minister, other important economic ministers, and representatives of the popular unions (farmers, workers, engineers, ...). At other times, decisions have to be approved by the 'Economic Committee', which has a similar composition but is chaired by the Deputy Prime Minister for Economic Affairs [see also Saigh, 1986: 459–461]. Ultimately, of course, power lies with President Asad and the top of the Baath party. It is noteworthy, though, that the Baath organisation has no role in the planning process [Wilson, 1983: 13]. Similar to the Egyptian case, the SPC has Planning Bureaus in every ministry and state organisation. The total number of professionals employed by the SPC, not including local planning directorates, is estimated at 180. ['SPC' and 'Supreme Planning Commission' are the not quite accurate English terms used by the Syrians themselves; the Arabic originals refer to the 'State Planning Organisation' for the former, and the 'Supreme Planning Council' for the latter].

In **Iraq**, (Figure 3.12), the Ministry of Planning is situated on the same formal level as other ministries, but by 1979 had acquired considerable influence due to its lengthy professional experience (planning in Iraq dates from 1950). This was reversed with the execution of Adnan Hamdani, the Planning Minister,in 1979 because of 'pro–Syrian sentiments'. The Ministry has since proved less powerful, less effective, and was damaged further by a bomb blast in 1983. As in Syria, real power lies with the President, and the Revolutionary Command Council (RCC). The RCC has a number of development–related committees (sometimes including non–Baath experts) where economic policy is hammered out — such as the Economic Planning Council, the Foreign Economic Relations Committee, the Higher Committee for Energy, and the Budget Committee. The Ministries of Planning and Finance are now mainly technical 'service' ministries, carrying out the technical work of drawing up the plans and the annual budgets [cf. Townsend, 1982: 267–271].

In **Jordan** (Figures 3.10 — 3.11), the Ministry of Planning is on a par with the other ministries, ever since it was elevated from the status of a 'Board' in 1984. It has little enforcing power. A striking aspect in Jordanian plan formulation is the direct involvement of the private sector. In the preparation of the latest five–year plan (published in 1986), consultation involved 24 special commissions representing all sectoral interests, in addition to the 'general commitee' (see Fig. 3.11) – a procedure which may be 'politically laudable but not perhaps the best basis for a tightly co–ordinated plan focused on key objectives' [*FT*, 22-5-87: 20]. Given the large role given to the private sector, moreover, the plan is in effect only indicative. Substantial power in formulating policies lies with the 'Supreme Planning Council', headed by the

Prime Minister and including, in addition to the most powerful ministers (Planning, Foreign Affairs, Industry),the Governor of the Central Bank and representatives from the Chamber of Commerce and Industry and the private sector. Within the Cabinet there is also a Ministerial Development Committee (or 'Planning and Finance Committee'). Crown Prince Hassan has a hazily defined role in overseeing the development process: he can be informally present at all levels. There is reason to believe that he is strongly influenced by private sector advisers.

In **Oman** (Figure 3.13), the Technical Secretariat of the Development Council (DCTS) is situated on the level of the other line ministries. In early 1986 the professional staff consisted of only 53 people. The Development Council itself — usually comprising about half the Cabinet — is one of the three powerful councils where policy formulation takes place, the other two being those of 'Financial Affairs' and 'Natural Gas and Petroleum' Between the mainly rich and powerful on these councils (sometimes present in more than one) and the Sultan and his advisers, resource allocation is decided. The Sultan heads all three councils. All Ministers concerned with developmental issues are members of the Development Council, with the Prime Minister as Chairman,and a continuous contact is maintained between the Technical Secretariat and individual ministries concerning both initial proposals and later specifics of projects. The access and trust which the DCTS's Egyptian Director, as a person, enjoys with the Sultan, is a special factor, with the policy implications referred to earlier. The finalised Plan needs approval of both the Development and the Financial Affairs Councils, is sometimes discussed in the Cabinet as a whole, and is then decreed by the Sultan. The private sector is of course not bound by the plan, nor, as indicated earlier, is the highest leadership.

Yemen's Central Planning Organisation (CPO) is headed by a Deputy Prime Minister who is also Minister of Planning (Figure 3.14). He is responsible to the Supreme Planning Council of the Cabinet, headed by the Prime Minister. CPO employs some 375 people, of whom professionals can be estimated as numbering between 130 and 200. In theory CPO stands above and is more powerful than other ministries. In practice it is perceived as being fairly weak, although Dr Al–Attar has President Saleh's support. As mentioned earlier, domestic political considerations sometimes have to take precedence, and ministers who disagree with al–Attar, may succeed in finding other channels to influence the President's opinion: e.g. other members of the military ruling group (especially those from a minister's own tribal group).

In **Algeria** (Figure 3.16), the status of the Ministry for Planning and Regional Development is not formally higher than that of other ministries, but its role in drawing up the plans is central. Discussions take place at several stages with relevant Ministers, the Ministry of Finance, and Parliament. Plan enforcement has the backing of the political leadership, as far as it can afford.

In the **PDRY** a similar organisational framework obtains (Figure 3.15). The system appears to allow for substantial participation by local authorities and sectoral organisations. The main impetus and direction come from the Yemeni Socialist Party's (YSP) Polit–bureau. The plans are worked out by the Ministry of Planning after consultation with line ministries, the Supreme People's Council (controlled by the YSP, as are the unions and federations), and the local councils. The Economic Secretariat of the YSP (consisting of the Economic Secretaries of the Local Party Branches in addition to six economic experts not affiliated with governmental bodies) works in a hazily defined tandem with the Ministry, both in the planning process and in monitoring plan implementation. After the plan has been drawn up, it needs the approval of the YSP's Central Committee, which, in turn, passes it on to the Cabinet via the Supreme Council for National Planning; the latter is chaired by the Prime Minister, with the Minister of Planning as his deputy. Finally, the Supreme People's Council provides its stamp of approval before the President signs it [see also Ismael & Ismael, 1986: 88–89]. In 1978, at the time of the World Bank mission to the country [World Bank, 1979: 74–75] the staff of the Ministry numbered only 34 professionals. The plan, once approved, becomes law and is considered the second most important document after the Constitution. As indicated before, however, tribal realities and power politics still play a large role — witness the fighting and 'revolution' in January 1986.

2. The Aid Administration and its Position

Egypt's aid administration is mainly situated in the 'International Co–operation' wing of the Ministry for Planning and International Co–operation (Fig. 3.1). The 'Foreign Donors Unit' is subdivided according to donors. A role is also played by the 'Economic Department' of the Ministry of Foreign Affairs, and by the Ministry of Finance. The latter prepares the investment budget. The delineation of functions is not wholly clear, however. Moreover, individual ministries such as the Ministry of Industry [cf. Abdel-khalek, 1984: 17] can sign loan agreements. Formally, these have to fit into the Plan, and the projects concerned should be approved by the General Authority for Investment and Free Zones (GAIFZ). Follow–up of financial input and results of projects is done by the Central Auditing Agency.

As indicated earlier, ministers in **Sudan** had a fair degree of autonomy, depending on their personal power, in deciding which projects to adopt and seek finance for. That situation seems to have changed since the overthrow of Nimeiri, but a longer time-span is needed to assess this trend. Formal resonsibility for acquiring and administering of foreign assistance lies with four bodies in the Ministry of Finance, Planning and Economy (Figure 3.2). In 'Finance', there is the Loans Repayment Section of the General Expenditure Department in the Central Budget Administration (c. 13 professionals); the 'Foreign Aid Administration' in the Planning Wing (with some 35 professionals); the Debt Management Department of the General Directorate for Foreign Financing (c. 30), and the General Directorate for Commodity Aid (c. 25), the latter two in the Economy Wing. This gives a total of just over one hundred professional staff. In December 1985 an amalgamation of the four was proposed, to form a 'Department for Foreign Co-operation' under the Economy Wing. In reaction to this suggestions were made, rightly in this author's view, to appoint instead a (Deputy) Under–Secretary for Foreign Co-operation, without actually amalgamating the departments and separating them from Planning.

Arab and especially Saudi assistance for Sudan has often been sought and acquired by the Head of State, such as during General Swar adh–Dhahab's visits to Saudi Arabia in the year of his interim administration.

The actual capacity of the Sudanese aid administration leaves much to be desired. From 1984 onwards attempts were made to establish computer and data processing system in the Ministry. The situation in late 1985 indicated that the initial (unrealistic) hopes have not been fulfilled. The consultants involved, in addition to describing the difficulties they encountered, also painted a bleak picture of the situation at the outset of their project [Calhoun *et al.*, 1986: 10]:

> neither the government of the Sudan nor anyone else had a cumulative database indicating what development projects were underway or in the planning stage ... Nei-

ther the Sudanese government nor anyone else attempted to keep accounts for the whole range of aid activity. The Sudanese Finance Ministry, indeed, was not in a position to say how far its lines of credit were drawn down at any one time, how much of last year's budget had actually been expended, or whether the statements of Sudan's debts proffered by particular lenders were accurate.

In **Ethiopia** (Figures 3.5 — 3.6) three bodies can seek aid: the ONCCP — more particularly the Department of Foreign Economic Relations (FER), manned by 15 professionals; the Ministry of Finance; and the Relief and Rehabilitation Commission (RRC). There is a general control by the ONCCP top officials and the Economic and Social Department of the Workers' Party of Ethiopia's (WPE) Central Committee. The management of aid and contracts — once acquired — are the responsibility of (1) the RRC (NGOs) and FER for relief aid; (2) the FER for government–to–government aid and multilateral assistance; (3) the FER and the Ministry of Finance for foreign loans.

For **Djibouti** the reader may consult Figure 3.7. The responsibility for management of assistance is diffuse. Important in acquisition and initial contracts are the Presidency and the *Direction des Relations Bilaterales* in the Ministry of Foreign Affairs and Co–operation. But since most specific development aid fits into the investment list made up for the 1983 *Conference des Donateurs*, one has to consider the importance of the parties that made up the list: the President, the Cabinet, the *Direction des Relations Bilaterales,* the Ministry of Finance and National Economy (including the Planning Bureau), and French and other foreign advisers. At present, control over aid that has been agreed upon, falls to the Ministry of Finance and National Economy, with desks for each donor.

In **Syria** (Figure 3.9), 'Arab front aid' is the direct responsibility of the President and Prime Minister. Other assistance is acquired and administered by the 'Directorate for Planning of International Economic, Scientific and Technical Co–operation' in the State Planning Council. It is staffed by some 25 professionals divided over three sections: OECD, other bilateral, and multilateral assistance. Requests for and distribution of assistance should match the Plan, and have to obtain the agreement of the Economic Committee and the Prime Minister's Office.

In **Jordan,** seeking and administering specifically development–oriented assistance is done by the 'Economic and Technical

Co-operation Department' (c. 20 professionals) in the Ministry of Planning. Other ODA and financing are administered by the Ministry of Finance as an executive agency for the highest political leadership. There is, however, no sharp distinction.

Iraq, of course, presents a special case in that until 1980 no proper administration for incoming aid was needed. Since late 1980 massive war assistance, as well as commercial loans and credits have become necessary. The Ministry of Finance and some individual ministries are responsible for rescheduling of loans on certain contracts and arranging credit from foreign companies; the Ministry of Finance also plays a role in managing international loans. However, overall control, political pressure on trade partners, and the absolute control over the more than $ 40 billion (*cf.* Nonneman, 1986: 95–104) in financial aid and oil–swaps from the Gulf states, is the domain of the highest political leadership.

In **Oman,** the Sultan and his Financial Affairs Council take the key decisions on foreign loans and assistance. Unless the Sultan is personally involved, the matter is formally initiated with the donor by the Ministry of Foreign Affairs, which then passes it on to the Ministry of Economy and Financial Affairs. Administration of American economic assistance is managed in a way quite different from anywhere else in the region. It is the responsibility of the 'Omani–American Joint Commission for Economic and Technical Co-operation' (OAJC), co–chaired by the Omani Under–Secretary for Foreign Affairs and the U.S. Ambassador. The OAJC's managing director is an official from the office of the Deputy Prime Minister for Economic and Financial Affairs, and the Commission is in fact lodged within the Omani Ministry of Economic and Financial Affairs, which virtually eliminates the problem of access (Figure 3.13).

In **Yemen,** reflecting the situation elsewhere, the budget and other direct grant aid from Arab Governments (Saudi Arabia !) is a matter for the highest political leadership (Yemen not only receives massive undocumented assistance from the Saudis, but also a stipend for the President). That aside, CPO gathers the most important aid administration functions in the 'General Directorate for Projects and Financing' (with 15 professional staff), and the 'General Directorate for Technical Co-operation' (no figure available). Every foreigner working in the country in connection with assistance needs CPO approval.

Algeria in its bilateral assistance relations usually works with general co–operation agreements, in the framework of which a Bilateral Commission for Economic (and technical) Co–operation is set up. Under this commission are installed Sectoral Committees (in each of which there is a group for trade and investment and one for technical co–operation), and Project Committees. On the Algerian side, the latter are composed of officials from the Ministry of Planning and Regional Development, the Ministry of Foreign Affairs, and the Ministry of Finance.

In the **PDRY** the political leadership holds the main role in acquiring development assistance. Technical administration and co–ordination with the Plan falls to the Economic Affairs Wing of the Ministry of Planning, and more particularly to the 'Bilateral Co–operation' and 'Co–operation with Arab and international Organisations' sections; and to the Technical Co–operation Departments in each ministry [World Bank, 1979a](Figure 3.15). In 1985, a new body was established to handle and redistribute aid in kind.

— — —

Figure 3.1 Egypt: Administration of Development and Aid

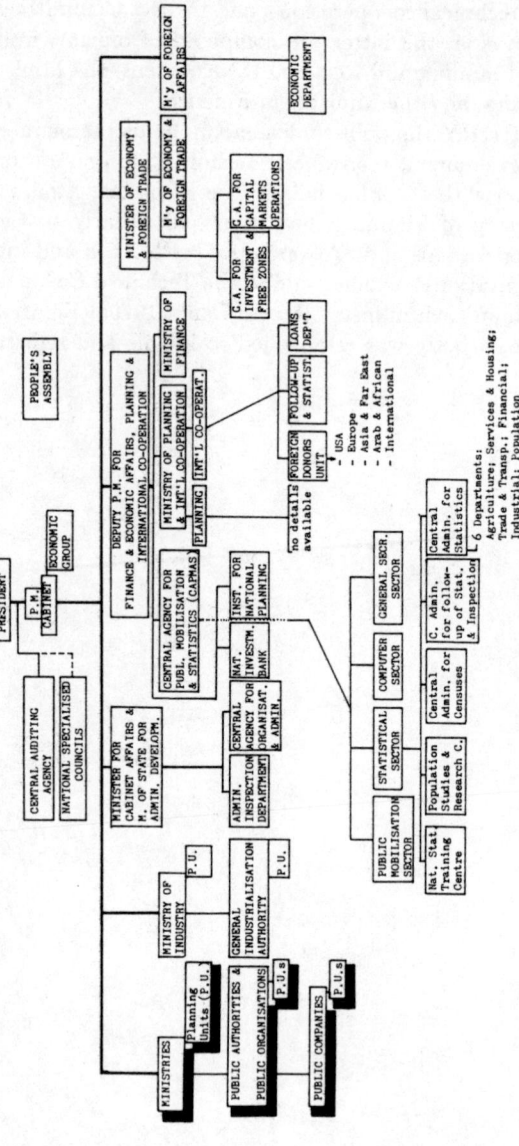

Notes: - Formal Planning Sequence: Info from line Ministries & CAPMAS goes to MPIC, which suggests Plan, taking into account availability of resources; feed-back to Line Ministries, who make up sectoral plans which are then fitted into the Plan. Discussion between MPIC & the Ministries is followed by the involvement of the Cabinet; finally, approval in the National Assembly is required. Implementation by the Ministries, Follow-up by Central Auditing Agency & MPIC.
- Situation on the ground: other influences have had fluctuating importance; follow-up was little more than financial accounting. Since 1983/84, MPIC appears in a stronger position; started collecting quarterly reports on implementation and producing annual follow-up report, more than just financial; however, by early 1986 the new style had not yet resulted in actual reallocations resulting from these reports.
- Note the focal position of the Minister for Cabinet Affairs/Minister of State for Admin. Development, who is supposed to 'pull the strings together'.

Figure 3.2 Planning and Development Administration in Sudan

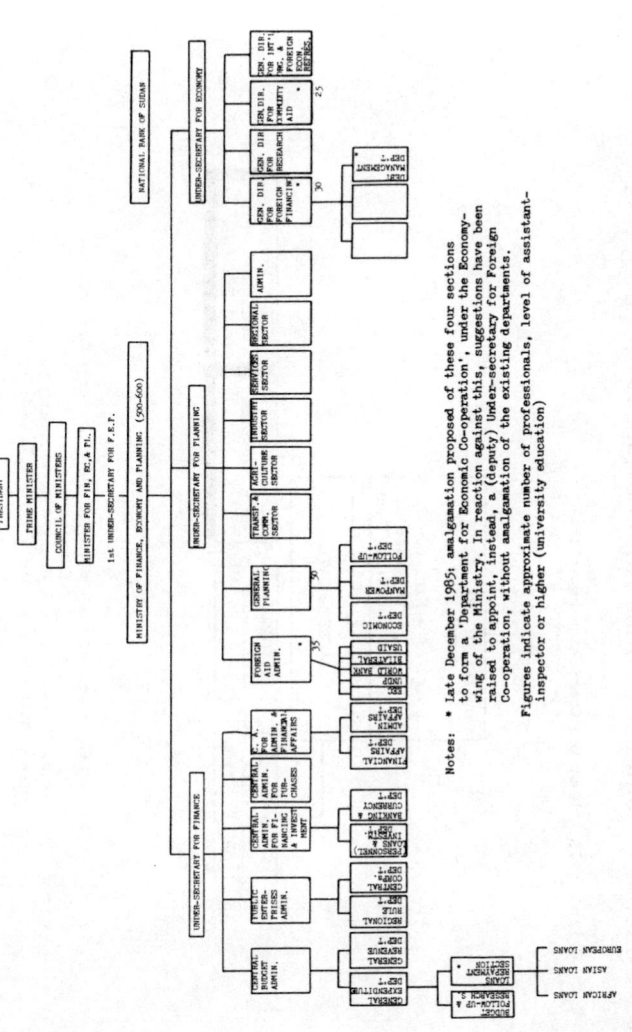

Notes: * late December 1985: amalgamation proposed of these four sections
to form a 'Department for Economic Co-operation', under the Economy-
wing of the Ministry. In reaction against this, suggestions have been
raised to appoint, instead, a (deputy) Under-secretary for Foreign
Co-operation, without amalgamation of the existing departments.

Figures indicate approximate number of professionals, level of assistant-
inspector or higher (university education)

Figure 3.3 Ethiopia's Planning Administration before 1979

(1) 1970: Planning Commission established

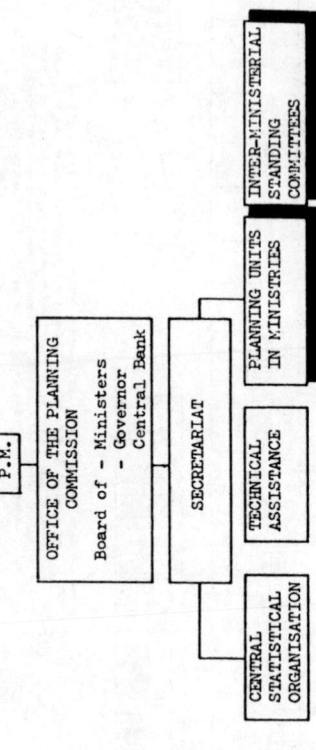

(2) 1977: establishment of the "National Revolutionary Operations
           Command"
           as an "organisational hierarchy embracing public
           organisation at all levels" (MULAT, 1985: 96).

Figure 3.4 1979: Ethiopia's Central Planning Supreme Council

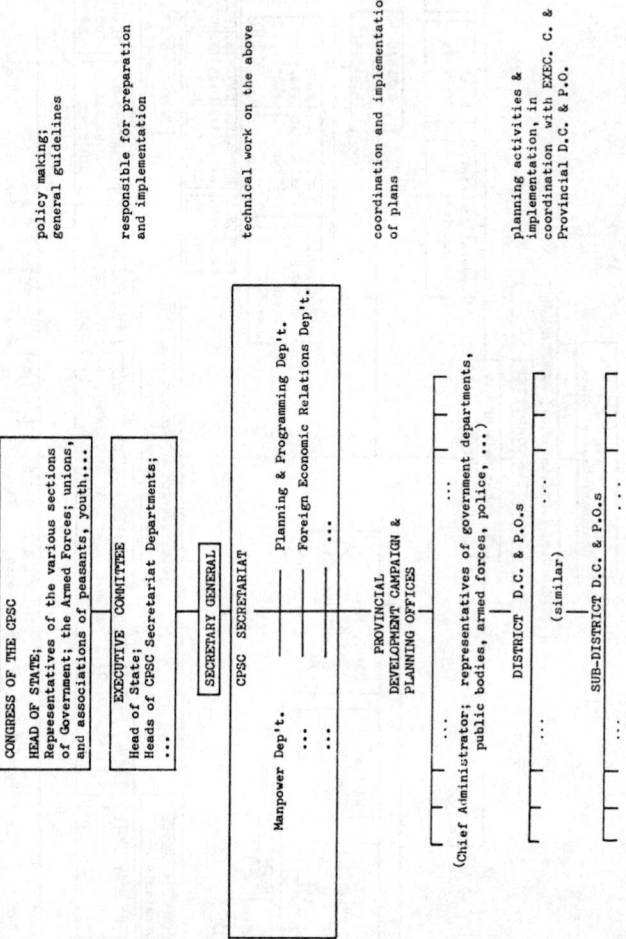

CONGRESS OF THE CPSC HEAD OF STATE; Representatives of the various sections of Government; the Armed Forces; unions, and associations of peasants, youth,...	policy making; general guidelines
EXECUTIVE COMMITTEE Head of State; Heads of CPSC Secretariat Departments;	responsible for preparation and implementation
SECRETARY GENERAL	
CPSC SECRETARIAT Manpower Dep't. Planning & Programming Dep't. ... Foreign Economic Relations Dep't.	technical work on the above
PROVINCIAL DEVELOPMENT CAMPAIGN & PLANNING OFFICES ... (Chief Administrator; representatives of government departments, public bodies, armed forces, police, ...)	coordination and implementation of plans
DISTRICT D.C. & P.O.s ... (similar) **SUB-DISTRICT D.C. & P.O.s** ...	planning activities & implementation, in coordination with EXEC. C. & Provincial D.C. & P.O.

Figure 3.5 Ethiopia: Planning Administration as from September 1984

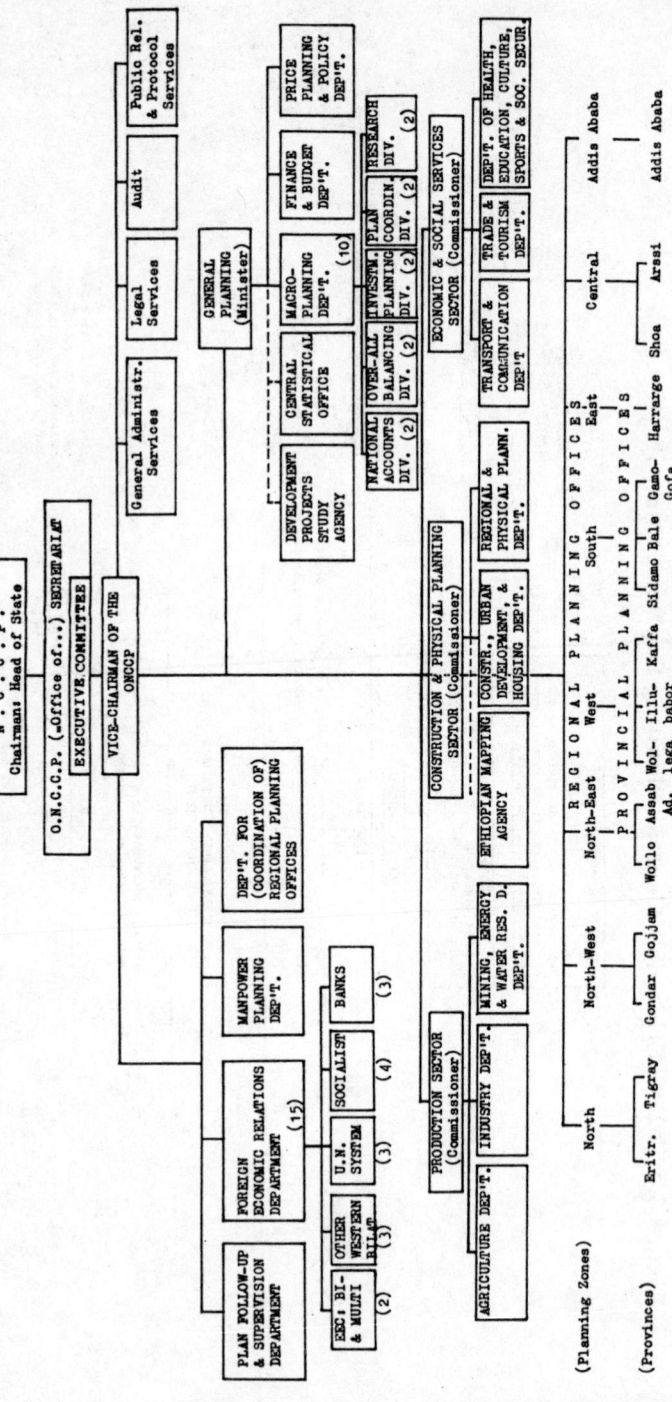

A W R A J A   D E V E L O P M E N T   C O U N C I L S

(Districts)

W O R E D A   D E V E L O P M E N T   C O U N C I L S

(Local)

Notes: – The three Agencies : Development Projects Study Agency;
Central Statistical Office; and
Ethiopian Mapping Agency,
are semi-autonomous, though under the ONCCP.

– The Plan Follow-up and Supervision Department follows up and
supervises the implementation of the annual plans by the
implementing agencies (Ministries, organisations,...). On the
basis of (1) regular implementation reports from those agencies
and (2) its own field work, the Department compiles quarterly,
half-yearly and annual plan implementation reports which it
submits to the Executive Committee.

– The actual plan documents are drawn up by the Macro Planning
Department, which is fed, by other relevant departments and
sectors.

– The F.E.R. Department is mainly responsible for :
1. Collection and processing of data on Ethiopia's Foreign
   aid, loans and grants. So far its performance in this respect has been less than satisfactory, partly due to under-
   staffing and deficient information available to the Dep't.
2. Projection of short- medium- and long-term loans and grants
   in co-operation with the Finance and Budget Department.
3. Supervision of preparation of foreign aid-financed projects,
   and following up their implementation.
4. Participation in the preparation and signing of economic,
   cultural and trade agreements with other countries.

Figure 3.6   Ethiopia: Overall Distribution of Responsibility for Central Development
Planning and Aid Administration

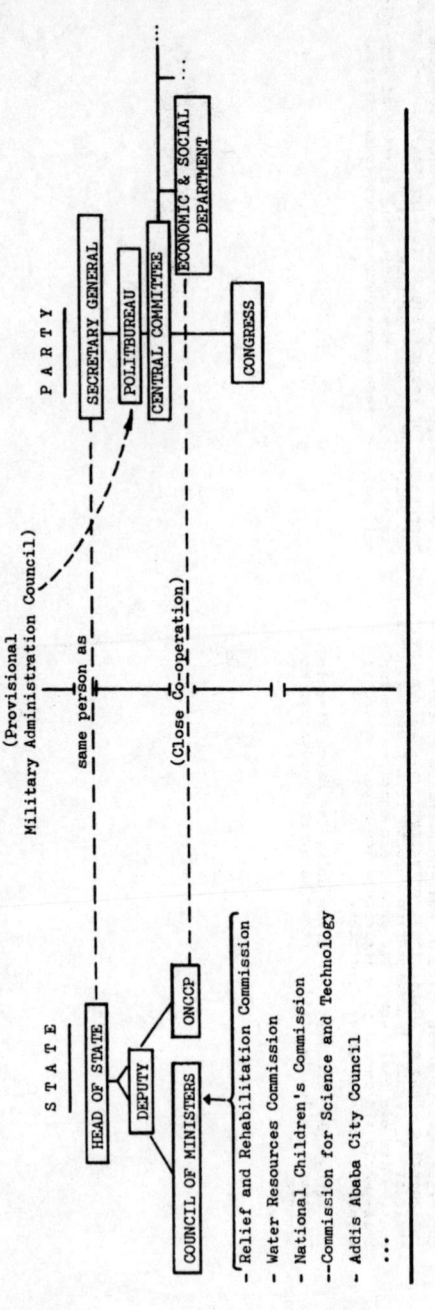

Can seek aid: - ONCCP
                - Ministry of Finance
                - Relief and Rehabilitation Committee

Management of aid
and contacts: (a) relief: R.R.C. (NGOs)
                           Foreign Economic Relations Department (ONCCP)

              (b) Gov't - Gov't and multilateral: F.E.R.

              (c) Loans: F.E.R. + Ministry of Finance

Figure 3.7 Djibouti: Planning and Aid Administration

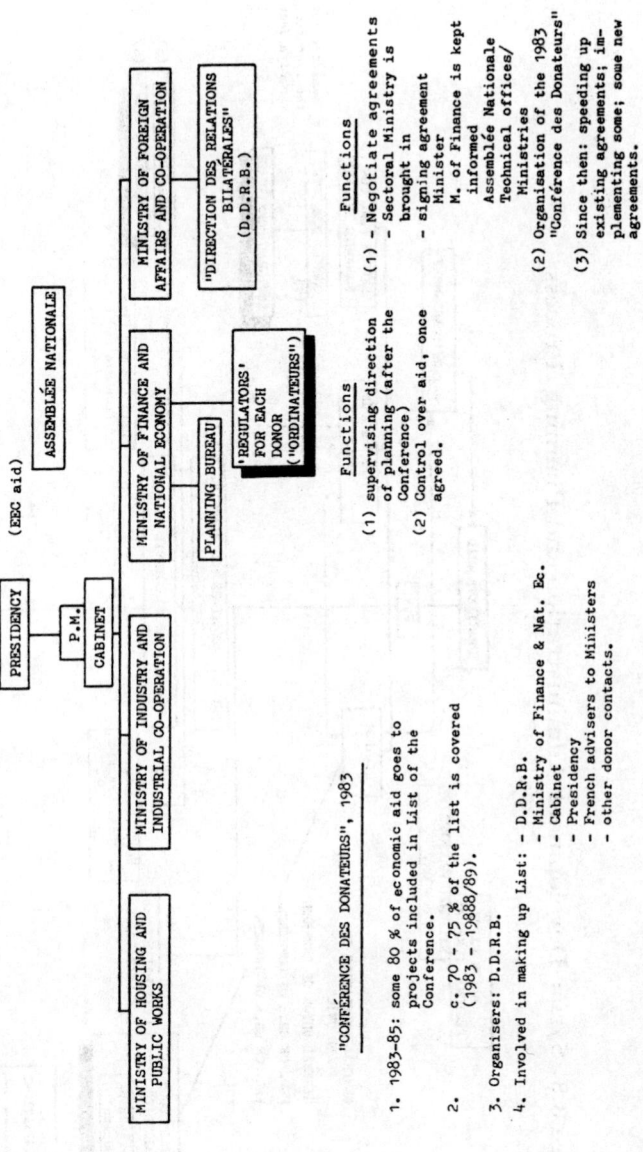

PRESIDENCY

(EEC aid)

ASSEMBLÉE NATIONALE

P.M.

CABINET

| MINISTRY OF HOUSING AND PUBLIC WORKS | MINISTRY OF INDUSTRY AND INDUSTRIAL CO-OPERATION | MINISTRY OF FINANCE AND NATIONAL ECONOMY | MINISTRY OF FOREIGN AFFAIRS AND CO-OPERATION |

PLANNING BUREAU

'REGULATORS' FOR EACH DONOR ("ORDINATEURS")

"DIRECTION DES RELATIONS BILATÉRALES" (D.D.R.B.)

Functions

(1) supervising direction of planning (after the Conference)
(2) Control over aid, once agreed.

Functions

(1) – Negotiate agreements
   – Sectoral Ministry is brought in
   – signing agreement Minister
   M. of Finance is kept informed
   Assemblée Nationale
   Technical offices/
   Ministries
(2) Organisation of the 1983 "Conférence des Donateurs"
(3) Since then: speeding up existing agreements; implementing some; some new agreements.

"CONFÉRENCE DES DONATEURS", 1983

1. 1983-85: some 80 % of economic aid goes to projects included in List of the Conference.

2.   c. 70 - 75 % of the list is covered (1983 - 19888/89).

3. Organisers: D.D.R.B.

4. Involved in making up List: – D.D.R.B.
   – Ministry of Finance & Nat. Ec.
   – Cabinet
   – Presidency
   – French advisers to Ministers
   – other donor contacts.

Figure 3.8 Syria: Development Administration and Planning Process

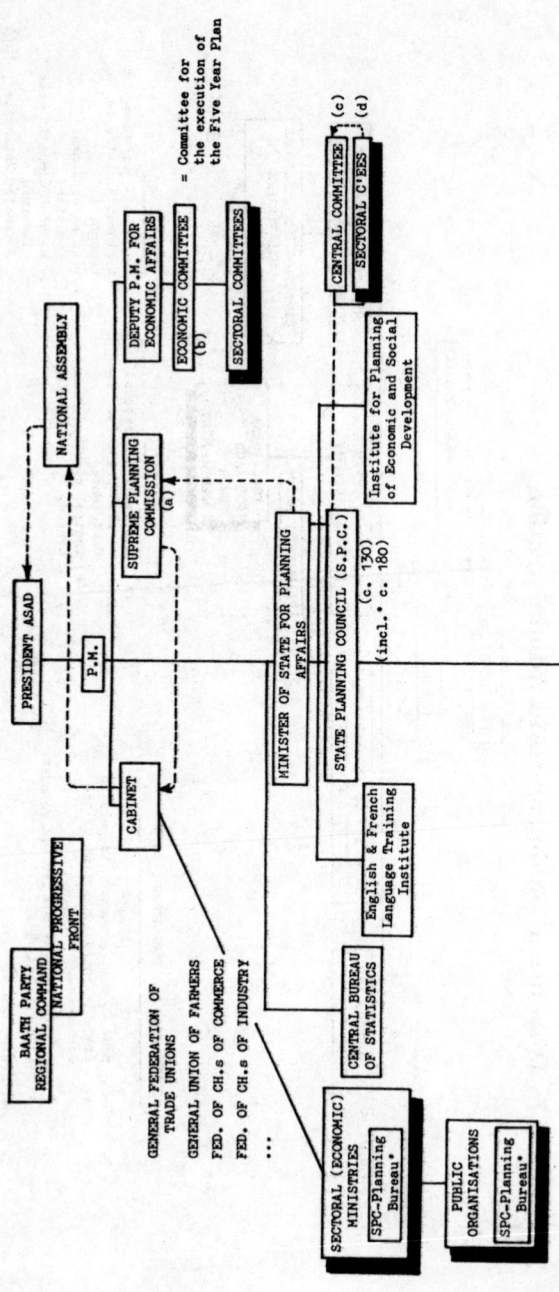

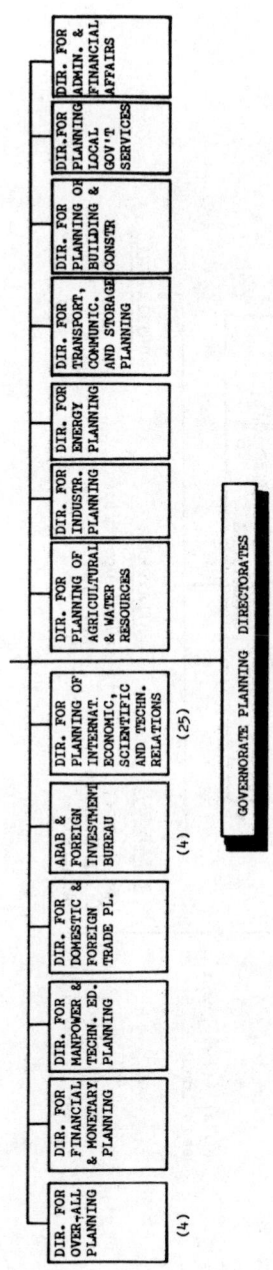

(4)   (4)   (25)

GOVERNORATE PLANNING DIRECTORATES

| DIR. FOR OVER-ALL PLANNING | DIR. FOR FINANCIAL & MONETARY PLANNING | DIR. FOR MANPOWER & TECHN. ED. PLANNING | DIR. FOR DOMESTIC & FOREIGN TRADE PL. | ARAB & FOREIGN INVESTMENT BUREAU | DIR. FOR PLANNING OF INTERNAT. ECONOMIC, SCIENTIFIC AND TECHN. RELATIONS | DIR. FOR PLANNING OF AGRICULTURAL & WATER RESOURCES | DIR. FOR INDUSTR. PLANNING | DIR. FOR ENERGY PLANNING | DIR. FOR TRANSPORT, COMMUNIC. AND STORAGE PLANNING | DIR. FOR PLANNING OF BUILDING & CONSTR | DIR.FOR PLANNING LOCAL GOV'T SERVICES | DIR. FOR ADMIN. & FINANCIAL AFFAIRS |

Notes:

(a) Chaired by the Prime Minister;
   Members: Ministers concerned with economy and development;
            representatives of the concerned Unions and/or Federations
            and/or Chambers.

(b) Chaired by the Deputy Prime Minister for Economic Affairs;
   Members: representatives from Trade Unions Federation and Farmers' Union;
            Crucial 'Economic' Ministers.

(c) Chaired by the Minister of State for Planning Affairs;
   Members: Sectoral Deputy Ministers; Deputy Planning Minister;
            representatives of Unions / Federations / Chambers.

(d) Chaired by the concerned Deputy Minister;
   Members: Deputy Minister of Planning;
            representatives of the concerned   SPC - Planning Bureaus in
            the Ministries concerned;
            heads or representatives of the concerned SPC directorate(s);
            representatives of the concerned Federations and/or Unions
            and/or Chambers.

Figure 3.9 Syria: Aid Administration

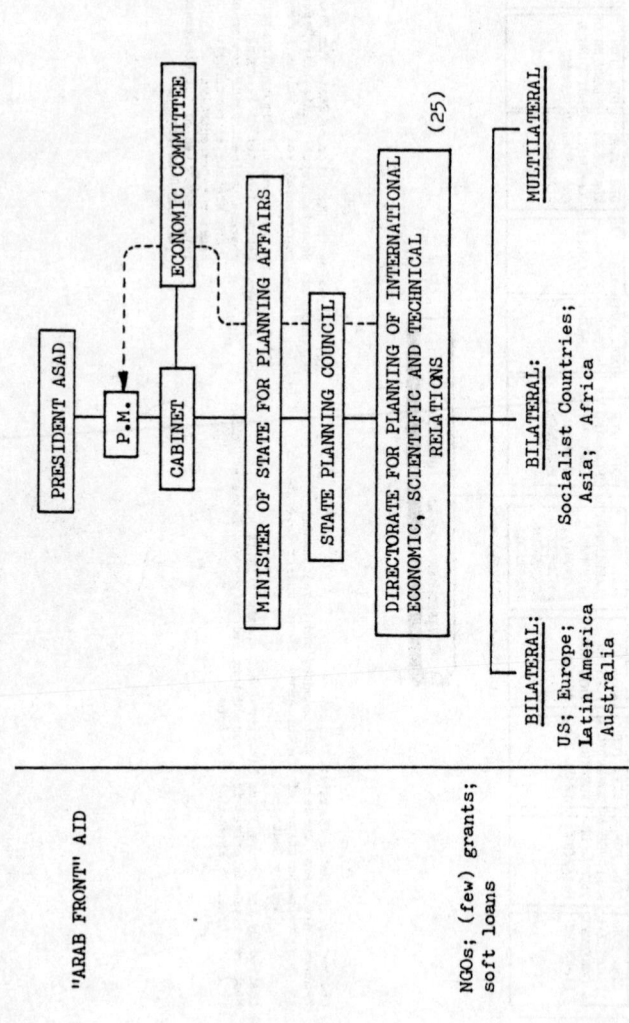

"ARAB FRONT" AID

PRESIDENT ASAD

P.M.

ECONOMIC COMMITTEE

CABINET

MINISTER OF STATE FOR PLANNING AFFAIRS

STATE PLANNING COUNCIL

DIRECTORATE FOR PLANNING OF INTERNATIONAL ECONOMIC, SCIENTIFIC AND TECHNICAL RELATIONS   (25)

BILATERAL:
US; Europe;
Latin America
Australia

BILATERAL:
Socialist Countries;
Asia; Africa

MULTILATERAL

NGOs; (few) grants;
soft loans

Figure 3.10 Jordan: Administration of Planning, Development and Aid

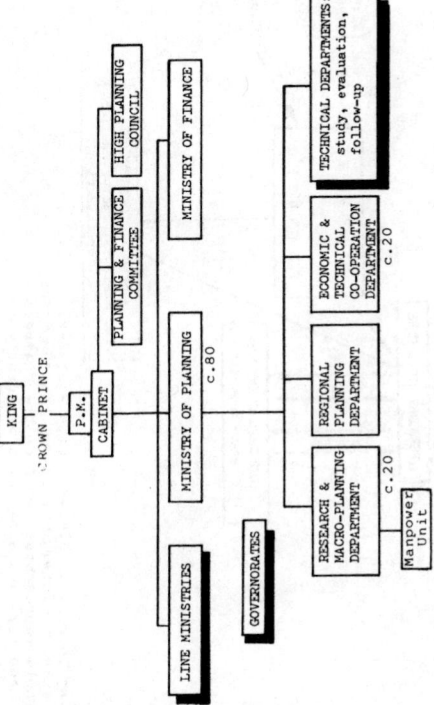

Notes: – figures indicate number of professional staff

Members of planning and Finance Committee:
at least P.M., Minister of Finance, Minister
of Industry, Minister of Planning.

Figure 3.11 Jordan: the Planning Process

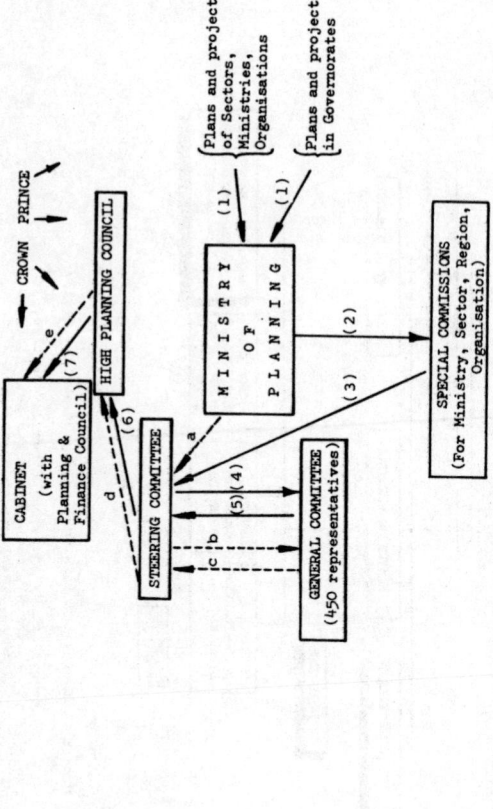

Notes: 1. The "High Planning Council": P.M., Foreign Minister,
        MinisterofIndustry, MinisterofPlanning, the Governor
        of the Central Bank, representatives from the Chambers
        of Commerce and Industry, and some private sector
        representatives.

       2. A FULL LINE indicates the sectoral planning process:(1)-(7)
          A DOTTED LINE indicates the Macro or overall planning
          process. a ... e

Figure 3.12   Iraq: Planning and Development Administration, as of 1982

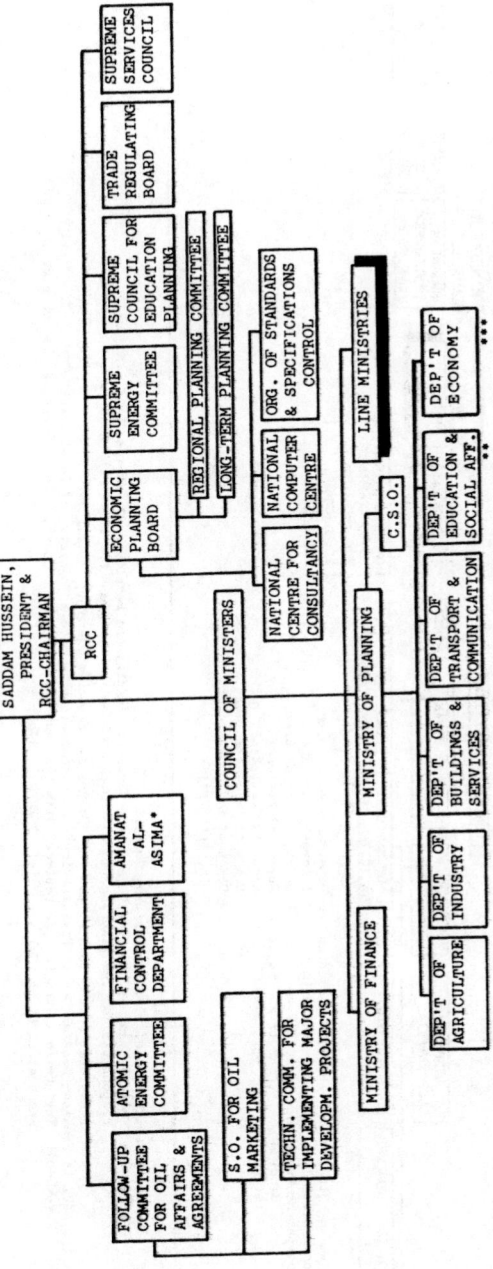

NOTES: * Amanat al-Asima is "Baghdad Municipality", responsible for sewerage, water supply and some infrastructure in the
            capital.
         ** Dep't studies needs and implications (resulting from planning decisions) regarding manpower and education.
         *** This dep't mainly does research for the other dep'ts : it has no coordinating function.
         - The Ministry of Planning is closely linked with the Economic Planning Board (headed by Saddam), for which
           it has in effect become a technical secretariat.
         - There are several more high-level committees, but they are not directly development-related.

SOURCES: Midland Bank International; TOWNSEND, 1982; author's information.

Figure 3.13   Oman: Development Administration

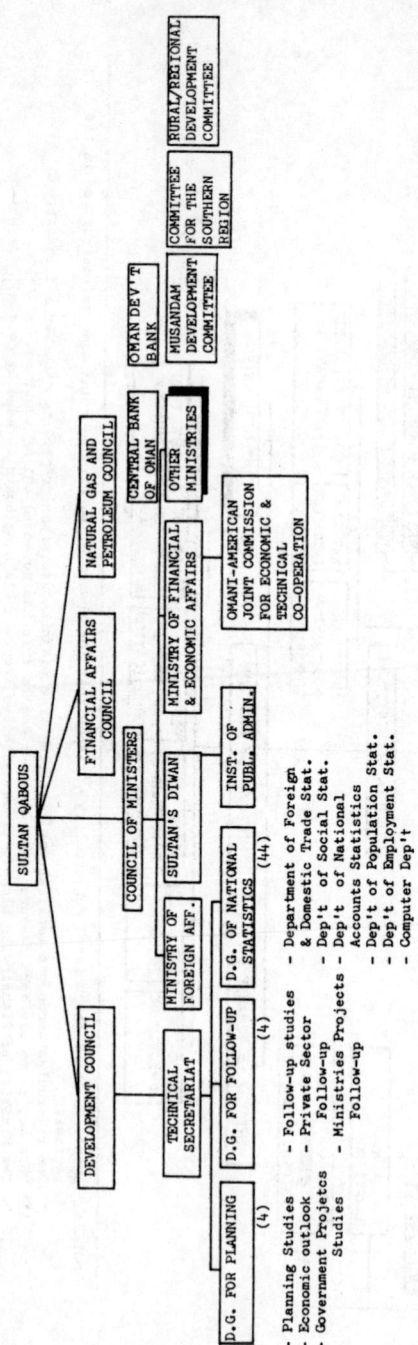

1972 : (March) Establishment of "Interim Planning Council"
     (September) Establishment of "Supreme Council for Economic Planning and Development", chaired by the Sultan,
                responsible for the planning and encouraging of Development, and for links with donors.

          Answerable to the Council was the "Centre for Economic Planning" (C.E.P.)
1973 : C.E.P. is renamed "General Dev't Organisation", in November, it is made a "Ministry of Development".
1974 : (November)   The previous structure is replaced with the "Supreme Development Council with a Technical Secretariat
                    and chaired by the Sultan. (cf. CLEMENTS, 1980: 71-73).

Figure 3.14 Planning and Development Administration in Yemen AR

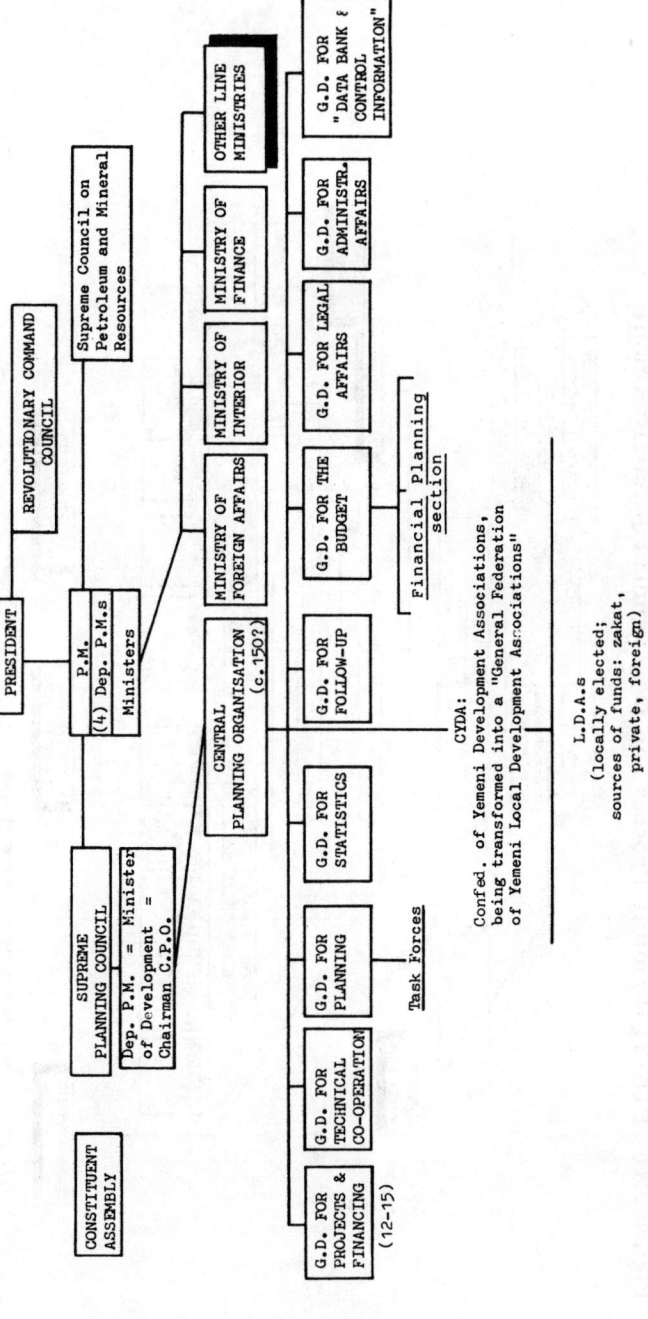

Figure 3.15 PDRY: Planning Process and Development Administration

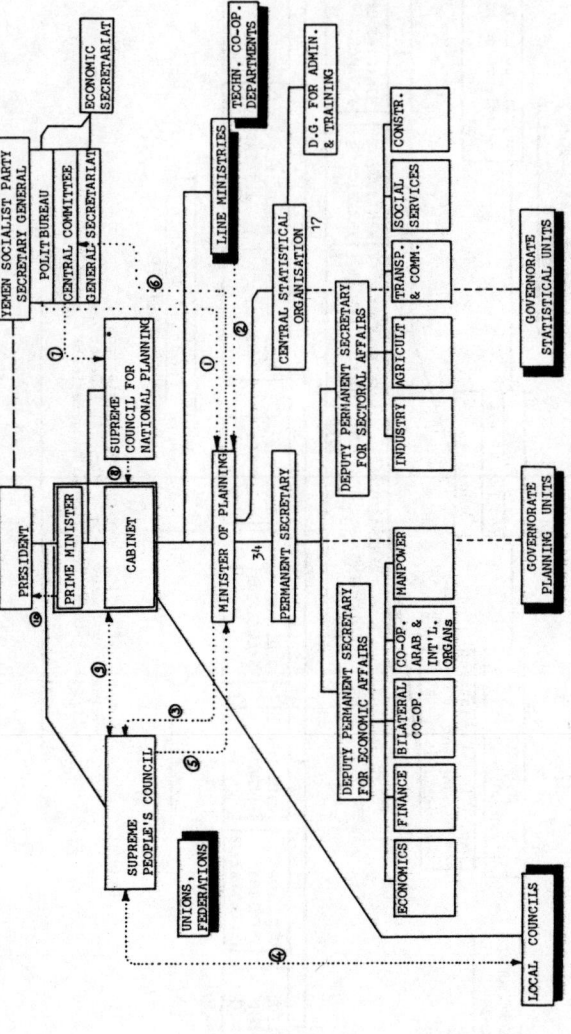

Note: figures indicate number of professional staff in 1978 (World Bank, 1979);
figures in circles indicate the sequence of the planning process
*SCNP Chair: PM, Deputy Ch.: M. of Planning

Figure 3.16 The Planning Process in Algeria

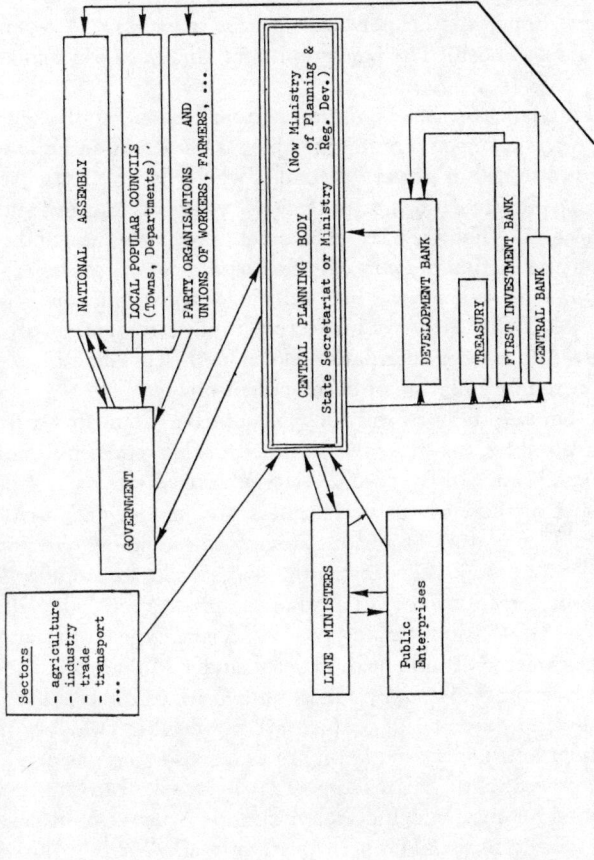

Source: Dirk Beke, Gent University

Participation and Decentralisation

In all Middle Eastern administrations real power and control lie at the top, often even outside the administration, with a few political heavyweights. The administrative structures are of a monolithic nature, in the sense that decentralisation of decision–making, if there is any, nearly always concerns ephemeral matters or is purely formal. Often, 'decentralisation' measures in fact strengthen the hold of central power, as happened in Egypt in the second half of the 1970s, by giving more power to local but directly government–connected officials, while eating away at the responsibilities of elected councils [Ayubi, 1984]. The lack of participation is situated at three levels: within the admnistration; from the administration proper to the political decision–makers; and from the population to both. The background for this has been explained earlier.

There is, nevertheless, an input from below. Firstly, regimes must always take some note of people's aspirations and opinions, if they are to retain power. Secondly, where formal participation is lacking, informal ways of putting views across and influencing policies can be effective. Tribal channels for information and complaints still function in many Middle Eastern countries. In Yemen, afternoon Qat–sessions can be a vehicle for conveying views to the influential. Lastly, however ineffective it may have usually proved, formally–organised participation can nonetheless sometimes play a role in the formulation of development policy.

In Oman, there is only a Consultative Council, with appointed notables, to advise the Sultan. But this represents one end of the spectrum. In Syria and Algeria, several unions or federations, such as those of workers, farmers, etc., are formally involved in policy formulation at various stages. These unions are party–controlled but they still constitute good sensors for popular feelings about certain topics. In Jordan the private sector has direct access to the decision–making process. The Egyptian parliament has a fair degree of influence (at least under Mubarak) although the views expressed usually reflect those of interest groups, such as the business community, which are powerful anyway. In Iraq, parliament and party function more as a sensor than as a vehicle for real power sharing. This appears true for all Arab one–party–dominated regimes, which does not exclude a degree of discussion within those parties. The party structure also tends to provide, unintentionally, informal channels of communication. In Sudan it would appear that the newly elected parliament will indeed be heard. Open discussion of development questions, in newspapers, journals, and in academic fora, is blooming in Sudan and Egypt, where it does have an influence. Such discussion in Algeria is comparatively open (within limits) and in Jordan and Yemen, where university departments have some input in the policy–making process.

Decentralisation as a means of achieving more participation and engagement on the part of the population at large deserves some further attention at this stage, and a few cases will be considered.

Local Development Associations in Yemen. Political traditions in Yemen always left room for local autonomy. This and the egalitarian ethos of tribal society seemed to provide a strong basis for the Local Development Associations (LDAs) which were first set up in the 1960s. In 1973, the *Conference of Yemeni Development Associations* (CYDA) was established to coordinate the associations' activities and act as a go–between with the government. Following the coming to power of al–Hamdi in 1974, government support to the scheme increased substantially and the number of LDAs grew quickly. By 1980 there were over 200 covering the whole country [Swanson, 1985: 133]. The LDAs are basically local cooperatives which sprang from local and/or government initiatives. Their goals were defined as the provision of clean drinking water, access roads and health care [ibid.]. Members of the LDA's General Assembly are democratically elected and they in turn elect their Administrative Board [ibid.: 138]. Coordinating Councils at the provincial level, headed by the governor, were set up and rules for financing were laid down. The LDAs can raise money locally, approach foreign donors (NGOs) — but only sign agreements with agreement of the CPO and usually the co–signature of the concerned ministry — and have a right to a 75 per cent share in the *zakat*, or local tax of 10 per cent on agricultural production. These taxes, it should be noted, are collected by officials of the central government, and subsequently the LDAs receive their share from the institutions of central government. The LDAs are also supported by technical and financial assistance from the CYDA. In 1979 the Yemen Cooperation Bank was created, linked to the CYDA, to play a role in financing LDA projects [Escher, 1982: 59].

The LDAs, on the whole, have built up a reputation of independence and acquired quite a respectable record of achievement. For example, by 1979 they had been responsible for constructing

5,000 km of roads, 850 drinking water projects, and 600 schools. [World Bank, 1979b: 83]. The reality of participation and committed involvement of the local population varies from one LDA to the other. Expatriates working with LDAs in the health sector, for example, speak of some of the elected groups of LDA 'officials' being genuinely representative, and of a growing involvement by at least some social groupings (on occasion the local women rather than the men). There are, however, also considerable problems. Two relate precisely to the 'causes for hope' referred to above. First, tribal egalitarianism does not preclude a tradition of effectively hereditary leadership by paramount families. Leadership of, and gain from, LDAs often ends up in those same families, while others may not always enjoy the advantages of their labour. The tradition of formal democratic procedures of LDAs, therefore, may be distorted by traditional power–centres [Swanson, 1985: 141–144]. Secondly,

> Yemen's history has been a tug–of–war between state power and local autonomy, with the result that the centre mistrusts the periphery almost as much as the periphery suspects the centre. The LDAs are situated squarely in the middle, representing the state to the villager and the tribesman to the state [ibid.: 145].

The combination of these two factors often leads local people to view the LDAs as somewhat suspect, both because of their government links and because the people in charge are perceived of as handling the money to their own benefit — which evidence suggests they sometimes do. Other factors limiting the success of LDAs are the limited funds, the dearth of available expertise and CYDA experts [Escher, 1982: 64], and the lack of effective institutionalised communication both within the local communities and between LDA and central government [ibid.: 65; Swanson, 1985]. The LDAs have mostly failed, moreover, to marshall migrant workers' remittances, although there are examples to the contrary [Swanson, 1985: 145]. In the latter respect, the conclusion Swanson comes to is telling. Considering that remittances are the most important income of many communities,

> the LDAs' obliviousness of their emigrant communities suggests that CYDA should develop a coherent emigrant policy. The umbrella organisation must provide the LDAs with both the tools and the direction necessary for involving migrants in the development process. Their inability to do so is a reflection of the Yemeni government's

own ambivalence towards the LDA movement. [ibid.: 145]

Overall, however, one must conclude that the LDAs have proved comparatively successful, and have great potential. The implication of the 1986 reorganisation is not clear at the time of writing, but the likelihood is that the LDA network will become more integrated with the government. This may reflect a greater governmental commitment, but more probably stems from the general Middle Eastern trend of strengthening central power.

Egyptian Local Government. (This section is mainly based on Ayubi, 1984; see also Asam, 1986). Up to 1975, 'the concept of local *government* — as distinct from local administration — had not really been fully accepted either by the traditional rural leadership or by the central and local bureaucrats' [Ayubi: 61]. With the 1975 Local Government Law, two types of local organisation came into being at the levels of province, county (or town with satellites), city or urban district, and village: (1) an elected local council (of which 50 per cent had to be 'workers and peasants'), and (2) an executive local commission. These local bodies were given the power to decide on the creation and management of public utilities and works, except those of a national or 'special' nature; their approval was needed for the use of public utilities or the exploitation of natural resources; their members were given a degree of 'immunity'; and they had the right to create and run their own funds to help finance their tasks. At the same time, however, the local official responsible to central government remained powerful. A coordinating role for the whole system was played by the Ministerial Committee for Local Government, headed by the Prime Minister. The provincial governors were considered the President's representatives.

After the political unrest of 1977 (the food riots) reforms were introduced into the system. These were made law by a presidential decree in 1979. Governors from now on had to be natives of the province they administered; they received the status of Minister; and they all had to be members of the National Democratic Party. 'The main thrust of the new elements introduced by this law related to two major areas': (1) 'the expansion of the 'developmental' functions and authorities of local units' — which were already considerable; and (2) the 'broadening of the executive and political power of the *appointed* local officers' [ibid.: 68]. In theory, therefore, a fair degree of decentralisation had now been obtained. In reality however, no significant shift of resources from the government to the local level occurred. Moreover,

> governors now have in their regions all the authorities that previously belonged to the various ministers (including the important powers of the Minister of Finance) as well as many of what used to be the authorities of the Minister of Local Government [ibid.: 69].

The system was supervised by a Governors' Council, which was headed by the Prime Minister and included in its membership the Minister of Local Government. The Council coordinated with the Ministry of Planning and, depending on the case, other ministries.

> Politically speaking, what has happened is that — in the name of decentralisation — governors (and to a lesser extent other leading officials) have been given quite extensive authorities while the local elected councils have been deprived of some of their previously–held rights (...) Members are no longer able to "question", investigate or to call to account ... the governor or the heads of public departments and corporations within the governorate, but can only "ask", enquire or seek information ... On the other hand, the governor has the right to "veto"the resolutions of the popular councils if he thinks they are not in agreement with the law [ibid.: 70–71].

Although 'one cannot rule out the possibility that [these changes]... may enhance certain aspects of rural development', Ayubi concludes that 'the main objectives were security– related' : the government, in the wake of the 1977 riots, 'has installed new ways and means of tightening its grip over the localities while promising them a measure of increased development' [ibid.: 72–73].

Syria's 1971 law on Local Government provides for two levels of local administration: (1) that of the governorates and (2) the lower administrative levels of city, township, rural unit, and village [see Akash, 1983]. Local councils are elected for four years. They each have an Executive Office. At governorate level the leading official is of course the governor, and it is also he who proposes the candidate to be 'elected' by the city council members as head of their Executive Office. The council president then appoints the members of his Office after they have been 'proposed' by the governor. Even though the local councils are said to have control of (a) security, (b) social and economic activities and administration of public services, and (c) the management of the local bureaucracy, it is clear that real control remains firmly in the hands of central government and its representatives. In fact, the councils have no say over matters of economy, education, industry, finance, electricity, oil, information, and defence. All that remains the exclusive domain of the central ministries [ibid.: 208]. The councils can only 'supervise' and carry out the plans of higher authorities; their power to initiate short– or long–term plans of their own is severely circumscribed. The Planning Directorates at governorate level are directly linked to the SPC and co–operate closely with the representatives of central government. There has, however, been conflict between the governorate planning directors and the central planning directors of SPC. Their respective responsibilities are not clearly delineated. To try to smooth these differences over, all governorate planning directors gather twice a month in Damascus with their counterparts at the SPC central office.

As mentioned earlier, in *Jordan* development efforts on the local level fall under the only vaguely delineated authorities of (1) local government, (2) the Regional Planning Department in the Ministry of Planning, and (3) the Directorate for Regional Planning, which comes under the umbrella of the Ministry of Municipal and Rural Affairs and Environment. Plans and projects framed at the governorate level are taken into account during plan preparation. An interesting example of local autonomy in development affairs is the Aqaba Region Authority, established in 1984 [*FT*, 24–5–85]. It is semi–autonomous and answers directly to the Prime Minister. The intention is that Aqaba, Jordan's only seaport, should become the country's major growth pole outside Amman. The Authority is self–financing. It does not itself invest public funds, but draws up its own regional plan which is then submitted to the government. It is not clear at the time of writing whether or not the intention to establish other such authorities will be followed up.

In *Ethiopia,* the smallest administrative unit is the peasant asssociation. The local people ('peasants') elect the membership of their councils, and the latter control the allocation of land. At this lowest level, as well as higher up (regional, etc.), projects can be initiated, according to the size and importance of the project. Major investments require higher or central agreement, but even peasant associations can suggest big projects. It is still too early to assess the overall success of this principle. Large parts of the rural population have not yet been integrated into the system. It is clear, however, that a very high degree of central control is maintained. The reorganisation of the planning offices and development councils at the regional, provincial, *awraja* and *woreda* levels is still proceeding in accordance with the new administrative structures introduced in 1984. Whether this reorganisation will make possible an upward flow similar in importance to the downward flow, remains unclear — but it seems improbable.

Lastly, *Sudan's* experience in decentralisation reveals the significance of the interaction between political and economic environment. It has long seemed clear to most observers that any solution to Sudan's political problems would have to include a fair degree of regional autonomy (particularly as regards the non-Muslim south). Measures to this effect were carried through, and comparative stability — the first necessity for any development effort — was achieved (see also Asam, 1986). Increasing economic difficulties, however, resulted in a severe 'cash-famine', and local government, left without adequate funds to carry out its functions, gradually lost both its developmental capacities and its legitimacy. In that sense, as Niblock [1985: 18] puts it, the 'problems faced by the Sudanese economy led directly to political disintegration'. This points to the futility of decentralisation measures if the resources for running those local administrations are not (made) available and cannot be locally extracted.

— — —

What emerges from the above is that, some partial exceptions notwithstanding, the flow of decision-making remains generally top-downwards. Middle Easterners mostly view their bureaucracies in a rather negative light, as somewhat ineffective instruments, whose primary object is to control them [Palmer & Nakib, 1981: 75-77]. This inevitably results in the administration having reduced developmental impact, partly due to the lack of co-operation on the population's part. The only way to reverse this situation is to bring about a much higher level of political participation. In that sense, the lack of participation remains (especially in the poorer Middle Eastern countries) a great impediment to effective development administration, and thus to development. This should not, however, be construed as an argument for the immediate introduction of Western-style parliamentary democracy, both because only gradual change can avoid chaos (and worse), and because different systems may well be better suited to the situation of some countries.

— — —

Conclusion

The practical effects which flow from the characteristics covered in this chapter have already been made clear. Inconsistent policies; the predominance of the legitimacy/ survival imperative; a growing trend towards *infitah* (excepting Ethiopia and to a lesser extent the PDRY); and generally the ineffectiveness of development administrations. To recapitulate, both international and domestic factors give rise to these characteristics. The international factors comprise (a) dependence on the developed economies and (for oil–poor countries) on the capital–surplus oil–exporting countries; and (b) the inherent outward rather than inward orientation of administrations in a 'charity economy' context. The domestic factors are (a) political underdevelopment; and (b) the fact that the physical and socio–economic framework is not 'ready', either for the technical tasks at hand, or for the socio–political implications of consistently planned change.

In the light of what has emerged so far, two major questions arise. The first is whether 'modern development' values, as adopted in the countries of the Middle East (and the rest of the Third World) are not themselves at fault. They reflect, it can be said, a basically Western, industrial value system, be it in its 'capitalist', 'socialist' or mixed embodiments. It would, however, be utopian to advocate a total rejection of that value system, both for international economic and political reasons, and because of the partial assimilation of many of those values by the majority of the politically articulate population. Moreover, no credible alternative 'autochthonous' model has yet been worked out in the Middle East – despite attempts in that direction in Iran. This leads on to the second question. Rather than seeking to adapt the environment to Western administrative principles (as most writers on public administration in the Middle East seem to want to do), would it not be potentially much more rewarding to start from the given socio–cultural situation and to use that as the basis on which to develop a better-adapted administration ? If this led to less alienation on the part of the societies which the bureaucracy is supposed to serve, a major improvement would have been achieved. Ayubi [1986] terms this the 'ecological–contingency approach'. The approach does not imply leaving everything as it is. It advocates, rather, learning from such successes as have been reached, and building on these [Paul, 1982; Ayubi, 1986: 214–217], instead of merely focussing on obstacles to a Western Weberian system.

Cases of managerial, organizational and developmental
sucess do occur in the Arab World, and the beginning of
wisdom should partly revolve around a stock-taking of
such cases. In Egypt, the same bureaucracy that failed in
promoting the agrarian reform ... succeeded in managing
the Suez Canal and in building the Aswan High Dam...
The same Egyptian people ... managed — in a society
notorious for its inability to keep a secret — to keep the
[1973] war as a total surprise... In Algeria and Iraq, the
bureaucracy seems to be managing the oil industry quite
effectively. The Lebanese banking system has actually
been expanding and improving during the difficult years
[of fighting]. [Ayubi, 1986: 214–215]

To the best of this author's knowledge, very little has so far been
done in active pursuit of this approach, apart from recommending
it and citing some examples (Al-Buraey's [1986] work is a heart-
ening exception). The task of actually drawing practical lessons
from the successes and failures, and on that basis recommending
practical measures to improve Middle Eastern bureaucracies, also
falls outside the scope of this study. Some elements relevant to
such an undertaking, however, emerged from the cases studied.

4 AID TO MIDDLE EASTERN COUNTRIES

Aid Reliance

Five Middle Eastern states are aid–givers, rather than recipients. These are Saudi Arabia, Kuwait, The UAE, Qatar and Libya. Bahrain and Oman, despite being significant oil–producers, have not ceased to be recipients of concessional assistance. The five 'non–recipients' have in the past sometimes been major recipients of mainly Arab assistance — e.g. Egyptian aid to Kuwait and the small Gulf countries; Kuwaiti aid to the other Gulf emirates; Qatari and Abu Dhabi's aid to the poorer emirates. But this, at least in its concessional form, belongs to the past and will not be treated further in the present study. Today, these countries buy the technical asistance and teachers they need: either commercially, from foreign consultants, and by paying good salaries to Egyptians, Jordanians and others to come and teach; or from the multilateral technical assistance agencies such as UNDP. They put at least as much money into the latter organisations as they obtain from them.

Middle Eastern aid recipients, as will already have become apparent, vary considerably in economic structure, wealth, and political posture. This naturally has implications for the type and scale of foreign aid which they require or receive. The Arab–Israeli dispute, moreover, imposes on some states an additional heavy burden of military expenditure. Only Sudan, Djibouti, Ethiopia and the Yemens suffer from the level of underdevelopment which afflicts most African countries, but others may require a similar or greater amount of external funding for reasons of defence spending. Egypt fits into the latter bracket. Equally dependent on foreign cash injections are Jordan and Syria, although their economies generate a much higher per capita income. In their case also, the main drain on reserves is due to defence expenditure related to a large extent with their position as frontline states in the struggle with Israel. Jordan, for instance, although not needing much in the way of technical assistance from the West, and despite

Table 4.1
Principal Aid–reliant Middle Eastern Countries:
average net ODA as % of GNP, 1970–71; 1982–83
(world rank in brackets); 1984[a]

Country	1970–71	1982–83		1984[c]
Jordan	12.7	20.1	(8)	18.5
Djibouti	32.6	18.6	(9)	24.3
PDRY	...	12.3	(21)[b]	14.1[d]
Sudan	0.4	10.8	(26)	7.7
Yemen	6.5	9.2	(29)	8.8
Ethiopia	2.4	5.9	(45)	11.1[e]
Syria	0.8	5.9	(46)	5.4
Egypt	1.9	4.8	...	5.5
Morocco	2.6	4.1	...	2.9
Bahrain	...	...	...	4.8

Notes: a. Only data for ODA from DAC, OPEC and multilaterals, with the exception of the figures for the PDRY and Ethiopia in 1984, which include CMEA–aid (the two countries are the main recipients of CMEA–aid in the Middle East). b. The PDRY's actual aid–reliance is much higher. This figure does not include CMEA assistance. Compare 1984. c. Calculated on the basis of OECD figures [OECD, 1985; 1986]. d. Assuming that total ODA to the PDRY in 1984 amounted to $ 166 million [Ismael & Ismael, 1986]. e. Including $ 155 million in CMEA–aid. *Sources:* see section on aid–flows to PDRY; OECD, 1985, 1986.

possessing a comparatively sound economy, is in fact the most aid–reliant country in the region — judging by the proportion of aid to GNP (see Table 4.1). In 1982–83 aid constituted over 20 per cent of GNP (which made it the eighth most aid–reliant country in the world). In absolute terms, Egypt is the main recipient of ODA in the Middle East (see Table 4.2), followed by Syria, Sudan and Jordan. Djibouti's high degree of dependence on aid is explained not only by its LLDC status and great need, but equally if not more so by strategic considerations. Oman's continued acquisition of aid, in the first place from the Gulf Arabs but also some from the USA, is also thanks to the strategic and political considerations of donors. Political and economic coordination in the framework of the Gulf Cooperation Council (GCC) is also of significance to Oman's position as an aid–recipient, as is also the case for the (mainly Saudi) aid to tiny Bahrain. Some countries have, in keeping with their political allegiances, openly opted for one 'camp' of donors: Jordan quite firmly chose the West; Bahrain directed itself towards Saudi Arabia; Djibouti stuck to the French connection; and the PDRY looked to the USSR (although gradually succumbing to the lure of Gulf money). Ethiopia, although not officially preferring any one donor over another, has by virtue of its political stance and the image it projected in effect forfeited its chances of obtaining substantial aid (other than famine relief) from certain Western quarters.

Donor Influence

It is evident that the use which recipient countries make of donor-provided resources is greatly influenced by the donors. Four main factors seem to play a role in this phenomenon.

(1) Where aid constitutes an essential element in covering development expenditure, government proposals to potential donors for the financing of certain projects, whether or not embedded in a 'Plan', are often shaped in accordance with what donors are prepared to give.

(2) Since there is usually a lack of indigenous expertise, the drawing up of priority lists and project definition often fall to foreign experts (who more often than not have ties with a donor country) or a multilateral assistance agency.

(3) Both during plan and project preparation, and during implementation, bureaucrats and decision–makers tend to be 'accessible' to foreign donors and/or investors for persuasion — genuine or less so — and, indeed, corruption.

(4) As indicated earlier, some countries consciously open the way for certain donors and thus, concomitantly, for their preferences.

The relevance of the above factors varies from country to country. The following combinations would appear to apply to the five most donor–influenced Middle Eastern countries:

– Egypt	(1)(2)(3)(4)
– Sudan under Nimeiri	(1)(2)(3)(4)
– after Nimeiri	(1)(2)(4), plus the local chaos
– Djibouti	(1)(2)(4)
– Yemen AR	(1)(2)
– Jordan	(4)

The above list merely indicates the major factors and is by no means exclusive.

In four countries donor influence is considerably less. They are Ethiopia, the PDRY, Oman and Syria. In the first two instances, economic aid from the non-communist world is rather

Table 4.2
**Total Net Disbursements of ODA to Selected Arab
Countries, (exc. CMEA), as % of GNP and
as % of total ODA**

	% of total ODA				% of GNP			
	60–61	70–71	82–83	84–85	60–61	70–71	78–79	83–84
Egypt	3.7	2.3	5.5	6.5	4.5	1.9	10.7	4.7
Syria	0.4	0.3	3.7	2.8	1.8	0.8	12.1	5.0
Sudan	0.5	0.1	3.3	3.2	1.8	0.4	6.9	9.8
Jordan	2.3	1.0	3.1	2.3	27.6	12.7	37.6	17.8
Morocco	2.1	1.7	2.2	2.2	4.2	2.6	3.0	2.6
Tunisia	1.8	1.7	0.8	0.6	8.5	7.1	3.9	2.4
Algeria	9.9	1.9	0.6	...	15.1	2.4	...	...

Source: OECD, 1985, 1986

Table 4.3
**Major Arab Recipients of Bilateral ODA from
DAC countries, in % of total DAC–ODA**

1960–61		1970–71		1980–81		1983–84	
Algeria	7.4	Algeria	1.4	Egypt	4.2	Egypt	5.1
Egypt	2.3	Morocco	1.4	Sudan	1.2	Sudan	1.3
Morocco	1.6	Tunisia	1.3	Morocco	0.8	Morocco	0.8
Tunisia	1.3	Egypt	0.8	Tunisia	0.7		
Jordan	1.3						
Libya	0.7						

Source: OECD, 1985, 1986

limited, and politico–economic orientations are compatible anyway with those of the main backer, the USSR. In the case of Syria,
its main dependence is not on Western investment, but on economically untied Arab aid and Soviet military assistance. Oman
is special in that it has of its own will, at least partially aligned
its economic development with the development aims of the GCC
region to which it belongs.

In the case of totally dependent and 'penetrated' countries
like Egypt and Sudan, the process seems irreversible. In Egypt
many are dissatisfied with USAID and the IMF, and there are
persistent 'irritants' in relations between the latter organisations
and the Egyptian government. Yet for the government to reject
the strongly–worded advice tendered by these organisations ap-

pears scarcely feasible. While it may be interesting to note the Sudanese government's break with the IMF in early 1986, caused by domestic political disaffection with the policies which that institution had presided over in the country, there seems to be no way for Sudan to survive financially without renewed IMF and (now also partially frozen) Western aid. After the resignation of the Minister of Finance and Economic Planning (who had reached agreement with the IMF) in December 1985 and the subsequent rejection of the IMF package by the government, there seemed to be the prospect of new policies being developed. The policies announced and taken by the new Minister, however, resembled in almost everything but name the measures for which the IMF had asked. Not surprisingly, there was speculation about a secret deal with the IMF [*The Middle East*, April 1986].

Donors' Motives

The major motives of US aid to the Middle East are clearly (1) those of a political nature and (2) those related to domestic economic concerns. The 'Food for Peace' programme (PL 480) says so in its name, but the same points apply to most American assistance except emergency famine relief. Weinbaum [1982: 118] points out that the 'legislative language of PL 480 left no doubt that the program was intended to cater to specific U.S. domestic interests and to further broad foreign policy objectives'. The domestic economic interests — higher market prices and quasi-guaranteed sales for US farmers; reduced storage costs for the US government; penetration of US firms into local markets — are obvious and have been attested to by Weinbaum [ibid.: 118–121] and others. This is reinforced by explicit conditions attached to a large share of assistance, for instance the obligation on countries receiving PL 480 aid, to also buy a considerable proportion of their food imports from the US on commercial terms [cf. ibid. and Abdel–Khalek, 1984]. Political considerations, however, remain paramount. The twin aims of (1) supporting and keeping in power of 'moderate' and 'friendly' regimes, and (2) encouraging regimes to start or continue aligning their foreign policy with US needs and wishes, have been evident in the allocation of aid to Morocco, Tunisia, Sudan, Jordan, Oman and Egypt. The case of Egypt — the US's main aid recipient — constitutes the best example. Aid was resumed after Sadat had turned away from the USSR, and initiated the Open Door Policy. In the period leading up to the Camp David agreements and until the present, US aid

was a major instrument in making Egypt stick to its American–
allied course. Weinbaum [1982: 121–128] presents extensive evidence to this effect, and he illustrates parallel situations for other
Middle Eastern recipients of US aid. The USAID Director in
Egypt from 1982 to 1984, Michael Stone, has been quite specific
about the political dimensions of US aid:

> The purpose of of the United States assistance program
> in Egypt is clear. We believe that a stronger Egypt is
> better able to do two things. One, to provide effective
> leadership in the peace process in the Middle East, and
> two, is better able to be a strong friend of its allies *(sic)*
> [Stone, 1984: 35].

His adding that those allies could be the US or other Arab or
European or Eastern nations carries little weight — at least not
when those nations might be pro–Soviet. The least one can say,
is that

> it may be that one major source of USAID's problems
> lies in the fact that it must follow both a geopolitical and
> a developmental agenda. These two agendas sometimes
> push the organisation in different directions [Sullivan,
> 1984: 5].

For one thing, 'development, which is by definition a long–term
activity, may be less important than a short–term perspective
which concentrates on solving immediate problems' [ibid.] and,
one might add, on high–visibility projects to boost legitimacy.

For West European donors, three kinds of factors seem to
be important: economic, political and historical. Needless to say,
they interlink and overlap. In nearly all of the European donors'
assistance, though less so in the cases of the Scandinavian countries, commercial considerations play a major role. Better access
is sought for national firms to Middle Eastern markets; and the
donors in many ways try to create a situation where the recipient
acquires a degree of dependency on the commodities provided.
France is probably the best example. In food assistance, domestic
economic considerations similar to those in the US have been important. However, a considerable share of assistance is a dubious
investment on commercial terms. Future hopes, of course, play a
role, but assistance also fits within the political posture of the Europeans towards the Middle East. The attitude of the countries
of Western Europe has become decidedly more 'pro–Arab' over
the last 15 years. The main rationale for this political stance, in
this author's view has been the safeguarding of Europe's future oil

Table 4.4
US Government Economic Assistance to Selected Middle Eastern Countries, 1982 — 1985, in US $ millions

Country	1982	1983	1984	1985
Egypt	936	1,019	1,139	995
Jordan	104	21	22	22
Morocco	40	55	68	91
Oman	1	15	15	20
Sudan	162	...	...	...
Syria	27	—	—	—
Tunisia	45	22	21	12
Yemen	—	30	33	41[a]

Notes: 1982: calendar year
1983 — 1985: financial year
1984: estimated
1985: proposed
(a) actual figure as reported in *MEED* , 19–4–86.

Other sources:
– US Department of Treasury; US Department of Commerce, *The 1984 Annual Report of the Chairman of the Development Coordination Committee.*
– USAID, Cairo.

supply from the region, through acquiring a foothold and creating good–will. In that sense, the attitude is an extension of and parallel to the Euro–Arab Dialogue. The historical factor is of course the colonial link, observable mainly in France's relations with the Maghreb. In the case of Djibouti, however, the one preponderant motive is of a strategic nature.

For the Arab donors, politics and ideology have mingled with the economics. Economic considerations of self–reliance were set in a framework of pan–Arabism in the case of the massive assistance plans for the Sudan, which was to become the Arab world's 'breadbasket'. The Sudanese regime was, however, also amenable to financial inducements for it to remain on its 'moderate' course. On the donors' part, the hope of maintaining domestic stability in Sudan by infusions of money and thus safeguarding the regime, was a powerful spur. Certainly Arab aid, especially when disbursed through bi- or multi–lateral development–oriented agencies, has a respectable record as far as its contribution to development is concerned. To an extent, indeed, South–South cooperation has been realised in the Middle East, particularly regarding

Table 4.5 US Assistance to Middle Eastern Countries, 1987-88

	Final allocations for fiscal 1987							Requested allocations for fiscal 1988		
	FMS	MAP	IMET	ESF	DA	PL480	Total	Military	Economic	Total
Afghanistan[1]	–	–	–	12,152	17,848	–	30,000	–	30,000	30,000
Algeria	–	–	100	–	–	–	100	100	–	100
Cyprus	–	–	–	15,000	–	–	15,000	–	10,000	10,000
Djibouti	–	1,000	135	1,900	–	–	3,035	2,135	3,000	5,135
Egypt	1,300,000	–	1,750	815,000	–	189,201	2,305,951	1,301,750	997,454	2,299,204
Ethiopia	–	–	–	–	–	4,311	4,311	–	3,389	3,389
Israel	1,800,000	–	–	1,200,000	–	–	3,000,000	1,800,000	1,200,000	3,000,000
Jordan	–	39,941[3]	1,800	14,000	–	–	55,741	53,800	18,000	71,800
Lebanon	–	–	475	500	–	–	975	475	300	775
Mauritania	–	370[3]	75	–	2,000	3,426	5,871	75	8,887	8,962
Morocco	2,000	32,000	1,525	10,000	16,370	44,427	106,322	51,450	79,664	131,114
Oman	–	–	150	15,000	–	–	15,150	5,300	20,000	25,300
Somalia	–	7,500	1,250	17,500	13,228	10,000	49,478	23,250	44,707	67,957
Sudan	–	5,000	1,000	–	22,472	40,587	69,059	11,000	78,739	89,739
Tunisia	–	32,500	1,525	16,203	–	–	50,228	41,450	25,000	66,450
Turkey	177,941	312,059[3]	3,300	100,000	–	–	593,300	788,500	126,400	914,900
Yemen (Sanaa)	–	1,000	1,150	–	22,000	5,000	29,150	4,100	27,000	31,100
West Bank/Gaza	–	–	–	8,500	–	1,603	10,103	–	1,547	1,547[5]
Other Middle East[2]	–	–	–	5,906	–	–	5,906	–	42,550	42,550
Middle East total	3,279,941	431,370	14,235	2,231,661	93,918	298,555	6,349,680	4,093,385	2,706,637	6,800,022
World total	4,040,441	853,750	55,044	3,550,000	1,493,991	1,462,993	12,083,311[4]	5,863,101	9,346,174	15,209,275

Other relevant funding
Middle East peace-keeping operations
Multinational Force & Observers (Sinai) – $24,377,000
UN Forces in Cyprus – $7,312,000
Anti-terrorism – $9,840,000

Other relevant funding
International peace-keeping
operations – $46,311,000
Anti-terrorism – $9,840,000

Notes
[1] Humanitarian assistance
[2] $5 million for Regional Co-operation in Middle East (Egyptian-Israeli joint projects) and $906,000 for project development and support
[3] Aid exceeds levels presented to congress
[4] Includes $627.1 million unspecified economic assistance
[5] Some of the $42.6 million in regional funds is expected to be allocated to the West Bank and Gaza Strip

FMS foreign military sales (concessionary or, for Egypt/Israel, payment forgiven); MAP military assistance programme; IMET international military education and training; ESF economic support fund; DA development assistance; PL480 food and commodity assistance

Source: MEED

Arab Solidarity. In fact, assistance from funds such as the Kuwait Fund for Arab Economic Development has often gone to countries whose policies are not in unison with those of the donor country. Since the major share in inter–Arab development assistance is, however, direct government–to–government (often undocumented) aid, it is clear that directly political considerations have played and continue to play an important role. The billions of assistance to Egypt up to 1978 were part of an effort to create in that country a growth pole for Arab strength, and more specifically an Arab arms industry. The aid was further justified on the grounds of Egypt's position as a confrontation state. When Sadat signed the Camp David agreements, this aid was suspended. Syria and Jordan, the major recipients of Arab financial aid since then (not including the mainly Saudi and Kuwaiti war aid to Iraq since 1980 — amounting to some $ 40 billion up to the end of 1985 [Nonneman, 1986: 104]) retained their frontline status and were treated accordingly. Clear political motives are also apparent in Saudi Arabia's assistance to the PDRY, by which the Kingdom has sought to loosen that country's ties with the USSR; and in its massive financial support of the Yemen AR government and economy, in addition to its subsidies to Northern Yemeni tribes. It is significant that Yemen is represented by its Foreign Minister in the Saudi–Yemeni Coordination Council, which is concerned with Saudi assistance to Yemen [Hofmann, 1984: 44]. Finally, Gulf assistance to Bahrain and Oman is to a very large extent motivated by political and strategic considerations. This is scarcely surprising, given the role which political factors played in creating the GCC. Further considerations on the motivations of Arab aid are put forward in Chapter 6.

Japan's aid policy in the Middle East seems to be determined by (1) short– and long–term commercial aims, and (2) the need to safeguard its oil supplies, as was argued for the case of Europe.

Weinbaum [1982: 130–131] presents an overview and interpretation of Soviet and East Bloc aid to the Middle East, particularly in agriculture. The aims of this group of donors appear to be (1) acquiring political support in the region and safeguarding (or possibly expanding) military facilities; (2) forging strong economic contacts with the recipient countries, involving long–term supply contracts for raw materials. Soviet and East Bloc assistance is usually embedded within a general framework of co–operation.

Chinese assistance to the Middle East, though much lower than that of other main donor groups, 'has been in direct competition with that of the Soviet Union and a prime instrument of Peking's foreign policy' [see evidence in ibid.: 131–132].

— — —

Aid Flows: Country Data

Algeria

Algeria has received rather limited concessional assistance. During the 1970s it borrowed heavily on the international market, and again so from 1983, but since the late 1970s repayments have outweighed new borrowing [MENA 86: 283]. The country has become very much less dependent on aid, thanks to its oil revenues. It is worth noting, however, that Algeria's total debt had reached over $ 17,000 million by the end of 1985 [*MEED*, 20-12-86: 34]. In 1960–61 (see Table 4.2) it relied on ODA to the tune of some 15 per cent of its GNP; in 1982–83 the equivalent figure stood at only 0.3 per cent. The initial assistance came mainly from France, but up to the end of 1986 over $ 1 billion in ODA had come from the Arab national and regional development institutions, mainly from the Islamic Development Bank and from the Arab Fund for Economic and Social Development (AFESD) [AFESD, 1987b]. French average annual ODA to Algeria in 1983–84 (gross) amounted to $ 47 million; ODA from Austria to $ 42 million [OECD, 1986]. In 1987 the World Bank came to Algeria's assistance, agreeing to provide three loans, for a total of $ 464 million, to finance water supply, irrigation and road maintenance work [*MEED,* 18-4-87].

Bahrain

Due to relatively small and falling oil revenues, Bahrain is quite dependent on Arab (mainly Saudi) assistance, both in the form of grants and loans, and as direct investment. In 1983 and 1984 the island nation received GCC grants of c. $ 150 million per year [MENA 85: 276]. The economically important causeway connecting Bahrain with Saudi Arabia, which opened in 1986, was paid for in full by the Saudi government. Total gross disbursements of Arab/OPEC aid to the country is listed by the OECD at $ 155 million in 1983, and 208 million in 1984 [OECD,1985].

Djibouti

Independent only since 1977, Djibouti is very aid–reliant (Table 4.1). In 1970–71, ODA represented 32.6 per cent of its GNP. Although the equivalent had fallen to 18.6 per cent in 1982–83, Djibouti was still the second most aid–reliant country in the Middle East (after Jordan), ranking 9th in the world. In 1984, moreover, the proportion rose again to over 24 per cent. The data in Table 4.6 must be viewed with care, because although they give a good general picture, they are not complete. Thus French ODA is really much higher. According to the Mission Française de Coopération in Djibouti, French civil ODA has amounted to some $ 65 million each year since independence, although OECD [1985] data indicate a somewhat lower annual average of c. $ 40 million for 1982–84. In per capita terms, the country is the prime recipient of French aid. Strategic considerations, together with Islam in the case of the Saudis, are the main rationale behind French and Saudi aid. In 1986 Djibouti was facing a deepening balance of payments deficit and an escalating debt service, while it appeared less certain than before that Arab donors would fill most of the gap. Still, the Kuwaiti, Saudi and Abu Dhabi Funds are to provide funds for the Djibouti Port Development Programme and the upgrading of Ambouli Airport in 1987, both vital elements in the country's hopes of economic development.

Table 4.6
ODA to Djibouti, 1984, according to
UNDP–gathered data ($ mn)

Country	Technical Assistance	Capital Financial Ass.	TOTAL
France	18.9	8.5	27.4
Saudi Arabia	—	75.0	75.0
USA	2.8	5.5	8.3
Italy	—	8.5	8.5
Kuwait	—	6.8	6.8
Libya	—	4.1	4.1
FRG	0.3	1.0	1.3
Japan	—	1.3	1.3
Egypt	0.9	—	0.9
Canada	0.4	—	0.4

Source: UNDP, Djibouti

Egypt
Egypt, on the evidence of figures for 1982–1985, has been the largest recipient of OECD bilateral assistance in the 1980s, as well as of overall ODA (ahead of Israel and India) (see Table 4.3). Upto 1978, Arab countries were important donors. Arab bilateral aid in 1975 amounted to more than US $ 2 billion, in 1976 to over

Table 4.7
Egypt's Foreign Sources of Funds,
1981–1984 (million current $)

	1981/82	1982/83	1983/84	1984/85[a]
Direct investment	250	247	250	275
Internat. assist.[b]	1,489	1,787	1,825	1,900
US	839	1,137	1,125	1,200
Other bilat.	400	350	400	400
Multilat.	250	300	300	300
Suppliers'credits	842	886	950	900
Banks (net pos.)	305	—	−100	−100
Errors & omissions	114	545	—	—

Notes: a. projected b. excluding US military assistance *Source:* American Embassy Cairo, 1985

Table 4.8
US Economic Assistance to Egypt,
1974 — 1987 (million current $)

financial yr	1974–1983 obligated	expended	1983 exp.	1984 obl.	1985 prop.	1987 obl.
ESF	6,454.5	3,982.9	867.4	868.0	750.0	815.0
CIP	2,823.9	2,211.3	302.1	...	...	...
Projects	3,629.7	1,771.5	565.3	...	...	...
PL–480	2,064.8	2,008.1	204.9	269.3	243.3	189.2
TOTAL	8,518.4	5,991.0	1,072.3	1,139.0	995.0	1,004.2

Notes: ESF: Economic Support Fund
        CIP: Commodity Import Programme
Sources: USAID Cairo, s.d.; US Department of Treasury,
        Department of Commerce.

$ 1 billion, and in 1977 to more than $ 1.7 billion [MENA 85: 323]. This aid was cut off after the Camp David agreements, and the US (which had already been giving Egypt some $ 1 billion annually since 1976) became Egypt's one major donor (see Tables 4.7, 4.8). In addition to this, Egypt has since 1981 received annual grants of c. $ 1.3 billion in military assistance from the US [Butter, 1987: 3]. In 1985 an agreement was reached for an extra $ 500 million over two years, but this has not been repeated. However, in order to avert Egypt's defaulting on its debts to the US, most of the capital assistance budget has been turned into cash transfers. This means that in fact, for a while at least, new US 'economic' aid to Egypt goes straight into repayment of (mainly military) debt. There are, however, sufficient previously committed USAID funds which are still to be used [ibid.: 6]. Far behind as bilateral donors come Japan, averaging some $ 200 million a year in the 1980s, West Germany and France, averaging some $ 150 million (Table 4.9). Other important donors are the EEC, which signed a financial protocol with Egypt for the period 1977–81 (170 million ECU) and again for 1982–1986 (276 million ECU)[*JOCE,* 27–9–78; 29–11–82]; and the World Bank, which has the largest share of multilateral aid (some $ 270 million in 1978, for instance). It is worth noting, also, that after arduous negotiations with the IMF Egypt obtained in May 1987 what has been termed 'the softest deal in the history of the IMF'— no doubt after heavy American pressure to that end.

Table 4.9
Main Bilateral Donors to Egypt, 1980 — 1984 ($ mn)

	1980	1981	1984
USA	1,100	1,000	1,139
Japan	181	221	204
FRG	149	136	189
France	190	176	115

Source: diplomatic sources in Cairo.

Note: the figures for the three West European countries should be seen as indicative rather than accurate data; in different sources different figures
will be found, but the general picture remains correct.

Ethiopia
Ethiopian officials never tire of pointing out that theirs is the country receiving the least ODA per capita among LLDCs. Mainly
because of Ethiopia's image abroad, Ethiopia does indeed obtain
far less assistance than its great needs would justify. In addition

to the civil war, one of the main obstacles to successful development policies today is precisely that lack of foreign financing. In absolute terms, most ODA comes from the multilateral organisations, in which the major input is Western. Bilateral aid comes predominantly from the East Bloc CMEA (Committee for Mutual Economic Assistance). ODA to Ethiopia mainly takes the form of technical assistance, contrary to the case of most other recipients. CMEA aid in 1983 and 1984 was put at the equivalent of $ 159 million and $ 155 million respectively [OECD, 1985: 116], mainly from the USSR. This has brought Ethiopia's aid–reliance figure for 1984 to over 11 per cent of GNP. Since 1982, the Soviets have supplied oil to Ethiopia on credit terms, for the equivalent of c. $ 30 million a year. Strategic considerations have made the country by far the largest recipient of Soviet and Eastern Bloc aid in Africa [ibid.: 117]. The World Bank has provided loans of $ 40 million in both 1983 and 1984. World Bank lending to Ethiopia is forecast to reach between $ 400 and $ 500 million by 1988. By 1984, some $ 150–200 million had been acquired from the IDA [*MEED*, 15–6–84; 20–12–86: 42]. The IDA has since further expanded its assistance, focussing on the agricultural sector and often in coordination with the EEC. In 1986 the IDA approved a $ 62 million loan for an electrification programme [*MEED*, 20–12–86:42]. UNDP also plays an important role. ODA from the EEC (as opposed to its individual member states) for 1983–1984 is put at 52 million the OECD [1985]. This made Ethiopia the second largest recipient of aid from the EEC. Under Lomé III, the EEC has allocated a further ECU 220 million ($ 228 million) to Ethiopia. Development asistance from the US is not expected to resume during the 1980s (barring a change in Ethiopia's political posture). Nevertheless, the US has been the country's largest relief donor, with supplies amounting to c. $ 300 million in 1985. As for other bilateral donors: in 1983–84 Italy provided an annual average of $ 31 million in ODA, Canada $ 18.5 million and Sweden $ 16.5 million. Italy has so far been the only Western bilateral donor offering assistance for large industrial schemes.

Jordan

Jordan in 1982–83 was the most aid–reliant country in the region and ranked as eighth worldwide, with an ODA equivalent to 20.1 per cent of its GNP (Table 4.1). This, as was pointed out before, is mainly due to the politico–military situation in the area. Before 1967 capital imports and subventions came mainly from the USA and the UK; since then, Arab assistance has acquired an increasingly important role. In 1978, the US was still the major single donor, providing $ 80 million out of the c. $ 500 million which the country received that year. This was also the year of the Baghdad Summit, at which Arab countries (read: the rich oil producers) decided to support Jordan, Syria and the PLO with large financial injections. Jordan was to receive the equivalent of $ 1,250 million annually. In fact, less than half the agreed amount had been disbursed by 1983, but Jordan in any case had not budgeted for the total to be received (see Table 4.10). Receipts of budget support assistance were halved in 1984, falling to c. $ 276 million; both Qatar and the UAE, coming under financial pressure themselves, stopped payments, and Kuwait reduced its grant by 40 per cent [MENA 86: 501]. Saudi Arabia was thus the only one of the initial seven Baghdad Summit–donors to still honour its pledge. In 1985 budget support rose again by over 70 per cent, however. This was largely due to a $ 156 million grant from Oman in the early summer [MEED 21–12–85]. Budget support remained above the $ 400 million mark in 1986. Arab aid has also included more directly development–oriented assistance (see Table 4.11). Although initially small in comparison with the budget support figures, the total value of development loans has caught up with that of budget support since 1984. Saudi Arabia, Kuwait and the US appear to have been the major bilateral donors of development loans to Jordan. Total Arab aid in 1983 was estimated by OECD [1985: 114] at $ 703 million. For 1984, the figure dropped to $ 613 million, before picking up again the following year. Jordan has been the largest recipient of assistance from the Arab national and regional development institutions, having been given some $ 1.6 billion up to the end of 1986 [AFESD, 1987b].

The US stopped its budget assistance in 1981, because of what the Americans considered King Hussein's unco–operative stance in the peace process (Camp David)[MENA 86: 501]. Other American aid, however, was still forthcoming. The USAID figures in Table 4.11 do not reflect the total US (non–military) contribution, which amounted to $ 104 milion in calendar year 1982; $ 21 million in financial year 1983; an estimated $ 22 million in FY 1984; and the same amount for FY 1985 [US Government figures]. This level was maintained through 1987, dropping to $ 18 million in 1988. From 1987 these amounts are likely to have been supplemented by 'extra economic assistance', as provided for in the US's 'supplementary budget legislation' of autumn 1985.

Table 4.10
Sources of Jordanian Central Government Funds in Current Prices (\$ mn)^a during the 1976–80 and 1981–85 Development Plans

	1.Budget Support	2.Surplus in Current Account (incl. 1)	3.Foreign Loans & T.A	4.Total Revenues
1976 actual	178.8	32.7	88.6	206.8
1977 actual	330.0	186.3	181.4	384.2
1978 actual	220.6	73.4	305.4	401.2
1979 actual	574.8	211.7	224.1	523.8
1980 estim.	580.2	307.0	202.0	517.9
Total 76–80	1,884.3	745.7	1,001.4	2,033.9
1981 budget	658.8	380.7	288.9	742.5
1982 estim.	658.8	429.3	407.7	926.1
1983 estim.	658.8	464.4	580.5	1,147.5
1984 estim.	658.8	548.1	791.1	1,420.2
1985 estim.	658.8	664.2	1,069.2	1,792.8
Total 81–85	3,294.0	2,486.7	3,137.4	6,029.1

Note: a. Calculated from JD–figures as in 81–85 Plan Document: 1 JD =\$ 2.7
Source: JORDAN, N.P.C., *Five Year Plan...1981–1985.*

Morocco

ODA to Morocco in 1982–83 was equivalent to 4.1 per cent of the country's GNP. In 1984 the equivalent share was lower at 2.9 per cent. In 1983–84, an annual average of \$ 239 million came from DAC countries, of which \$ 114 million was from France and some \$ 30 million from West Germany [OECD, 1986]. Aid from the US has been rising, from \$ 40 million in 1982, to \$ 55 million the next year, \$ 68 million in 1984, and a proposed \$91 million for 1985 [US Gov't figures]. In October 1983, the 'Club of Paris' countries agreed to reschedule Morocco's debt for 1983/84, and a new IMF–sponsored programme through to 1985 was agreed [MENA 86: 612]. A new agreement with the IMF was reached after considerable delay in late 1986 [*MEED* 20–12–87: 56]. Subsequently, about \$ 900 million in repayments to Paris Club countries was rescheduled in March 1987. The World Bank has been an important lender to Morocco. In 1985 a \$ 200 million World Bank programme to reform industrial and trade policy was begun. In the first half of 1987, the Bank approved a further \$ 485 million in loans for public sector reform, water supply, sewerage, and telecommunications [*MEED*, 10–5–86; 6–6–87; 13–6–87].

Table 4.11
Foreign Receipts of Jordan's Central Government, 1980 — 1986, in $ mn

Source	1980	1981	1982	1983	1984	1985	1986
TOTAL	942.9	853.5	751.4	754.1	643.4	956.3	868.7
Arab Budget Supp.	680.9	624.3	566.2	541.7	276.0	475.9	410.6
Econ. & T.Ass.	21.7	—	—	1.0	—	—	—
Developm. Loans	240.2	229.2	185.2	211.6	367.4	480.4	458.1
Kuwait	39.3	25.4	9.4	43.3	27.7	33.2	22.8
Saudi Arabia	16.8	21.3	7.1	26.4	28.5	29.5	29.4
Iraq	16.5	15.3	13.0	—	28.1	34.2	22.9
AFESD	8.1	12.0	4.8	1.7	5.4	3.1	8.2
UK	7.9	13.1	1.5	1.1	10.6	—	—
FRG	15.8	17.2	6.7	5.2	1.7	16.0	13.0
USAID	58.8	15.6	18.2	23.7	8.8	6.5	9.4
IDA	8.7	4.3	10.7	6.0	—	—	—
Japan	6.5	11.1	15.3	8.6	15.1	11.8	43.4
Other	61.6	93.9	98.5	95.6	241.5	346.1	309.0

Source: Central Bank of Jordan,
    Monthly Statistical Bull., Jan 198

Notes: Calculated on the basis of figures in JD 1000. Conversion
    rates: JD1=$3.357 (1980); $3.026 (1981); $2.837 (1982); $2.754
    (1983); $2.601 (1984); $2.534 (1985); $2.857 (1986) (average
    middle prices).
    Figures for 1984–1986 are preliminary.

Aid from Arab countries became very important after 1979, although it is now dropping again. In 1980, for instance, Saudi assistance was estimated at over $ 1 billion [ibid.]. Morocco has been the second largest recipient of Arab national and regional development institutions' aid, having received c. $ 1.4 billion through to the end of 1986 [AFESD, 1987b].

Oman

Oman occupies a crucial place in the strategic and political considerations of the the US and the Arab Gulf States. Its large defence expenditures are supported by the GCC and to a lesser extent by the US. In July 1983, the richer GCC members agreed

Table 4.12
Oman's Grant and Loan Receipts ,
1975 — 1984, in US $ millions

	1975	1980	1981	1982	1983	1984
Total grants & loans (net)	350.6	104.8	291.0	161.3	618.1	647.1
Net grant receipts	...	101.9	144.8	42.0	147.0	...

Sources: Grant receipts: IMF,

International Financial Statistics

Figures for total grants and loans calculated from

RO figures,[OMAN, 1985] (1 RO = $ 2.89524 until Feb. '86).

to give Oman an annual grant of $ 150 million for defence expenditure, until 1995. US military aid in 1985 and 1986 stood at $ 40 million and $ 78.5 million respectively [*MEED*, 17–6–85]. Non–military aid stems from a similar motivation. Oman receives economic asistance from the GCC, the World Bank, and the US. US economic assistance is channelled via the Omani–American Joint Commission, which has a 1981–1985 budget for grants and technical assistance, of $ 25 million, and another $ 45 million for soft loans [OAJC figures]. In June 1986 $ 5 million were added to the $ 25 million budget [*MEED*, 7–6–1986]. The Arab Funds (mainly KFAED and ADFAED) had provided Oman with c. $ 540 million by the end of 1986 [AFESD, 1987b].

Sudan

The extent of Sudan's dependence on the external world has been highlighted earlier. The ODA it received in 1982–83 was equivalent to 10.8 per cent of its GNP, dropping to 7.7 per cent in 1984 (Table 4.1). The average annual amounts of ODA from DAC and Arab/OPEC countries and from the World Bank and IDA, in 1982–83, are listed in Table 4.13. The Arab group, the USA, and the World Bank/IDA emerge as the most important donors. The World Bank group in 1984 offered $ 126.4 million [World Bank, 1985]. It should be noted that the OECD figure for Arab/OPEC aid listed in Table 4.13, is most probably considerably exceeded by real flows because of further Saudi aid (including

Table 4.13
DAC, Arab/OPEC and World Bank/IDA assistance
to Sudan, 1982–83 (in US $ millions)

DAC	**Total**	**409.5**
	USA	147.1
	FRG	62.7
	UK	58.7
	EEC	39.4
	Netherlands	30.3
	Italy	21.0
	Canada	12.0
	Denmark	8.6
	Switzerland	5.2
	Others	24.5
Arab/OPEC (1983)		**361.0**
World Bank + IDA (1983, net)		**130.0**

Source: calculated on the basis of OECD [1985] data

official and unofficial budget support) for which no precise data are available. In late 1984, the USA, Saudi Arabia, West Germany, the UK and others suspended aid programmes because of arrears in repayments. The rescheduling arrangement of Spring 1984 had collapsed as the economy continued to worsen. Saudi Arabia in early 1985 unfroze some $ 35 million in the form of oil supplies. In May 1985, a new rescheduling arrangement was agreed with the 'Club of Paris' [MENA 86: 696 — 697]. Provisional agreement to reschedule an estimated $ 145 million in arrears on Arab loans was reached in Riyadh in October of that year, and the following month a joint delegation from KFAED, the Saudi Fund and AFESD held talks in Khartoum 'aimed at finalising a spending programme for $ 300 million — 330 million in frozen project loans'. This appears to have been ratified in early 1986 [*MEED* 23–11–1985; 20–12–86: 62]. In 1986, Saudi Arabia released another 6 months' oil supplies [*FT* 7–6–1986]. Assistance from the Arab national and regional development funds as of end 1986 stood at over $ 1 billion [AFESD, 1987b]. Since Sudan was declared ineligible for further assistance by the IMF in February 1985, discussions have taken place but at the time of writing IMF asistance had not yet been resumed.

It seems clear that assistance to Sudan was mainly motivated by the desire to keep the country and thus the regime afloat [see Brown, 1985]. Genuine long–term development aims, however, were present in much of the Arab assistance, partly in connection with the 'breadbasket' scheme. The strategic importance of the country makes it unlikely that Saudi and American assistance will be stopped, Sudan's loss of economic credit–worthiness notwithstanding. This could change, however, if the Sudanese regime allows Libyan and radical influence to replace that of the country's traditional allies.

Syria

Syria's aid–reliance, exclusive of Iranian oil and CMEA–assistance, amounts to c. 6 per cent of its GNP (1982–84). This reliance is mainly due to the regional political situation and the country's frontline status (see the section on Jordan). Syria was in fact the main recipient of Arab/OPEC bilateral aid in 1983 and 1984. Gross disbursements of that aid, amounting to $ 690 million in 1975 and $ 355 million the next year, rose steeply after the Baghdad Summit, to an average of $ 1.5 billion in 1979 and 1980. In 1982 it dropped to $ 1.2 million, sliding further back to $ 922 million and $ 834 million in 1983 and 1984 respectively [MENA 85: 672–673; OECD, 1985]. The main donors, as in the case of Jordan, have been Saudi Arabia and Kuwait. For several years, Kuwait's contributions of budget support for Syria have been hotly contested by the Kuwaiti Parliament, but the Cabinet has consistently overturned resolutions hostile to the continuation of such contributions. Since 1984, nonetheless, Kuwaiti subventions have nevertheless been cut substantially, as was the case for Jordan. In 1985, Kuwait's Foreign Minister declared that Kuwait would give KD 53 million (c.$ 180 million) to Syria in that financial year ('84/85)[*EIU QER* Kuwait, 1985,4]. Since then, however, there has been uncertainty over Kuwait's contribution, leaving only Saudi Arabia as a reliable source of hard currency. Saudi assistance has come to some $ 600–700 million annually, which is 'about all that stands between Damascus and bankruptcy in terms of its foreign exchange requirements' [*FT*, 2-6-86]. As of end 1986, the Arab development institutions had provided Syria with some $ 755 million (mainly from the Saudi Fund, AFESD and KFAED) [AFESD, 1987b]. Except from Arab sources, Syria receives very little capital assistance. During the Fifth Five–Year Plan (1981–85), 9.3 per cent of the total investment of $ 26 billion was planned to come from foreign sources. Of these foreign receipts, only $ 8 million were expected to be in the form of grants or other concessional assistance [Syria, 1981].

Assistance from United Nations agencies from 1977 to 1984 averaged some $ 27 million annually [UNDP, 1985a]. The main Arab funds offering assistance have been AFESD, the Saudi Development Fund, and the Islamic Development Bank. Worth mentioning, too, is Iran, which — in compensation for Syria's loss of income due to the closure of the pipeline from Iraq — has provided some 6 million tonnes of oil annually on favourable credit terms since 1982. The agreement held the Iranians to supplying 1 million tonnes free, and the remaining 6 million at a $ 2– 2.5/barrel discount. However, Syrian failure to repay and the suspected breakdown of a rescheduling agreement in 1984, led to Iran's halting of these oil shipments in 1985 [*FT*, 2-6-86]. The collapse of the oil price in late 1985 and 1986 caused further disagreement over the price for the 6 million tonnes (which was now no longer 'cheap'). Only in June 1986 was the agreement renewed for six months; the Iranian government showed itself flexible, with a view to discouraging Assad from pursuing his rapprochement with Jordan and possibly Iraq. By 1987 it was clear that, whereas the 1 million tonnes free oil were still being supplied for use by the army, the Syrians were obtaining the remainder of their oil requirements at market prices from Saudi Arabia, Kuwait and others.

Available data show two other significant bilateral donors. West Germany gave c. $ 30–40 million a year until 1980, when it virtually stopped aid; yet in 1984 the German government again committed itself to providing $ 62 million [UNDP, 1985a]. The US gave $ 27 million in 1982, but no US aid has been forthcoming since then [US Gov't figures]. Capital investment is also provided by the World Bank and the EEC/European Investment Bank.

Tunisia

The Tunisian government was able to attract concessionary loans for development projects in the frame of the 1982–86 Plan. The most important bilateral donors in recent years have been the USA, West Germany, France, Saudi Arabia and Kuwait. From Arab regional and national development institutions, the country had received almost $ 1.4 billion by the end of 1986 [AFESD, 1987b]. The US reduced its economic assistance from over $ 40 billion in the early 1980s to about half that amount in 1983 and 1984, and a figure of only $ 12 million was proposed for 1985 [US Gov't figures]. Since then, however, the volume of US assistance has risen somewhat again. The most important multilateral donor has been the World Bank group [MENA 86: 752–753]. Due to the oil price collapse, Tunisia in 1986 was 'forced ... into the arms of the IMF'. After the dismissal of the long–standing Prime Minister Mzali, negotiations with the IMF and the World Bank were begun and a $ 260 million IMF deal was signed in November of that year. The World Bank agreed to provide a $ 150 million loan to support trade reforms, followed by a similar loan for the same amount in 1987. In all, some $ 300 million of Tunisia's 1987 financing gap was expected to be covered by concessional assistance [*MEED*, 20–12–86; 28–2–87; 18–4–87].

Yemen Arab Republic

Yemen's largest donor by far is Saudi Arabia, accompanied by the GCC as a whole. Up to 1975 Yemen was more reliant on Eastern Bloc aid, but since then a clear shift has occurred. Saudi and Gulf aid to the country is motivated largely by the desire to keep Yemen away from the USSR and also to strengthen it against any potential threat from South Yemen. On the basis of official, unofficial and diplomatic sources, this author believes that Gulf grants to Yemen from 1979 onwards have come to c. $ 400 million a year, with c. $ 600 million in each of 1981 and 1982 (of which some $ 300 million was from Saudi Arabia). This excludes Saudi Arabia's military aid and grants to tribes. In fact, total annual Saudi transfers have been estimated by some observers at up to $ 1 billion [see for instance *The Economist*, 16–1–82], but the level had without doubt dropped by the mid–1980s. Official estimates, it should be stressed, consistently grossly undervalue Gulf grants. From such figures as are available, however, it appears that grants in 1986 were considerably higher than the previous year. The rise was mainly due to increased Saudi assistance, and has compensated for the estimated 30 per cent drop in remittances from Yemenis working abroad [*MEED* 13–12–86]. On top of this, Yemen has received considerable development aid (in the more narrow sense of the word) from the Arab world — again mainly from the oil producers. Up to the end of 1986, over $ 1.2 billion had been obtained from the Arab national and regional development institutions. The Iraqi Fund emerges as the largest contributor: the $ 353 million provided to Yemen over this period make the country the largest recipient of the Iraqi Fund [AFESD, 1987b].

In 1981, the respective annual contributions of other donors were put at : the World Bank/IDA c. $ 35 million; West Germany c. $ 20 million, the Netherlands $ 13.5 million, the USA $ 13 million; The USSR c. $ 4 million; the UK $ 3 — 4 million; UN–agencies c. $ 11 million [*MEED*, 10–4–81]. From the UNDP–collected figures about development aid to Yemen in 1984 [UNDP, 1985c], several points emerge. Firstly, ODA is heavily dominated by capital rather than technical assistance. Secondly, after the Arab countries (particularly Saudi Arabia and the UAE: the latter gave at least $ 88 million), the most important donors are the UN system (c. $ 58 million); Japan (c. $ 54 million); and the USA (c. $ 18 million according to the UNDP listings, but $ 33 million according to more reliable US government sources). US economic assistance (including PL 480) rose to c. $ 41 million in 1985 before falling back to $ 33 million the next year, and a proposed $ 31 million for 1987 [*MEED*, 19–4–86]. Also to be mentioned are the Netherlands, with recorded ODA of some $ 12 million in 1984 (OECD figures indicate an annual average of $ 29 million in 1983–84); and the USSR with about $ 10 million.

So as to maintain the flow of assistance, the government of the Yemen AR has tried to keep its status as an LLDC. So far it has largely succeeded. But in view of the country's large income from remittances, and recently its success in the quest for oil, several donors have begun to rethink their aid policies in Yemen. Some may scale down their assistance — the Netherlands being a case in point. However, the extreme dependence of Yemen on these 'subsidies', and the politico–strategic importance of the Yemen for the West, make it probable that, in the medium–long term, the country will have to suffer only a modest decrease in its favoured status.

People's Democratic Republic of Yemen

Over the period 1974–77 seventy–five per cent of development investment was funded from external sources [World Bank, 1979a: 106]. In the 1981–85 Plan, foreign assistance was projected to cover c. 70 per cent of the budget. Of this aid, c. 60 per cent has come from the Communist countries : mainly from the Soviet Union, but also from China and most others. Most of this has gone to technical assistance and to infrastructure. A further 30 per cent has been provided by Arab countries and regional funds, largely in the form of budget and balance of payments support. The final 10 per cent has been contributed by the international organisations: their share has mostly taken the form of technical assistance, but the IMF and World Bank have also provided balance of payments support. The World Bank lent some $ 150 million from 1970 to 1984 [author's interview with semi–official sources; MENA 85:

793–794; MENA 86: 855]. In 1984, the aid–reliance of the PDRY accounted for the equivalent of 14.1 per cent of its GNP (Table 4.1). Project work has been largely aid–financed. Total foreign aid in 1984 is thought to have stood at c. $ 166 million [Ismael & Ismael, 1986: xviii].

A shift has taken place in the direction of the country's aid–reliance. The USSR, since 1970 its main development partner, remains in that position. Indeed, it is the Soviet Union which in 1987—1988 was funding and carrying out the development of the newly–discovered oil fields in Shabwa and the construction of the pipeline to the coast. But since 1975, the Arab countries' share has risen steeply. This has been caused not only by the accumulation of oil wealth in the Gulf states, but also by the PDRY government's desire to break out of its isolation. Simultaneously another shift occurred: by 1982, Kuwait and Abu Dhabi had replaced Libya and Algeria as the country's main Arab sources of aid. Assistance from Arab national and regional development institutions by the end of 1986 amounted to some $ 639 million (about half the amount for the Yemen AR), the largest share in which came from the AFESD ($ 205 million) and the Islamic Development Bank ($ 137 million), followed by the Kuwait Fund for Arab Economic Development (KFAED)(c. $ 114 million) [AFESD, 1987b].

— — —

Donor Coordination

The need for coordination between donors and the ways of achieving it have become a significant point of discussion in recent years. The 1985 DAC Report [OECD, 1985: 195–209] devotes a chapter to it, which the reader may consult for a general discussion and overview.

When describing the kinds of coordination arrangements in the Middle East, one must distinguish between official, government approved arrangements on the one hand, and such other coordination and consultation between donors which is not officially sanctioned. As regards the former, three main kinds of arrangements are discernible: (1) a Consultative Group arrangement, with the IBRD as the 'lead' agency: Egypt, Sudan, Morocco; (2) 'Round Table' arrangements with the UNDP taking the lead: Djibouti, and, since 1985, Yemen AR, although in the latter the government, represented by CPO, hosts and chairs the meetings; and (3) a situation of governmental monopoly over any official coordination, as in Ethiopia, Syria, Jordan and the PDRY, though in the latter country a round–table arrangement has been proposed by the donor community.

Reality in many cases tends to look somewhat different. In Egypt, the official arrangement is effective, but because of the US's large share in total ODA to the country, USAID in effect took over as the main coordinator, from the late 1970s to 1982. Great apprehension grew amongst Egyptians about a perceived 'plot' by the Americans to take charge of the economy, in connivance with the IMF. The matter became a big issue in the local press. USAID's dominant role in coordination has since become less visible, and the IBRD has re–emerged as at least the official lead agency. An 'interest' has developed between the US and the UK in each other's projects. This apparently *ad hoc* consultation and coordination is mainly based on the personal initiative of the respective representatives and has no institutional basis. UNDP plays a limited, informal role, and seeks to perform a catalysing function in bringing others together. It also acts as the coordinator for UN agencies, although it has not always been able to fulfill that function fully.

This UNDP role is, with some variations, mirrored in the other countries under consideration. In Sudan, donors appear to wish to push the agency into the role officially performed by the IBRD, but its small capacity (under–staffing, as nearly everywhere else) makes that impracticable. In Yemen, UNDP (with a

seconded World Bank expert) has played a crucial role in bringing donors together and in suggesting a round–table arrangement
(which the government initially rejected although it subsequently
had to agree to a modified formula under the pressure of circumstances and donors).

Another general feature of donor coordination in these countries — and presumably elsewhere — is the official policy of the
EEC on the subject. In 1984, it was decided that information
about the member states' development assistance should be exchanged between the individual representatives in the country
concerned. Both at Ambassadorial level and the level of First
Secretary regular meetings have been instituted. The mission of
the EEC–Commission in the country usually plays an important
role as a focal point. Much depends, however, on the personality
and initiative of the representatives concerned. Actual coordination between the members states is often inadequate.

There is, moreover, considerable coordination between Arab
donor–institutions, through a Coordination Secretariat located in
the Arab Fund for Economic and Social Development (AFESD).
This includes the co–financing and joint administration of some
projects (for further details see Chapter 6).

Although relief aid is not really the subject of this study, the
coordination in relieving the Ethiopian famine merits attention.
Under the impulse of the UNDP, some 60 donors (bilaterals, multilaterals and NGOs) in 1984 established a more institutionalised
contact among themselves, and a Steering Committee was created
in which 2 bilaterals (EEC, Canada), one UN agency (WFP) and
2 NGOs were represented (the latter in turn assuming a coordinating role within the NGO community). Also, an 'Informal Coordination Committee of Bilateral Donors' (ICCBD) was formed. All
Western donors met regularly and discussions filtered through to
the Committee via Canada and the EEC. When in November 1984
Kurt Janson was appointed 'Assistant UN–Secretary General for
Emergency Operations in Ethiopia', the Steering Committee became an 'Advisory Council' to him. The ICCBD was subsequently
expanded to include Eastern Bloc donors, Japan and India. In addition to the above, Western Ambassadors would meet from time
to time with Janson, to discuss policy issues. At times, Janson
would call a meeting of all three groups (NGOs,the ICCBD, and
the Advisory Council), which would be attended by the Relief and
Rehabilitation Commission. This system existed until July 1985.
Canada provided the Chairman of the ICCBD for one year, but

on expiry of that term, no other country was prepared to take over. Because of this, no more meetings of either the ICCBD or the Advisory Council took place. It was thought probable at the time of the author's visit to Addis Ababa (January 1986) that the newly created function of 'Deputy Emergency Coordinator' of the UN (the assistant to Janson's successor Priestley) would replace this chairmanship. At present, however, channels of communication are partly blocked; also, the UN cannot take over the 'go–between' role of the Advisory Council.

Some Notes on NGOs in Development Aid to the Middle East

Insufficient evidence was available to the author to make possible a comprehensive account of the activities, impact and procedures of NGOs. Some brief points will be offered. NGOs are active in development assistance in most of the recipient countries under consideration. In all cases the NGO must have a contract with, or permission from, the government of the country concerned. In Yemen, many NGOs work with the LDAs, under government–LDA–NGO contracts. In other cases elsewhere in the region, particularly in the field of relief assistance, many work almost without any interference once the contract is concluded, although government control is always present. A typical example is Ethiopia: within certain limits, the organisations do their work as they see fit, but there is a constant supervision by and consultation with the authorities. NGO assistance varies considerably, from food relief (Ethiopia and Sudan), to providing expertise in research and planning, and training programmes (e.g. the Ford Foundation in Egypt, the Maghreb, Jordan and Lebanon [Weinbaum, 1982: 139]), to scholarships such as those of the Ford Foundation and Humphreys in Syria (where this is overseen by the SPC).

Concerning NGO coordination, only in the cases of Ethiopia and Sudan does this rise above an otherwise extremely limited level. This is partly explained by the emergency conditions in these two countries. In Ethiopia, coordination among NGOs is organised by the 'Christian Relief and Development Association' (CRDA), which has functioned since the mid–1970s and is in effect Ethiopian. Most NGOs are members of CRDA; the organisation's function is to provide several services to its membership. It can, or can help, solicit funds from overseas; it provides tax–free import and clearing facilities; and it can act as a channel for negotiations with the government. Some NGOs, like the huge 'World

Vision' organisation, approach donors themselves. A donor like 'Band Aid', (not a member, since it is not an active field organisation) prefers liaison through CRDA. The Organisation, it must be pointed out, also has non–Christian members. Members have to be accepted: CRDA will examine their track record and their proposed project(s), and normally also check if they have an agreement with the authorities (usually with the RRC, which is the immediate superior body to CRDA).

In Sudan, December 1985 saw the first serious efforts to achieve NGO coordination, when 21 NGOs met and agreed to start regular meetings. The first of these was held on December 12, and was chaired by the 'Save the Children Fund/USA' representative in Khartoum. It appears that his organisation is the main promotor of the idea. Results have to be awaited.

'Is Aid Harmful ?'

The academic battle between the pro- and anti–aid lobbies has been raging for years. This author cannot hope to settle the debate, but can only aim at stating and briefly reviewing the positions before considering their relevance for the case of the Middle East. Donors in general simply assume that their activities have been, in principle and in general, positive. Since 1980 some soul–searching has been done as to the modalities and procedures of the aid effort, but this has not affected the essentially postive conclusion [see OECD, 1985: 251–260]. Apart from exhortations that more aid should should be made available, the 'traditional' aid–lobby follows basically the same philosophy. This is clear, for instance, in the reports of the Brandt–Commission [Brandt, 1980; 1983], or in the positions put forward at UN fora. There may be discussion about the kinds of aid provided and about priority areas, or even about the potentially negative effects of excessive donor–influence, but the principle of transferring substantial financial resources in one form or another to the Third World has not been questioned by this school, nor has the record of aid up to the present been fundamentally challenged by them. The academic buttress of this approach is constituted by the 'two–gap' school. The argument goes that the developing countries suffer from a foreign exchange gap and a savings/investment gap; foreign asistance can fill both of these, in addition to the 'manpower gap', and thus put these countries on the road to development. It is assumed that this intervention will allow the economy to grow until the recipient no longer needs such assistance [Rosenstein–Rodan, 1961; Fei & Paauw, 1965; Chenery & Strout, 1966; Papanek, 1972].

This school of thought is now radically opposed both from right– and left–wing circles. The 'right' (e.g. Bauer, 1970: 280–284; 1976] has argued that the whole principle is objectionable, both on grounds of economic 'morality' and in its effects. Free enterprise is stifled because of growing state intervention, which is intrinsically wrong and produces bad results; rather than stimulating national savings, Bauer argues, aid tends to reduce them. Others have been content to argue that aid has at best been irrelevant. Case as well as cross–national studies by Rahman [1968], Griffin & Enos [1970], Weisskopf [1972], and Bornshier *et al.* [1978], among others, indicate an non–significant correlation between foreign asistance and economic growth. These findings have in turn been challenged by Papanek and others, however. It would appear that it is really an empirical question, varying from one case to another — a point to which we will return later.

The above arguments have been partly taken aboard by 'progressive' or 'radical' writers. But they go further. They point out that not only does aid often produce disappointing results; it also has some outright negative consequences: creating intra– and inter–country imbalances, fuelling corruption and maintaining unequitable socio–political systems. The most fundamental criticism, however, is structural: aid, it is argued, has functioned as a complement to commercial international economic relations in integrating the Third World economies into the international economic system, and creating a situation of dependency [Amin, 1971; Lappé *et al.,* 1980; Hayter, 1971, 1981]. This criticism is not only aimed at bilateral aid, since it is argued that the multilateral institutions, too, are instruments in the hegemonic strategy of the developed world [Hayter, 1981; Payer, 1974, 1982].

Common sense and the sifting of the evidence suggests that (a) neither of these two ends of the spectrum offer the way to salvation — they only become truly valuable in juxtaposition; and (b) much depends on the kind of aid given, and on the specific situation of the country concerned. This may be illustrated by re-considering the various arguments. The two–gap theory has been confirmed in several cases, in that correlations have been found between foreign asistance and savings and/or economic growth [see also Khatib, 1987]; success stories exist. On the other hand, the approach has been proved invalid (in its own terms) in other countries [Rahman, 1968]. Moreover, a non–theoretical perspective also throws doubt on the theory. In the successful cases of Pakistan, South Korea and Taiwan, not only was the volume of aid massive, but other factors such as effective private enterprise and mineral development were also important. In Mexico and Thailand, growth was achieved without much aid. And elsewhere aid demonstrably did *not* lead to significant growth [Spero, 1985: 189]. Even when the two–gap theory is confirmed, however, it only concerns the quantitative aspect of growth in GNP. This can not be identified with genuine economic development which would eventually become self–sustaining.

Radical writers support their claim that aid is detrimental *in se* since it is merely an instrument of imperialism, by pointing (a) at the obvious motivation from the donors' side, which in turn is clear from the modalities and the direction of their aid; and (b) at the many instances where a situation of dependence has been created. As argued earlier, altruism indeed features low on the list of donors' motives. Who receives aid has often been determined by political/strategic interests. However, the conclusion that aid is, therefore, *merely* a tool used in a grand imperialist strategy, is not necessarily correct. Moreover, the 'logical' link between hegemonic intent and the allegedly inherently negative nature of aid, is less than watertight. The dependence–argument is stronger. It has been explained earlier how most donors have tried to create a degree of dependence, on the part of the recipients, on some of their exports. This is true for manufactures as well as for food — particularly grain in the case of the US. In addition to the commercial dependence thus created, there is no doubt that aid has often been used to make the recipient politically dependent. Senator Humphrey of the US in 1957 openly defended this: 'If you are looking for a way to get people to ... be dependent on you, ... it seems to me that food dependence would be terrific' [Hayter, 1981: 86]. The actual use of food as a weapon has been dramatically illustrated by Sobhan [1979, 1983] for the case of Bangladesh.

The dependence–argument overlaps with the criticism that foreign assistance tends to have negative structural effects on the economy of the recipient. In some cases, the inflow of funds from abroad has substituted for, rather than supplemented domestic savings and investment. Moreover, the focus on the 'modern' sector, and the overall development philosophy (or lack thereof) accompanying assistance, have helped to bring about the dual economy phenomenon that has so often been decried in development literature. In addition, the restructuring of the economy and the reorienting and expansion of consumer tastes have both reinforced the element of dependency in the relationship between many LDCs and their donors or the developed world at large. Crucially, the relative neglect of agriculture, in combination with the populaton explosion (itself partly a result of aid) has led to a food crisis, dramatically increasing LDCs' dependence on food imports. Finally, the loans which this situation made necessary (and which often had only a small grant element) eventually contributed to creating severe balance of payments problems for many LDCs as a result of their rising debt repayment obligations.

Without doubt, foreign assistance has in many instances been a factor in the widening gap between rich and poor, both intra– and inter–LDC. This has been due to, *i.a.*, the channels which were used; the sorts of projects chosen; the urban bias; the structural effect on the recipient economy; and the bias in recipient allocation. Aid has, moreover, been used to avoid political transformation — a fact which hardly needs illustration [see Spero, 1985: 191–193]. Military assistance, of course, has been attacked on moral grounds, and because it, too, often contributed to bolstering unpopular regimes, and increasing political and economic dependence.

Finally, there is the case of the multilateral institutions. Hayter [1981] and Payer [1974, 1982] have argued that these institutions were established with the intent of serving the developed world's interests, that they remain controlled by it, and continue to fulfill their role in support of First World hegemony and international finance capital. It can hardly be denied that the main voice within the IMF is that of the West, and the US in particular. The latter has succeeded in slowing down or blocking reforms which have been demanded by the LDCs and supported by, for instance, the Brandt reports. However necessary external financing became for LDCs as a result of the combination of food crisis, oil crisis, and anti–inflationary policies in the developed world (in addition to debt repayment problems resulting from previous aid), it is nevertheless true that, on the whole, the IMF programmes 'forced debtor countries to shift the focus of their economic policy from development to financial stability' [Spero, 1985: 205]. In Mexico, the financial results of the IMF programme were spectacular by 1983, but 'from a development perspective ... the effects of the austerity program were devastating' : GDP was down, wages were down, and unemployment was high; exports had not been increased. 'Domestic austerity policies combined with external constraints led to a decline in all of the less–developed countries' economic activity ... The decline in economic activity was also reflected in unemployment' [ibid.: 205– 206].

To each of the above points, however, more positive rejoinders can be made. In some cases, aid did help lead to growth. Not all donors have been equally self–interested; not all aid has been motivated by domestic economic or political considerations of the donor. Aid *has* at times gone to recipients at loggerheads with the donors; this has *a fortiori* been the case with multilateral ODA such as assistance from IDA. Moreover, it is not because aid is motivated by self–interest, that it could not contribute to the development of the recipient. A donor who wishes to see an ally–recipient remain stable, will find it in his interest to promote genuine development at least to some extent. As to the depen-

dence debate, there is not sufficient evidence to support the claim
that aid must lead to dependence. Donors have certainly had that
objective in mind, and on the whole LDC economies have become
more intertwined with, and dependent on, the First World. But
there are success stories contradicting a 'logical' link. Moreover,
such dependence as was created can be attributed largely to specific kinds and modalities of aid (conditional, tied, etc.). This
says little about aid *in se*. The Third World's indebtedness, in
addition, can to great extent be blamed on the food and oil crises
of the 1970s, combined with the West's anti–inflationary policies;
other factors than aid thus played a major role. As far as the
structural effects of aid are concerned, these have again not always been negative, nor do they necessarily have to be so. True,
many donors' self–interest has often inevitably had that result, but
there are many exceptions, both bilateral and multilateral (think
only of Arab aid, for instance). The growing interest of at least
part of the aid community for agriculture, small–scale projects
and local development points in that direction. It also provides
a counterweight to the claim that aid fuels inequality and actual
impoverishment. Again, this *has* happened, but it is by no means
a general rule. Here, too, specific aid policies may be beneficial.
As to military assistance, even that may free resources for development. Finally, the case for the multilateral institutions. The
specific criticisms made earlier stand. But they do not justify the
radicals' conclusion. For one thing, World Bank and IDA assistance has made possible countless genuine development projects;
IMF loans and the facility to draw on SDRs have bridged vital
gaps; and the International Fund for Agricultural Development
(IFAD), to give but one example, has proved of very real value to
the Third World. For another, the negative connotations of the
Bretton Woods institutions are mostly due to the specific power
structure within them; the conditions and modalities of aid provided; and the reluctance of the US to expand or even maintain
the institutions' ODA budgets. In no way does this justify advo-
cating these insitutions's abolition: on the contrary, it requires a
continued campaign to improve them.

In conclusion, therefore, it appears that the question 'is aid
harmful?' needs rephrasing and de–coupling: does one discuss (1)
aid as it has been; (2) aid *in se;* or (3) the question of aid today
and in the future, given the existing situation ? It was argued
that even in the first case, the answer was by no means a straight-
forward 'yes'. Aid *in se,* it was suggested, is not harmful; one

may rather expect it to be beneficial. Specific policies, modalities and conditions are responsible for failure or worse. Untied aid, preferably in grant form, when part of a clear development strategy/philosophy which is not unduly biased towards urban and/or large scale projects and which allows a degree of local autonomy, this author would suggest, is highly likely to be a positive contribution towards an LDC's development. This leads on to the third version of the question: can aid be useful from the present onwards, given the realities of the present? The previous answer would already imply a positive answer to this question. That is reinforced by practical considerations. Many of the poorer LDCs would not politically or even physically survive a cut–off of aid. Things being as they are, and the LDCs having made the choices which they have, there is at present no alternative to continuing to assist them. Also, food and relief aid can not now be ended without causing unacceptable suffering and famine. Finally, it would appear to be perfectly possible, in theory, to make aid a really constructive excercise, by adapting its modalities and carefully considering the recipient's interests holistically and in consultation with him. As for the multilateral institutions and the IMF in particular, their long–term effectiveness for development as well as their image would be greatly enhanced by taking more account of socio–political realities and needs, and by expanding Third World participation in decision–making (for a start, this would lead to more SDRs being issued). One may doubt the realism of such expectations, however, given the fact that many donors in the past were shown to provide aid mainly out of self–interest. It is likely, therefore, that the effects of aid will very much remain 'a mixed bag'.

The Case of the Middle East

With the evidence of the previous chapters in mind, some comments on the case of the Middle East may be offered. Before considering the general question of the link between aid and development in the Middle East, however, the more specific one regarding the effect of aid on development administration will be examined.

Relationship between aid and development administration

Negative links may be observed in three interrelated areas. First, as argued earlier, the 'charity economy' phenomenon has had a direct impact on development administration, albeit more in some countries (highly dependent, with low domestic economic production) than in others. To a greater or lesser extent, indeed, the bureaucracies in the recipient countries of the region have been shaped through the aid effort. The Sudan is a case in point. The result, inevitably, has been that such bureaucracies have acquired an outward rather than inward orientation. In as much as it is shaped by external aid, the bureaucracy is not organically linked to the domestic economy nor tuned in to its problems. Secondly, the countless different procedures and rules of the various donors, and the attention which donors' representatives demand from the recipient's bureaucrats, has deprived the latter of time and/or energy which could have been devoted to tackling the real development problems. Thirdly, with aid and advice have come values which more often than not were alien to the prevailing culture. It is not surprising that bureaucracies shaped in this way will not automatically function as they would in the socio–economic and political context where those values originated: instead, people within and outside these bureaucracies have interpreted their functions in their own way. This not only affects the efficiency of development administration; the new symbiosis may also in return negatively affect the coherence of indigenous value systems.

It is within this framework of possibly negative links, that the positive contributions of aid and assistance to development administration must be found. Many administrative assistance projects, for example, may appear positive in their own right but still have a negative effect on a macro–level. At the same time, it is no doubt possible to avoid this pitfall precisely by being aware of its presence and 'working from within'. Given that one is confronted with a situation where many of the new values have been absorbed, however imperfectly, while the old framework has been irretrievably damaged (in other words, 'the clock cannot be turned back'), aid and administrative assistance have a role to play in helping to achieve the requirements imposed by this new situation. They may be, and indeed at times have proved, very helpful and even indispensible. It cannot be stressed enough, however, how carefully one must tread.

Relationship between aid and development

As to the aid — development relationship in the Middle East, the earlier general discussion can be applied quite straightforwardly. There have been definite successes in Egypt, Yemen, and even the Sudan. the same can be said for the less dependent cases of Algeria and Oman. In Jordan, to give one more example, the evidence shows a correlation between foreign asistance and economic growth. Often, however, the successes came at a high price. For the Sudan, the results (though not *solely* of aid) have been utter dependence on the donor community; a virtual bankruptcy due to astronomical debt servicing requirements; and in many ways a loss of control over the national economy. Egypt's case is not much less alarming. A concise survey of the aid debate for Egypt is given by Sullivan [1984: 95–101], in his conclusion to a symposium on the impact of aid on the country. He notes the contribution of aid to industry, infrastructure, and feeding the people, but finds that agriculture has been relatively neglected; 'food aid appears to have had a negative effect on Egyptian food production'; and the external debt situation has become 'worrisome'. 'At the macro level', he adds, 'foreign aid has helped Egypt, but it has been a mixed blessing'. Too much of the economy's growth occurred in the service sector. There is a real danger, Sullivan recognises, that Egypt will become 'hooked on foreign aid, unable to manage life without it and unable to invest in the future' [p. 96]. Some further assessments of the impact of aid in the region may be found in Bishai [1984] (Egypt); Zubir [1983] and Wohlmuth [1983] (Sudan); Hammad [1981] and Khatib [1987] (Jordan); Hofmann [1984] (YAR). The whole question of 'Food Aid, Trade and Development Assistance' is treated admirably by Weinbaum [1982; 115–155].

The earlier considerations on the more specific Aid — Bureaucracy link are of course directly relevant in the present discussion, too. Not only can, for many of them, the 'bureaucracy' –part of the equation be replaced by 'development'; it need hardly be stressed that the impact of aid on the development administration in its turn has an impact on development. Specific examples have been treated in previous chapters. Suffice it to point out, here again, that an absolute verdict on the positive or negative impact of aid for the Middle East and North Africa seems impossible: 'it all depends' on the kinds and modalities of aid provided, and on the recipient's specific circumstances. It is, in brief, an empirical question. As in the rest of the Third World, given that 'the clock cannot be turned back', aid undisputably has an important positive function to fulfil. With the modern development values which all of these countries have adopted, and from which there is no turning back, both financial and technical assistance will remain an essential requirement for a long time to come. Controversy will persist with reference to recipient regimes and politics, and to the general question of dependency. But without aid, countries such as Egypt and Sudan can only go under in a chaos of human

misery and violence. In addition, maintaining political stability
in particular states can be a perfectly legitimate reason for providing aid — but that discussion lies outside the scope of the
present study. If the balance of the aid effort is to be clearly positive, it is crucial to proceed carefully from a consciousness of the
above caveats, always starting from the realities and underlying
nature of the recipients. Some concrete characteristics of ODA in
an ideal world would be (1) the absence of political or commercial
ties; (2) a high proportion of grants and highly concessional loans;
(3) the integration into an overall development strategy; (4) close
consultation with, and large autonomy for, the recipient; and (5)
attention for rural development and small–scale projects, in addition to those sectors which already receive more than their due.
The scepticism of the present writer as to the likelihood of such
a scenario, however, has already been expressed. But whenever
there is a move towards fulfilling one or more of these conditions,
the chances of aid contributing to development increase.

5   THE REGIONAL FOCUS

In the first chapter reference was made to the salience of the concept of an Arab Nation and the contrast with reality. The Arab World might be thought to possess exceptional potential for regional, south–south integration in view of the presumed existence of such a nation, but divisiveness has appeared stronger. Attempts at some such form of integration have been made, however, and have not been completely fruitless.

The Arab League 'Agreement on Arab Economic Unity' (AAEU, 1957) had by 1964 produced a twin offspring: the Council for Arab Economic Unity (CAEU) and the Arab Common Market (ACM) — the latter being the first stage in the evolution towards the CAEU's aim of full economic unity; the establishment of a customs union was to be the first step. By 1975, 14 countries had ratified the AAEU, but actual membership in the ACM lagged behind. The initial four (Egypt, Syria, Iraq and Jordan) were eventually joined by Libya and Mauritania, while Sudan was on the point of becoming a member but never completed the ratification of the required formalities. Since the Camp David agreement Egypt has been expelled; the PDRY has joined, and Somalia and the Yemen AR have expressed interest but seem to feel that present membership conditions need to be relaxed further. The further stages of integration (free movement of factors of production, employment and ownership; coordination of various national policies, etc.) were never realised, although on a specialised, restricted level of functional institutions, bilateral agreements and joint ventures, some achievements were made. The common external tariff system still has not been established and only in 1973 were the tariff barriers between the 4 core states abolished. Intra–trade between 1965 and 1969 showed a noticeable though slight rise. But intra–imports between the four core members had declined to 3 — 4 per cent in 1975 and dropped further to 1 per cent the next year [ECWA 1979: 80]. Taking a broader view, covering the whole ECWA region, we find that the intra–ECWA exports ratio remained approximately constant over the 1975–1981 period,

but that the share of intra–imports in total imports declined from
13 per cent in 1975–77 to 10.1 per cent in 1981 (although for the
non–oil economies over the same period it rose from 13.6 per cent
to 19.8 per cent [ECWA 1983: table IV–A.4]. The overall figures
for the region, therefore, indicate a declining relative importance
of intra–trade, which is understandable when one considers the
value of oil exports on the one hand and the import need resulting from the countries' development plans on the other. Still,
the share of Middle Eastern intra–regional trade in world trade
has actually risen, but Poulson & Wallace found in 1979 [470]
that 'This increase ... is accounted for entirely by the Asian Middle East trade. The share of world trade accounted for by the
African Middle East and the Arab Common Market trade has
declined since 1973'.

Clearly, the ACM can be considered a failure in terms of its
own aims. The Amman declaration of 1980 which was intended
to revive and enlarge the ACM, was soon overtaken by political
developments in the region and lost its momentum. What were
the causes for this lacklustre performance? First of all there was
the political element: the jealous guarding of their sovereignty
by the various regimes and the continuing political tension which
obstructed effective coordination and at times even blocked all
cooperation (cf. Chapter 1). Second, Arab governments have been
worried by the possible negative effects of market integration, in
the short as well as in the long term. Short–term interests could
be harmed by the loss of customs revenues and because trade
diversion was expected to be more imporant than trade creation.
Domestic industry could be affected, and in the long term the
less developed partners could expect to suffer from the skewed
distribution that might follow in the overall development pattern.

In the light of the fact that trade diversion (TD) was and
probably remains more important than trade creation (TC) [see
Wilson, 1977: 95], the predominance of the element of market
integration in the ACM scheme already goes a long way in ex-
plaining why the latter's results were so poor. But there were
many additional factors (some of which are part of the cause for
this TD/TC ratio). One cannot overlook the geographical element, i.e. the non–contiguity of the African and Asian parts of the
ACM, overland trade being obstructed by the presence of Israel.
It was indeed noticeable that trade between the Asian partners
was far more important than that between them and Egypt and
the Sudan [ibid.: 93]. This accentuated existing bottlenecks —

though by no means all of them were caused by it — which in turn inhibited trade flows.

Among further causes for the ACM's failure were the differences between the economic systems of the countries. There were, moreover, plenty of exceptions to the free trade agreement, while tariff cuts — only applied in 1973 — were not very effective 'because quotas and exchange controls played a more significant role in restricting trade than tariffs in any case' [ibid.]. In addition, the links with the Gulf Arab economies, where tariffs remained low, in effect created great gaps in the common external tariff barrier.

Another important factor was the low stage of development, coupled to a lack of funds, which not only made the initial costs of integration that much more difficult to bear but also lessened the value of trade agreements. The exports of these countries, moreover, were and are mainly geared to the developed world due to the limited need of the countries within the region for the raw materials originating in the region (an orientation which colonial policies played not a small part in bringing about).

A last group of factors relates to the institutional aspect. There were no proper follow–up instruments regarding implementation of the agreements and there was a lack of accurate information. Such information as existed, moreover, was seldom exchanged. Generally, there was no serious framework for integration. Only recently have there been positive developments in this respect: one now has the Arab Monetary Fund, there is an Arab central statistical organisation, several other data processing and coordinating institutions are being set up, and many joint ventures, private as well as state–run, sprang up. Still, the ACM is not performing any better — which again confirms the importance of the political factor.

Political divisiveness versus functional cooperation

Starting with the Egyptian–Syrian–Jordanian Unified Army Command of 1956, seventeen unification or federation agreements between two or more Arab countries have been made, the latest (at the time of writing) being the unification agreement between Libya and Morocco which was revoked by King Hassan in 1986. Of all these, only the creation of the United Arab Emirates (1971) and of the Gulf Cooperation Council (GCC, 1981) can be considered as bearing more long–term significance. The rest either collapsed or withered away in a short time. The UAE has survived as a surprisingly stable federation, and during the 1980s developmental coordination among its component emirates has improved. The

GCC, too, has proved comparatively successful: a fair degree of political coordination has been achieved; the customs union stage has been reached, leading on today to arrangements which carry some features of a common market and even of what is termed an 'economic union'; and there is a strong socio–cultural trend towards integration. The causes for this success appear to lie in (1) the characteristics of the six states making up the GCC; (2) the links between the states before the actual creation of the GCC; (3) the similarly perceived external threat (mainly Iran); and (4) the apparently right choice of a loose confederational model, coupled to the realistic and thorough handling of GCC affairs since its creation. If one considers the creation and survival of the UAE one finds exactly the same factors at work.

In contrast, the failures of the other schemes were mainly due to (1) political tensions; (2) the characteristics of the states / regimes concerned; (3) the choice of 'model'; and (4) ill–advised policies once the scheme was initiated. The last two of these could have been controllable, the first two were not. Most of the obstacles which have so far inhibited integration in that part of the Arab world specifically covered by this study (i.e. excluding the rich Gulf), persist. Hopes for advanced forms of integration remain therefore wishful thinking.

This negative picture is to some extent belied, however, by functional co–operation in many fields. The role of the Arab League in promoting economic and socio–cultural co–operation has been considerable. Departments of its General Secretariat provide a forum for coordination in most fields of the economy and socio–cultural affairs. The Economic Council of the League, composed of the ministers of economy from the member states, aims to coordinate the economic policies of these states. The CAEU, in addition to fathering the ACM, has sponsored an array of agreements intended to help the growth of intra–regional investment. Particularly important among the latter, at least potentially, was the 1973 agreement on investment guarantees against non–commercial risks in host countries. All Arab League members belong to some fifteen specialised autonomous agencies, such as the Arab Academy for Maritime Transport; the Arab Centre for the Study of Arid and Dry Lands; the Arab Industrial Development Organisation; the Arab Satellite Communications Organisation — under whose auspices ARABSAT was set up; the Arab League Educational, Cultural and Scientific Organisation; the Arab Labor Organisation; the Arab Telecommunications

Union; the Inter-Arab Investment Guarantee Corporation; and, as a last example of special relevance for this study, the Arab Organisation for Administrative Sciences. The latter, beginning activities in 1969, aims at cooperation in furthering administrative science in the Arab world and at improving Arab administrations. It sponsors research and publishes a journal, is a member of the International Institute of Administrative Sciences, and organises conferences of official and academic experts regarding questions of administration in the Arab world. Unfortunately, although some of the research which is produced — often by outside contributors — is of good quality, on the whole the organisation tends to take on the characteristics of most Arab regional official bodies. It suffers from a lack of commitment among its staff, partly due to a lack of genuine support from the respective governments. Many appointments are political, and member governments are rarely prepared either to open their activities to objective criticism or to co-operate fully by providing the required data.

In addition, many Arab League members belong to some dozen Arab Specialised Unions and Federations: for instance, the Arab Federation of Engineering Industries; the A.F. for Shipping Industries; the Arab Seaports Union; the Arab Union of Food Industries; the Federation of Arab Chambers of Commerce, Industry and Agriculture; and (probably the best-known) the Organisation of Arab Petroleum Exporting Countries (OAPEC).

Intra-Arab aid flows have been significant, both bilaterally and through multilateral Arab institutions. The Arab Fund for Economic and Social Development (AFESD) merits mention here, in view of its focus on regional projects and Arab integration. All Arab League states enjoy membership in AFESD. This and other development institutions, as well as Arab aid in general, will be treated in more detail in Chapter 6.

From the 1970s onwards, many transnational joint ventures have been set up, often sponsored by the CAEU. Among these are the Arab Company for Drug Industries and Medical Appliances, the A.C. for Industrial Investment, the A.C. for Livestock Development, the Arab Mining Company, and the Arab Investment Company. Bilateral ventures also help to prevent duplication, as in the case of the Syrian-Jordanian textiles venture. Some of these joint ventures have been government-financed, some are mixed, some totally private. OAPEC's ventures include an Arab Shipbuilding and Repairs Yard, an Arab Maritime Petroleum Transport Company, an Arab Engineering Company, and others. Although many of the above joint ventures and organisations have proved ineffective or failed, others have been succesful. In addition, there is a plethora of specifically Gulf–related organisations and ventures, but they fall outside the scope of this study [see Nonneman, 1986: 194–195].

This type of functional co–operation under the auspices of the Arab League, OPEC, OAPEC, or otherwise, thus covers almost all conceivable fields, from industry, agriculture, transport and communications, through to the scientific and educational sectors. The United Nations Economic Commision for Western Asia (ECWA) — since 1985 named ESCWA (...Economic and Social...) — has played an important supporting role by gathering data and conducting studies into each of those aspects. ESCWA is now based in Baghdad, and has been advising several governments in the region about development policies in the widest sense of the word, attaching particular importance to the regional integration aspect. For detailed information about these organisations, ventures, services and activities, the reader may consult the annual *The Middle East and North Africa* (the section on 'Regional Organisations'), and the yearly issues of ECWA's *Studies on Development Problems in Countries of Western Asia* and *Survey of Economic and Social Develoments in the ECWA region*.

In addition to all the above, the region also provides examples of transnational co–operation on specific development projects or relief action. The most spectacular example is probably the Sudanese–Egyptian Jonglei Canal Project. This aims to reduce the massive evaporation, spreading and seepage of the Nile waters when they are passing through the swamps of the Upper Nile, by channelling most of the water straight through them. The Canal is meant to be navigable and thus also saves about 300 km on the previous route between Malakal and Juba. The extra water yield of about 4 billion cubic metres annually is to be divided equally between Egypt and Sudan. Work started in 1976, but excavation and other works in the 1980s have been obstructed by the rebellion in Southern Sudan. The upsurge in the guerilla and sabotage activities of John Garang's SPLA eventually caused work to be stopped altogether. Co–operation between Egypt and Sudan, however, still proceeded within the framework of the 1982 Complementarity Pact between the two countries. The Pact stipulated the creation of a Nile Valley Parliament and several joint institutions of government, as well as comprising agreements on mutual investment, equal treatment of citizens of the two countries, and a range of projects. The pact was to have been implemented in three phases, of which the first, preparatory, phase would end in 1984. This schedule was upset by the revolution in Sudan, and progress was 'frozen' pending the establishment of a new permanent government. One project which had passed the stage of feasibility studies, however, was continued. It provides for an area of 400,000 acres in central Sudan to be planted by a joint company. So far only 25,000 acres have been planted — with soya, cotton and dhurra. The pact was expected to be reactivated during 1986.

Djibouti, Ethiopia, Sudan, Kenya, Somalia and Uganda in 1986 established an Intergovernmental Authority for Drought and Development (IGADD), to be based in Djibouti. Its first major projects will be to develop drought–resistant grains and promote fisheries.

Another striking co–operative project is the agreement between Djibouti and Ethiopia jointly to upgrade the Ethiopia–Djibouti Railway. Djibouti has persuaded the Ethiopian government to accept the French offer of aid for this project, Czech competition notwithstanding.

A final example is Ethiopia's linking–in (after Djibouti's intervention) to a direct–dialling and television network which includes Djibouti, both Yemens, Somalia and Saudi Arabia. This illustrates, once more, how ideological postures often pose no obstacle at all to functional co–operation.

Joint development planning, however, has not achieved any significant results to date, even though the idea enjoys a degree of official support. Under the aegis of the Arab Economic and Social Council, tentative moves were made towards creating the basis for an 'Arab Development Plan'. An ECWA study commented in 1981:

> Certain steps have already been taken to facilitate plan harmonization, such as the agreement to formulate all development plans with a common time horizon and the adoption of a common overall strategy. Consultants are currently at work attempting to identify some joint projects that could become the common regional components for different but co–ordinated national plans. Nevertheless, considerable skepticism has been expressed within both private and government circles about the practicability of such efforts. Bearing in mind the caveats ... concerning the harmful long–term consequences of formalizing agreements which cannot be succesfully im-

plemented and adhered to [because of political realities and different basic economic philosophies], it might be appropriate to expect some doubts about the wisdom of such efforts.

The author added, however, that these doubts

apply only to substantive or binding planning. ... [The] objections would [not] apply to planning of the indicative type ... On the contrary, the information generated in any indicative planning excercise ... could be very valuable [for each individual country]. [Nugent, 1981: 57]

ECWA's 1984 Survey indicates how even the vague initial efforts have collapsed in the face of the deteriorating economic and political situation:

The implementation of the resolutions adopted by the Amman Summit in 1980 came to a virtual stand–still ... Ambitious plans for economic co–operation ad integration were set aside in favour of more attainable targets. Overall or comprehensive planning and harmonization of plans, like the Pan–Arab Development Plan, gave way to sectoral planning and the establishment of joint ventures [ECWA, 1985: 152].

In the face of these dificulties, the role of the Arab Institute for Planning, in Kuwait, can only be very modest. It may be of symbolic significance, however, that it is housed in Kuwait. It is indeed the GCC region which stands the best chance of establishing an effective joint development planning infrastructure, but even there it remains to be seen whether the imperative of long–term economic survival will be able to predominate over other political factors. Given the conclusions reached in previous chapters about the nature and context of national development planning, this regional lack of success does not come as a surprise.

6 THE ARAB DONORS

Much has been written in recent years about the role and nature of Arab (or OPEC) aid, and the institutions involved. Rather than duplicating those efforts, this chapter will be limited to a brief background and appreciation of Arab aid, and will then focus on the specific aid efforts and administrations of the most important donors: Saudi Arabia, Kuwait and the United Arab Emirates. Attention will also be given to the Arab Fund for Economic and Social Development (AFESD) as an example of a multilateral development institution with a coordinating function.

Some recent publications have provided valuable information on Arab/OPEC aid. An OECD report [1983] provides the statistical data and 'detached' assessment which has formed the basis for subsequent work. An update of basic facts and figures is provided in the annual *Development Cooperation,* published by the OECD. Porter [1986] gives a lucid and concise account and appreciation of the issues involved. UNCTAD in 1985 also published a report on the development assistance of OPEC members and institutions. A collection of valuable insiders' accounts and views, complemented by academic papers and a wealth of statistical material, is provided in the book edited by Achilli & Khaldi [1984]. A highly critical, detailed study of OPEC aid and its politics is found in Hunter [1984], while Imady [1984], until 1985 Director of AFESD, offers a sympathetic account and analysis with extensive statistical data. Further there are OPEC's own overview [OPEC, 1985] and the encyclopaedic work of Selim [1983]. Up-to-date figures about all of the Arab regional and national development institutions can of course be found in the quarterly and annual reports of AFESD's Coordination Secretariat (for instance AFESD, 1983, 1985a, 1986).

General Overview

Middle East aid donors have comprised the Arab members of OPEC (Saudi Arabia, Kuwait, UAE, Qatar, Iraq, Algeria, Libya) in addition to Iran and Oman. Other Arab countries have extended technical assistance and have, for instance, provided paid teachers (particularly Egypt prior to the oil boom), but they will not be covered here. The bulk of the funds, since 1973, has come from just six states: Saudi Arabia, Kuwait, The UAE, Qatar, Iraq and Libya. Iran was an important donor only between 1974 and 1978. Due to the Gulf War, Iraq turned from a donor into a net aid importer by 1983. When reference is made, henceforth, to OPEC assistance, it should be noted that Iran, Nigeria and Venezuela are included in the figures, and that this is therefore not co–terminous with Arab aid, although the latter does account for the lion's share in OPEC aid: 98 per cent after 1978. Saudi Arabia and Kuwait alone, which in 1980 provided 70 per cent of OPEC aid, accounted for 96 per cent by 1985 [OECD, 1986: 78]. 'Arab aid' will include the Islamic Development Bank.

Prior to 1973 and the quadrupling of oil prices, Kuwait had already been extending aid for many years, and at its independence in 1961 had set up the Kuwait Fund for Arab Economic Development (KFAED) This model was followed by the Abu Dhabi Fund for Arab Economic Development (ADFAED) in 1971, at the independence of the UAE, and, in 1974, the Saudi Development Fund (SFD) and the Iraqi Fund for External Development were established. From 1973–1974 onwards the Arab aid effort grew at a momentous pace, for three reasons. First, the countries concerned were now faced with a volume of funds which their economies could not absorb. Second, they perceived the need to justify their wealth and independence to the other Arab countries and the Third World at large. Thirdly, a genuine feeling that 'now the chance had come for the Third World' influenced the thinking of some governments.

The four bilateral Gulf donors (Saudi Arabia, Kuwait, UAE and Qatar) together in 1973 provided ODA to the equivalent of over 12 per cent of their GNP. This had dropped to 2.38 per cent by 1985 due to falling oil income and greater domestic absorptive capacity. From 1982 onwards Qatar's aid became comparatively insignificant (one fifth of that in the previous year), and the UAE followed suit in 1983–1984. Saudi Arabia in 1984 still gave some 3.3 per cent of its GNP to aid, Kuwait 3.8 per cent; by 1985 these figures had dropped to c. 2.9 and 3.2 per cent respectively. Specialists often question whether or not the massive assistance to the frontline states should be counted as ODA [see Porter, 1986: 146–149]. But even if it is excluded the proportion to GNP still remains significantly greater than the OECD's ODA (although this is no longer true for Qatar and the UAE individually). It must be pointed out, moreover, that the ratio to GNP in the case of the oil producers indicates something quite different from what it does in the industrialised countries. The former are not really *producing* goods but rather selling off irreplacable reserves in the form of oil. Aid from the oil–producing states therefore represents a long–term 'sacrifice'. Secondly, whereas aid from the OECD always offers the potential of a reverse flow — since goods, services and expertise usually have to come from the developed world — this has not been the case for the Arab donors. The latter have little to offer by way of such goods, services or expertise, although Kuwait has recently been changing that picture. A new trend appears to be indicated, however, by the huge rise of the share of oil grants and credits in total OPEC–ODA, from 6 per cent in 1984 to 22 per cent the following year [OECD, 1986].

In Tables 6.1 to 6.19 trends in volume, distribution, conditions and relative shares in Arab aid are shown. Table 6.15 shows the main OPEC aid institutions. Briefly, the following points may be noted:

(1) More than half of Arab aid goes to Arab countries.
(2) Within this, the most important recipients are the 'confrontation states' : Egypt (until 1978), Syria, Jordan and the PLO.
(3) The aid referred to under (2) is mainly 'general support assistance' (GSA) in grant form. The 1985 figures for total OPEC aid, however, indicate a clear shift, accounting for 16 per cent of total ODA, from GSA to oil grants and credits.
(4) If the 'political' aid to the 'confrontation states' is excluded, the conditions which accompany Arab ODA (as far as it is recorded) are harder than for OECD aid, and are hardening further.
(5) There has been a widening in the geographical scope of Arab / OPEC aid. As of 1986, aid had gone to 100 countries.
(6) As to the sectoral distribution of other than GSA, infrastructure has remained the main focus. The figures for 1985 again show a change, however: the share of agriculture rose from less than 2 per cent in 1984 to over 5 per cent.
(7) The major part of Arab aid has been bilateral. The share of multilaterally channelled assistance, however, roughly tripled since the mid–1970s to over 26 per cent in 1981. By 1985 it had dropped again to c. 17 per cent of total ODA. Co-financing has increased considerably.

(8) The share of the main Arab donors' national development
agencies in the total ODA which these countries have provided, has grown. Nevertheless, it remains relatively low.
By 1985, 47 per cent of Kuwaiti ODA was administered by
KFAED, but in the case of Saudi Arabia, SFD's share in 1984
was halved from the level it had reached in the early 1980s,
dropping to 3.7 per cent by 1985. The share of ADFAED–
administered aid in total ODA from the UAE had risen to
over 16 per cent by 1983. Its further sharp rise (over 50 per
cent in 1985) is merely the result of the equally sharp drop
in total ODA from this state (these figures include aid which
the funds administer on behalf of other bodies). In fact, more
than a third of Arab aid — mainly from Saudi Arabia — has
taken the form of government subventions to unspecified recipients. In 1984, less than 44 per cent of all OPEC ODA
was channelled through the funds. This still represents a significant rise: the share of the funds was only just over 28 per
cent of total ODA provided over all years (including 1984).

Data on the Arab national and regional funds' ODA up to the
end of 1986, and divided by fund, recipient region, and sector, are
given in Tables 6.16 to 6.19.

In the remainder of this chapter, the foreign aid of Kuwait,
Saudi Arabia and the UAE will be considered, as also will the Arab
Fund for Economic and Social Development (AFESD), which has
acted as a coordinator in addition to providing its own ODA. The
chapter concludes with some observations on the nature, trends
and motivation of Arab aid.

Table 6.1 Concessional Assistance by Arab OPEC Members 1974-1985

net disbursements in $ million [b]

	1970	1974	1975	1976	1977	1978	1979	1980	1981	1982	1983	1984	1985[a]
Gulf States													
Kuwait	148	631	910	706	1,302	1,001	971	1,140	1,163	1,161	997	1,018	749
Qatar	-	185	307	180	127	95	282	277	246	139	20	10	-2
Saudi Arabia	172	2,153	2,699	2,791	2,900	5,250	3,941	5,682	5,514	3,854	3,304	3,212	2,646
UAE	-	510	929	1,028	1,091	889	968	1,118	805	407	348	84	58
Sub-total	320	3,479	4,846	4,706	5,420	7,236	6,161	8,217	7,729	5,562	4,668	4,324	3,452
OTHER ARAB													
Algeria	1	47	31	11	35	39	281	81	55	129	37	48	45
Iraq	-	423	265	123	103	123	658	864	207	52	-30	-33	-26
Libya	64	147	275	98	130	132	145	376	257	44	144	20	151
Sub-total	65	617	571	232	267	294	1,084	1,322	519	225	151	135	170
TOTAL	385	4,096	5,417	4,938	5,687	7,530	7,245	9,539	8,248	5,787	4,819	4,359	3,622

Notes: a. Provisional
b. at current prices and exchange rates

Sources: OECD, 1983; OECD, 1985; OECD 1986

Table 6.2 Concessional Assistance by OPEC members in 1983

$ million

Donor country	Commitments			Net disbursements			
	Bilateral	Multilateral	Total	Bilateral	Multilateral	Total	As % of GNP
Gulf States							
Kuwait	1 141.2	197.5	1 338.7	757.7	247.5	1 005.2	3.84
Qatar	2.0	6.3	8.3	-4.3	14.9	10.6	0.13
Saudi Arabia	3 365.7	429.7	3 795.4	3 132.3	528.6	3 660.8	3.29
UAE	308.7	63.3	372.0	324.8	39.5	364.3	1.44
Sub-total	4 833.4	684.3	5 517.7	4 232.1	809.9	5 042.0	2.95
Other Arab donors							
Algeria	28.5	37.6	66.1	26.5	34.5	60.9	0.13
Iraq	8.7	33.3	42.0	-42.9	6.0	-36.9	-0.11
Libya	101.2	87.7	188.9	58.0	83.8	141.8	0.49
Sub-total	138.4	158.6	296.9	41.6	124.3	165.9	0.15
Non-Arab donors							
Iran	195.0	-	195.0	2.6	12.4	15.0	0.01
Nigeria	1.3	1.1	2.4	1.1	33.7	34.9	0.05
Venezuela	37.4	36.9	74.3	11.7	128.9	140.6	0.22
Sub-total	233.7	38.0	271.7	15.4	175.1	190.5	0.08
Total	5 205.4	880.9	6 086.3	4 289.1	1 109.2	5 398.3	1.03

Source, OECD, 1985.

Table 6.3 Concessional Assistance by OPEC members in 1984

$ million

Donor country	Commitments			Net disbursements			
	Bilateral	Multilateral	Total	Bilateral	Multilateral	Total	As % of GNP
Gulf States							
Kuwait	988.7	201.4	1 190.2	810.4	203.9	1 014.3	3.79
Qatar	2.0	7.5	9.5	2.0	10.6	12.6	0.16
Saudi Arabia	3 593.3	285.9	3 879.1	2 887.9	427.1	3 315.1	3.29
UAE	132.0	59.1	191.1	37.1	6.3	43.3	0.17
Sub-total	4 322.5	480.8	4 803.4	3 745.7	643.4	4 389.1	2.73
Other Arab donors							
Algeria	0.7	41.4	42.1	-2.0	44.3	46.48	0.09
Iraq	-	29.9	29.9	-50.0	2.2	-47.88	-0.14
Libya	74.2	89.3	163.5	0.6	16.4	17.08	0.06
Sub-total	74.9	160.6	235.5	-47.4	62.9	15.6	0.01
Non-Arab donors							
Iran	200.0	0.1	200.1	-	-	-	-
Nigeria	-	15.2	15.2	-	51.0	51.0	0.07
Venezuela	57.4	71.7	129.1	15.5	74.2	89.7	0.12
Sub-total	257.4	86.9	344.3	15.5	125.1	140.6	0.06
Total	4 654.8	728.4	5 383.2	3 713.8	831.4	4 545.2	0.86

Note: Bilateral data for 1984 are provisional

Sources: OECD, 1985: 371, except for Kuwait: calc.KFAED

Table 6.4 Concessional Assistance by OPEC members in 1985

$ million

Donor country	Commitments			Net disbursements			
	Bilateral	Multilateral	Total	Bilateral	Multilateral	Total	As % of GNP
Gulf States							
Kuwait	554.2	144.7	698.9	558.0	190.9	749.0	3.16
Qatar	5.1	10.6	15.7	-6.7	5.2	-1.5	-0.03
Saudi Arabia	2 462.8	321.9	2 775.8	2 283.1	363.2	2 646.3	2.88
UAE	46.9	55.0	101.9	51.7	6.4	58.0	0.24
Sub-total	3 069.0	523.3	3 592.3	2 886.1	565.7	3 451.7	2.38
Other Arab donors							
Algeria	49.9	39.7	89.6	7.0	37.8	44.8	0.08
Iraq	-	29.5	29.5	-26.1	0.2	-25.9	-0.08
Libya	171.9	84.4	256.3	137.7	13.6	151.2	0.59
Sub-total	221.8	153.6	375.4	118.6	51.5	170.1	0.15
Non-Arab donors							
Iran	199.6	0.2	199.8	-171.3	0.1	-171.2	-0.11
Nigeria	5.6	27.5	33.1	5.6	39.8	45.4	0.06
Venezuela	76.2	8.4	84.6	19.1	12.8	31.9	0.07
Sub-total	281.4	36.1	317.5	-146.5	52.7	-93.9	-0.03
Total	3 572.2	713.0	4 285.2	2 858.1	669.8	3 528.0	0.65

Note: Bilateral data for 1985 are provisional
Source: OECD, 1986.

Table 6.5
ODA as % of GNP: the Gulf States
and DAC compared, 1970–1985

	70	71	72	73	74	75	76	77
GULF STATES								
Kuwait	6.19	3.38	5.10	8.13	5.33	7.26	5.00	8.19
Qatar	—	—	0.13	15.51	9.26	14.59	7.35	6.79
Saudi Arabia	5.59	5.04	6.57	14.60	8.94	7.50	6.22	4.94
UAE	—	5.36	5.10	12.53	7.03	11.69	8.95	7.39
Sub–total	5.16	4.27	5.64	12.48	7.67	8.33	6.43	5.94
Other Arab	0.64	0.57	0.62	1.15	1.77	1.44	0.50	0.43
DAC	0.34	0.33	0.35	0.29	0.33	0.35	0.33	0.33

	78	79	80	81	82	83	84	85
GULF STATES								
Kuwait	5.48	3.52	3.52	3.63	4.60	3.84	3.79	3.16
Qatar	3.29	6.07	4.28	3.74	1.66	0.13	0.16	−0.03
Saudi Arabia	8.00	5.20	4.95	3.49	2.54	3.29	3.29	2.88
UAE	6.36	5.08	3.82	2.60	1.34	1.44	0.17	0.24
Sub–total	7.18	4.85	4.50	3.40	2.58	2.95	2.73	2.38
Other Arab	0.46	1.18	1.21	0.56	0.22	0.15	0.01	0.15
DAC	0.35	0.35	0.37	0.35	0.38	0.36	0.36	0.35

Source: OECD, 1985, 1986, except for Kuwait 83–84: KFAED–supplied figures.

Table 6.6
Comparison Financial Conditions of ODA
from DAC, OPEC and CMEA

	Share of grants			Grant element in loans			Overall concessionality		
	1975	80	81	75	80	81	75	80	81
OPEC	48	60	58	47	49	52	72	80	80
DAC	69	75	75	63	59	58	89	90	90
CMEA	20	28	31	50	52	57	52	65	70

Source: OECD, 1983: 16

Table 6.7   Composition of Aid Commitments from OPEC, DAC, CMEA

(In per cent of total)(a)

	OPEC			DAC			CMEA(b)		
	1975	1980	1981	1975	1980	1981	1975	1980	1981
Bilateral aid	93	88	74	76	72	70	99	99	99
General support assistance	45	69	56	4	3	5	12	21	24
Other non-project assistance	11	6	3	24	14	14	4	5	8
Project Assistance	37	13	15	48	55	51	83c)	73c)	67c)
Multilateral Contributions	7	12	26	24	28	30	1	1	1
Of which: to organisations with restricted membership(d)	4	10	21	5	7	7	-	-	-
Broad membership	3	2	5	19	21	23	1	1	1

a) Excluding debt reorganisation; for DAC countries project assistance also includes assistance allocable by sector.
b) Partly estimates.
c) Contains probably some current import financing.
d) Arab OPEC agencies for OPEC donors, EDF and EIB for DAC donors.

Source: OECD, 1983: 18

Table 6.8 Comparative Geographic Distribution of Net Bilateral Disbursements from OPEC, DAC, CMEA

	OPEC				DAC				CMEA(a)			
	1975	1980	1981		1975	1980	1981		1975	1980	1981	
LLDCs	12	15	20		20	20	19		13	20	21	
Other LICs (b)	60	14	4		37	36	37		47	51	46	
MICs (c)	26	70	76		37	40	38		25	29	34	
NICs (d)	x	x	x		4	3	5		3	1	1	
OPEC (e)	2	1	x		2	2	2		13	-1	-2	
3 largest recipients	65	51	47		24	18	18		70	83	88	
6 largest recipients	79	69	70		37	32	31		82	98	100	

Note: For about one-third of OPEC bilateral aid no data on its geographic distribution are available. For DAC countries about one-tenth is geographically unallocated.

a) Rough estimates.
b) Other LICs (low-income countries) include countries with per capita incomes in 1980 below $600, according to the IBRD Atlas, excluding China and the least-developed countries. The fall of OPEC aid to these countries is primarily due to the sharp decline of aid to Egypt.
c) MICs (middle-income countries) are those developing countries, other than NICs and OPEC countries, with per capita incomes exceeding $600 in 1980.
d) NICs (the newly-industrialised countries) are Argentina, Brazil, Greece, Hong Kong, Korea (Rep.) Mexico, Portugal, Singapore, Spain, Taiwan and Yugoslavia.
e) Here OPEC includes all members of OPEC other than Indonesia (a LIC) and Nigeria (a MIC).

Source: OECD, 1983: 17

Table 6.9
Net Bilateral Disbursements of Concessional OPEC Aid by Recipient Country

	1974–8 $m.	%	1979–83 $m.	%
Arab countries	13,689.6	75.92	17,917.5	86.03
Front Line				
Jordan	1,275.3	7.07	4,405.3	21.15
Syria	2,646.5	14.68	6,329.7	30.39
Egypt	5,307.7	29.43	110.4	0.53
Total	9,228.5	51.18	10,845.4	52.07
Bahrain	278.2	1.54	570.6	2.74
Lebanon	321.9	1.78	709.8	3.41
Oman	599.7	3.33	763.2	3.66
YAR (North Yemen)	785.7	4.36	1,098.7	5.27
PDRY (South Yemen)	303.5	1.68	209.9	1.01
Morocco	310.1	1.72	1,417.3	6.80
Tunisia	129.9	0.72	184.1	0.88
Mauritania	402.2	2.23	405.9	1.95
Somalia	477.0	2.65	438.8	2.11
Sudan	623.2	3.46	1,130.8	5.43
All other Arab	228.9	1.27	143.0	0.69
Other Islamic countries	2,530.8	14.04	2,041.0	9.80
African countries	325.7	1.81	506.7	2.43
Asian countries, of which:	2,175.4	12.06	939.6	4.51
Bangladesh	299.4	1.66	339.0	1.63
Pakistan	1,683.5	9.33	440.3	2.11
Other Asia	192.5	1.07	160.3	0.77
Europe (Turkey)	29.7	0.10	594.7	2.86
Other countries	1,811.7	10.05	867.6	4.17
European countries	11.6	0.06	53.6	0.26
African countries	184.6	1.02	625.4	3.00
Asia & Pacific, of which:	1,573.8	8.73	−54.2	−0.26
India	1,291.0	7.16	−267.1	−1.28
Other countries	282.8	1.57	212.9	1.02
Caribbean & Latin America	41.7	0.23	242.8	1.17
Total allocated	18,031.7	100.00	20,826.1	100.00
Total unallocated	5,657.2		11,358.7	
Grand total	23,688.9		32,184.8	

Source: OECD, *Development Co-operation*, Annual.

As in PORTER, 1986: 58.

Table 6.10 Sectoral Distribution of Bilateral Concessional Commitments by OPEC Donors

(In per cent of total)

	1973	1975	1977	1978	1979	1980	1981
Non-project assistance	88.3	60.8	56.1	79.8	76.4	84.9	79.8
Of which:							
General Support	85.5	48.7	49.2	76.9	65.4	78.5	75.2
Emergency Relief	0.8	2.4	0.8	0.4	6.5	2.3	2.6
Oil Credits	-	9.5	1.8	1.9	4.4	3.1	0.2
Other	2.0	0.2	4.3	0.6	0.1	1.0	1.8
Project assistance	11.7	39.2	43.9	20.2	23.6	15.1	20.2
Of which:							
Agriculture	0.3	1.6	0.4	0.4	1.7	0.5	1.4
Extractive							
Industries	0.2	8.2	1.2	0.9	2.3	-	0.8
Manufacturing	2.6	2.0	8.7	3.4	2.7	1.1	0.8
Energy	1.1	1.6	10.5	1.4	5.1	1.9	4.6
Transport, Storage							
and Communications	0.2	4.9	14.5	8.1	4.1	7.2	6.2
Education	0.4	1.5	1.0	1.0	1.2	1.0	0.5
Health	0.4	0.4	1.3	0.3	0.5	0.6	1.2
Other and							
Unspecified	6.5	19.0	6.3	4.7	6.0	2.8	4.7

Source: OECD, 1983: 35

Table 6.11   Geographic Distribution of Total Disbursements of Arab/OPEC Aid
(bi- and multi-lateral), 1982-85

$ million

	Gross				Net			
	1982	1983	1984	1985	1982	1983	1984	1985
Middle East and North Africa	2 874.1	2 478.0	2 195.2	2 117.0	2 711.4	2 266.9	1 963.3	849.1
of which:								
Syria	909.2	932.3	844.6	635.6	880.3	898.5	825.9	596.3
Jordan	717.0	708.5	661.1	508.9	744.0	686.9	614.5	462.8
Morocco	495.6	148.8	97.4	483.4	486.2	133.6	74.7	461.2
Yemen AR	282.1	215.0	212.4	168.5	276.0	203.0	197.6	151.3
Bahrain	94.1	225.0	208.4	83.8	90.2	214.8	197.3	70.8
Oman	136.7	79.0	73.4	75.3	124.9	63.5	57.6	60.8
Other	239.4	169.4	97.9	161.5	149.8	66.0	-4.3	45.9
Sub-Saharan Africa	1 018.6	911.8	634.1	762.2	960.2	834.7	555.8	658.3
of which:								
Sudan	199.9	367.5	122.0	216.3	185.5	357.6	116.5	215.2
Mauritania	98.3	73.7	66.3	80.8	93.8	68.3	62.1	61.5
Senegal	21.8	59.0	62.6	47.3	20.8	57.0	61.0	45.6
Somalia	184.2	46.1	30.1	45.2	183.1	43.3	29.3	38.3
Mali	52.2	49.0	12.3	40.0	51.1	45.9	10.1	30.9
Kenya	14.1	11.4	33.6	24.5	13.8	8.9	31.2	22.2
Djibouti	4.0	13.7	43.3	20.1	4.0	13.4	43.2	19.1
Other	444.1	291.4	263.9	288.0	408.1	240.3	202.4	225.5
Asia	469.7	410.6	305.9	227.9	196.2	113.3	-12.3	-88.7
of which:								
China	-	35.7	49.4	25.1	-	35.7	49.4	21.9
Bangladesh	158.0	123.1	41.1	30.2	148.4	109.0	26.3	2.1
Pakistan	108.3	110.1	50.1	21.0	28.0	19.9	-48.0	-65.6
India	78.3	27.3	52.8	57.5	-75.4	-125.6	-107.4	-91.3
Other	125.1	114.4	112.5	94.1	95.2	74.3	67.4	46.3
America, Europe and Oceania	135.3	77.2	73.4	93.3	122.9	56.8	60.0	66.3
of which: Turkey	102.8	32.7	34.4	43.1	95.3	24.9	30.1	26.4
Unallocated[a]	875.7	949.3	1 234.7	516.0	875.7	949.3	1 234.7	516.0
TOTAL	5 373.4	4 826.9	4 443.3	3 716.4	4 866.4	4 221.0	3 801.5	3 001.0

a) Mainly grants and loans from the Saudi Arabian Finance Ministry.
Note: Countries are ranked according to 1985 net disbursements.

Table 6.12 Share of Individual OPEC Countries in Arab/OPEC Multilateral Aid Agencies

(in per-cent)

	AAAID	AFESD	AMF(a)	BADEA(b)	GODE	IslDB	OFID(c)	OTHER(d)
Algeria	1.5	8.8	14.4	4.1	-	3.5	3.0	3.4
Iraq	15.0	8.6	14.4	14.2	-	1.4	4.8	12.5
Kuwait	19.5	23.0	9.5	14.9	35.0	13.9	10.9	19.1
Libya	-	13.0	3.5	16.3	-	17.3	6.1	10.8
Qatar	7.5	1.2	3.8	8.1	10.0	1.4	2.7	6.3
Saudi Arabia	22.5	21.6	14.4	24.4	40.0	27.8	30.4	31.2
UAE	15.0	5.9	5.7	12.2	15.0	10.7	5.0	16.0
Iran	-	-	-	-	-	-	15.5	-
Nigeria	-	-	-	-	-	-	7.3	-
Venezuela	-	-	-	-	-	-	13.5	-
Total above	81.0	82.1	65.7	94.2	100.0	76.0	99.2	99.3
Total subscribed capital $m	360	2655	931	738	2000	2148	3324	203

Notes:

a) Not an aid agency under DAC definitions, but included for the sake of completeness.
b) Including SAAFA.
c) Including IFAD.
d) AFTAAAC, Islamic Solidarity Fund and OAPEC Special Account.
Note: With the exception of GODE the above percentages do not add up to 100 since membership in these institutions is not limited to the ten countries listed.

Source: OECD, 1983: 40

Table 6.13
Annual Disbursements of OPEC Countries to International Multilateral Organisations: 1973–1981 average, 1984, 1985 (in US$ millions)

	1973–81	84	85
IDA	73	230.8	198.2
IFAD*ª*	71	65.3	13.6
African Development Bank*ᵇ*	31	37.8	42.2
African Development Fund*ᵇ*	9		
World Food Programme	23	22.2	31.3
World Bank	22	51.9	1.6
Inter–American Dev. Bank (non–Arab)	13	16.4	6.8
UNDP	11	7.8	5.6
UN Works and Relief Agency	9	7.5	3.4
Arab multilateral aid agencies*ᶜ*	...	312.1	301.6
Opec Fund	...	62.1	52.2

Notes: (a) beginning 1977; (b) counted together for '84 and '85 (c) AFESD, BADEA, IsDB, AGFUND
Source: OECD, 1983: 42; 1986

Table 6.14
Share of National Aid Agencies in Total Aid Disbursements of Donor Country, 1975 — 1985 (in per cent)*ª*

	Kuwait	Saudi Arabia	UAE
1975	5.6	—	0.2
1976	28.6	2.3	7.4
1977	12.9	6.4	12.4
1978	18.6	4.5	16.5
1979	40.0	9.8	8.7
1980	31.1	8.6	12.1
1981	23.8	10.4	12.7
1982	28.0	10.2	17.6
1983	34.0	8.6	16.2
1984	39.2	4.7	65.0
1985	47.0	3.7	50.3

Note: (a) Figures for 1975–1979 are from OECD, 1983: 26; those for 1980–1985 from OECD, 1986: 79. There is a discrepancy for the overlapping years 1980 and 1981. This is insignificant for Saudi Arabia and the UAE, but the figures for Kuwait in the latter source are about 25 per cent lower.

Table 6.15 Profile of Arab/OPEC Development Institutions, as of end 1984

	Base	Established	Started	Capital Authorized	Paid-in	Cumulative financing Comm.	Disb.
				in millions of US dollars			
MULTILATERAL							
Arab Fund for Economic and Social Development (AFESD)	Kuwait	Dec 1971	Jan 1974	2,800	1,822	2,229	1,078
Islamic Solidarity Fund	Jeddah	1974	1975	n.a.	n.a.	n.a.	n.a.
Arab Fund for Technical Assistance to African and Arab Countries (AFTAAC)	Tunis	1975	1976	n.a.	n.a.	n.a.	35[1]
Arab Bank for Economic Development in Africa (BADEA)	Khartoum	Nov 1975	Mar 1975	988	985	863	527
Islamic Development Bank	Jeddah	Oct 1975	Oct 1976	2,010	1,281	4,686	3,771
OPEC Fund for International Development (OFID)	Vienna	Jan 1976	Aug 1976	3,435	2,513	2,034	1,418
Arab Authority for Agricultural Investment and Development	Khartoum	Nov 1976	May 1978	540	340	67[2]	50[2]
Arab Gulf Fund for United Nations Development Organisations (AGFUND)	Riyadh	Apr 1981	1981	n.a.	167[3]	133[3]	n.a.
BILATERAL							
Kuwait Fund for Arab Economic Development (KFAED)	Kuwait	Dec 1961	Mar 1962	6,900	2,952	4,508	2,682
Abu Dhabi Fund for Arab Economic Development	Abu Dhabi	July1971	Sep 1974	544[4]	581	1,065	865
Iraqi Fund for External Development	Baghdad	June1974	Jan 1977	1,009	723	1,484	694
Saudi Fund for Development	Riyadh	Sep 1974	Feb 1975	7,163	5,300	4,510	2,291
Libyan Arab Foreign Investment Company[4]	Tripoli	Feb 1981	1981	1,700	887	n.a.	1,033[5]

Notes: 1) end 1983
2) Equity participation. In addition, AAAID has guaranteed loans from other sources to its subsidiary ventures for around US$ 86 m.
3) as of May 1985
4) Investments 'on a profitable basis' in all sectors
5) investments

Source: OPEC, 1985; individual institutions and their annual reports.

Table 6.16 Financing Operations of Arab National and Regional Development Institutions by Year and Institution, to end 1986

(\$ million)

Inst.	No. of countr.	No. of Oper.	1962-1973	1974	1975	1976	1977	1978	1979	1980	1981	1982	1983	1984	1985	1986	TOTAL	%
IsDB	38	454	-	-	-	-	119.3	188.7	498.7	475.4	649.1	519.8	571.2	836.6	671.9	724.9	5255.6	22.1
ADFAED	42	88	-	64.3	44.2	163.7	138.8	216.0	145.1	100.6	69.9	65.7	25.8	28.6	16.9	15.1	1094.6	4.6
OPEC Fund	81	409	-	-	-	42.7	243.0	155.0	212.8	250.8	400.9	323.7	212.9	94.4	51.2	87.7	2075.0	8.7
Saudi Fund	58	238	-	-	282.8	432.6	770.0	561.7	447.0	331.9	348.6	611.3	372.3	351.7	372.1	263.8	5145.8	21.6
Iraqi Fund	31	69	-	30.0	-	15.0	26.3	101.2	406.3	743.3	373.3	37.7	-	-	-	-	1733.0	7.3
AFESD	17	187	-	114.9	193.4	331.6	362.6	-	70.2	111.7	148.4	232.8	309.7	283.4	176.3	361.2	2696.2	11.4
KFAED	65	314	342.9	138.9	327.1	318.7	411.0	200.2	353.7	268.7	741.4	763.1	390.0	252.6	213.9	317.5	5039.5	21.2
BADEA	38	119	-	-	79.4	77.0	66.9	20.2	81.0	69.7	80.0	67.2	68.3	71.3	62.3	743.3	3.1
TOTAL		1878	342.9	348.0	847.5	1383.7	2148.1	1489.6	2154.1	2363.3	2801.2	2634.1	1948.9	1915.4	1573.6	1832.4	23782.9	100.0

Source: AFESD, 1987b

Table 6.17 Financing Operations of Arab National and Regional Development Institutions by Region and Sector, to end 1986

($ million)

REGION	No. of countries	No. of Operations	Transport & Telecomm.	Energy (El, Oil, Gas)	Water & Sewerage	Agriculture & Livestock	Industry & Mining	Others (a)	TOTAL	%
1) Arab countries	19	806	2781.9	2839.3	807.8	2338.0	2414.0	1260.9	12441.9	52.3
2) African countries	39	610	1519.7	748.8	175.2	888.7	451.0	606.4	4389.8	18.5
3) Asian countries	23	387	1132.6	2891.3	95.0	929.3	1059.3	369.8	6477.3	27.2
4) Latin American c. b	17	64	25.12	101.0	18.9	27.7	50.0	146.5	369.3	1.6
5) Other countries	2	11	53.7	10.8	26.5	13.6	-	-	104.6	0.4
TOTAL	100	1878	5513.1	6591.1	1123.4	4197.3	3974.3	2383.6	23782.9	100.0
Percentage			23.2	27.7	4.7	17.7	16.7	10.0	100.0	

Notes: a. Including financing operations, for supprt of national development institutions, Health, Education, Training, Housing, Tourism, Balance of payments support.

b. Largely from the OPEC Fund

Source: AFESD, 1987b.

Table 6.18   Financing Operations of Arab National and Regional Development Institutions by Sector and Institution, to end 1986

(in $ million)

Institution	No. of countries	No. of Operations	Transport & Telecomm.	Energy	Water & Sewerage	Agriculture & Livestock	Industry & Mining	Others[a]	TOTAL	%
IsDB	38	454	227.7	2552.4	93.6	425.7	1783.3	172.8	5255.6	22.1
ADFAED	42	88	182.4	395.2	40.2	118.2	333.5	25.2	1094.6	4.6
OPEC Fund	81	409	243.5	582.6	58.3	191.2	164.7	834.4	2075.0	8.7
Saudi Fund	58	238	2014.2	998.8	382.1	1072.2	350.0	328.5	5145.8	21.6
Iraqi Fund	31	69	220.8	124.2	5.0	320.7	186.3	876.1	1733.0	7.3
AFESD	17	187	767.5	463.2	309.5	828.1	245.5	82.5	2696.2	11.4
KFAED	65	314	1522.8	1393.7	208.8	1065.5	810.5	38.2	5039.5	21.2
BADEA	38	119	334.3	81.1	25.9	175.4	100.6	26.0	743.3	3.1
TOTAL		1878	5513.1	6591.1	1123.4	4197.3	3974.3	2383.6	23782.9	100.0
Percentage			23.2	27.7	4.7	17.7	16.5	10.0	100	

Note: a. see note (a) for previous table (6.18).

Source: AFESD, 1987b.

Table 6.19 Financing Operations of Arab National and Regional Development Institutions by Sector and Institution, to end 1986

($ million – Number of operations in brackets)

	Arab World	Africa	Asia	Latin America	Other	TOTAL	%
No. of countries	19	39	23	17	2	100	
IsDB	2834.5 (234)	526.2 (82)	1894.6 (138)	---	---	5255.6 (454)	22.1
ADFAED	831.3 (50)	100.2 (25)	155.9 (12)	---	7.2 (1)	1094.6 (88)	4.6
OPEC Fund	335.0 (57)	762.6 (200)	753.0 (93)	224.4 (59)	---	2075.0 (409)	8.7
Saudi Fund	2140.6 (90)	998.1 (87)	1914.5 (57)	59.9 (2)	32.7 (2)	5145.8 (238)	21.6
Iraqi Fund	1099.0 (33)	314.1 (17)	229.9 (15)	85.0 (3)	5.0 (1)	1733.0 (69)	7.3
AFESD	2696.2 (187)	---	---	---	---	2696.2 (187)	11.4
KFAED	2505.3 (155)	944.9 (80)	1529.6 (72)	---	59.8 (7)	5039.5 (314)	21.2
BADEA	---	743.3 (119)	---	---	---	743.3 (119)	3.1
TOTAL AMOUNT	12449.9 (806)	4289.8 (610)	6477.3 (387)	369.3 (64)	104.6 (11)	23782.9 (1878)	100.0
Percentage	52.3	18.5	27.2	1.6	0.4		

Source: AFESD 1987b.

Kuwait

Already before independence, Kuwait had been giving aid to the then Trucial States, Oman, Bahrain and the Yemens. In 1965 this was brought under the umbrella of a General Board for the South and the Arabian Gulf (GBSAG). The Kuwait Fund for Arab Economic Development was set up at independence in 1961. The Fund (see Table 6.15 and Figures 6.1 — 6.2) is semi–autonomous under the minister of Finance and Economy and has its own Board of Directors. Its funds come from an initial capital injection by the government, which was followed by further grants in 1974 and 1981, in addition to fixed yearly subventions of KD 30 million. With this capital it has functioned roughly on the lines of the World Bank, adding to it by investment. Under the General Directorship of Abdellatif Yusuf al–Hamad (now Director–General of AFESD) KFAED acquired an international reputation for good management and became a model for other Arab Funds. It bears repeating that less than half of Kuwaiti ODA is administered by KFAED. But the Fund has had an impact beyond its own contributions. Because of its reputation, its commitment to a project has often catalysed other donors into contributing. KFAED's criteria are the economic viability of a project, its socio–economic value, availability of additional funds (at least 51 per cent of the cost), and, in principle, the credit–worthiness of the recipient country. Independent follow–up is required and the Fund often sends its own field–missions.

Table 6.20
Kuwait's ODA in 1984, in US$ (rate KD 1 = $ 3.381)

Type	Amount	Repayments	Net
BILATERAL			
Grants	499,852,879	—	499,852,879
Soft Loans	408,214,069	97,689,214	310,524,855
MULTILATERAL	203,900,952	—	203,900,952
	(grants and capital subscriptions)		
TOTAL	1,111,967,900	97,689,214	1,014,278,686

Source: KFAED

Figure 6.1 Kuwait: the Administration of Aid

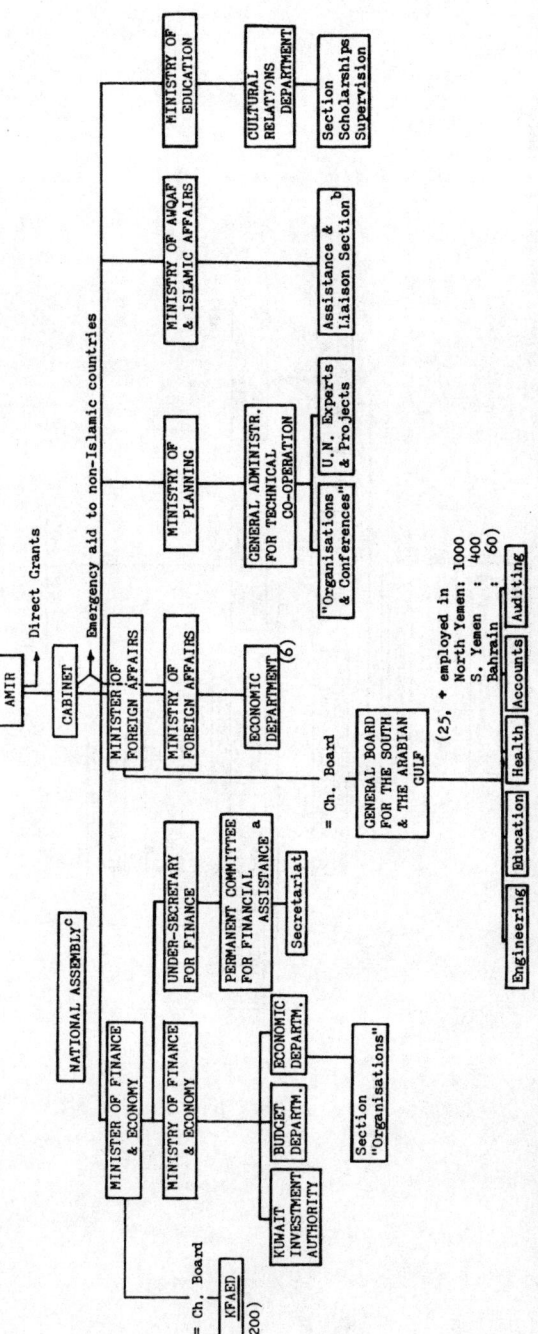

a. Members: Deputy D.G. of KFAED; Dir. Technical Co-operation (M. of Planning); Rep. Foreign Affairs; Rep. M. of Education; Rep. M. of Awqaf; Rep. GBSAG.

b. Responsible for religious assistance and emergency aid to Islamic countries.

c. Had to approve aid-flows (except KFAED and Amiri assistance) until its suspension in July 1986.

Figure 6.2 The Kuwait Fund for Arab Economic Development

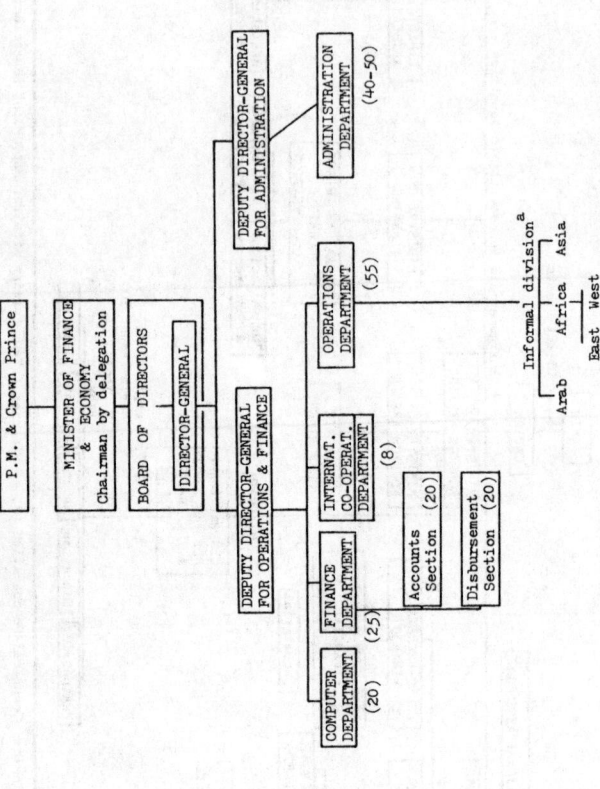

a. Blurred lines: task force approach.

Kuwait has been and still is among the top donors in the world. (See also Tables 6.1 — 6.5). In 1982 its net ODA disbursements amounted to about US$ 1.2 billion. They remained around US$ 1 billion in 1983, and again in 1984 when this amounted to almost 3.8 per cent of GNP. Net disbursements for 1984, according to KFAED calculations, amounted to $ 1014 million, or 3.82 per cent of GNP (see Table 6.20). Due to falling oil income, the figure for 1985 was considerably lower, reaching only $ 749 million. This lower trend had already been visible in 1982/83 in the assistance channelled via KFAED (comprising some 40 per cent of total Kuwaiti ODA in recent years). The level of the Fund's assistance continued downwards until the trend was reversed in 1986, with a 48 per cent rise to $ 317 million (from $ 214 million in 1985) (see Table 6.16). GBSAG has continued to allocate c. KD 16 million (US$ 55.2 million) to Bahrain and the Yemens. Calculations based on figures collected by KFAED indicate that in 1984 Kuwait's bilateral ODA went to 74 countries, the most important among which were Jordan (KD 67.3 million/$ 232.1 million), Bahrain (KD 35.2 million / $ 121.4 million), Syria (KD 27 million / $ 93.1 million), Oman (KD 14 million / $ 48.3 million), Yemen Arab Republic (KD 10.4 million / $ 35.9 million), China (KD 14.6 million / $ 50.3 million: no grants, only loans), and India (KD 13.3 million / $ 45.9 million: also mainly loans). Arab countries (including the PLO) received 69.4 per cent of the total, African countries 9.1 per cent, and Asian countries 19 per cent.

An overview of the administration and official bodies involved in providing aid and technical assistance is given in Figure 6.1. Responsibilities are widely spread, but the Minister of Finance and Economy oversees the largest part of the flows. He is also the chairman (by delegation from the Crown Prince) of KFAED. Decision–making for non–KFAED financial aid takes place in the Cabinet and Parliament (until the latter's dissolution in mid–1986). The Amir may give some direct grants himself but aid to the front–line states (as well as the 'loans' to Iraq since 1980) needed approval from Cabinet and Parliament. The Cabinet can also intervene directly in cases of emergency (famine etc.) in coordination with the Ministry of Foreign Affairs. The latter Ministry also provides overall direction and evaluation, as well as covering aid of a political nature, but it does not have its own ODA budget. GBSAG is semi–autonomous under its own Board, chaired by the Foreign Minister.

The Ministries of Finance and Economy were merged in 1985.

The functions of the Economic Co-operation Department, in Finance, were taken over partly by the Economic Department and partly by the Kuwait Investment Authority (KIA) which is linked to the Ministry. In addition to managing commercial investment, KIA also formally channels subscriptions to multilateral organisations, the funds for which come from the General Reserve. The procedure on multilateral aid is confused, however, with responsibilities divided between the General Administration for Technical Co-operation (GATC, in the Planning Ministry), and KFAED, in addition to KIA. Contributions to the Arab League, the United Nations, the Islamic Conference Organisation and GCC bodies are part of the budget of the GATC, which advises the Cabinet on the level of contributions and membership in multilateral organisations. According to the Director of KFAED's International Co-operation Department it is in fact the Fund which administers most multilateral contributions such as to the UN, IDA, IFAD, the Opec Fund and the Islamic Development Bank. On behalf of the Ministry of Finance and Economy, KFAED contributes out of its own capital to AFESD, the African Development Bank, the African Development Fund, the BADEA and the Inter-Arab Investment Guarantee Corporation. It would seem that KIA mainly acts as an accountant in keeping track of all contributions and as an intermediary between the Ministry of Finance and Economy and other bodies which receive their aid funds from it or the General Reserve. Direct administration of multilateral contributions is in fact divided between KFAED and GATC.

Actual disbursement of non-KFAED bilateral financial aid is done by the Budget Department in the Ministry of Finance. All of this aid, as well as that provided via the Ministry of Awqaf ('Religious Endowments') and the scholarships offered by the Ministry of Education, are in grant form. (The 'loans' to Iraq during 1980-82 and the oil-swaps from then on may well turn out to be grants, but they are not counted as ODA).

The Permanent Commission for Financial Assistance, which comes under the Under-secretary for Finance and was enlarged in 1985, is beginning to play a larger role in coordinating all the above forms of ODA. This coordination is meant to cover, by 1986/87, all institutions and all contributions.

KFAED provides only loans, not grants (apart from some technical assistance). But KFAED does administer some of the cash grants from the Ministry of Finance and Economy, as well as some of the multilateral contributions. The Fund also has responsibility for collecting all of Kuwait's ODA data and passing them on to the Coordination Committee of the DAC, where it represents Kuwait. In addition, KFAED represents the Kuwaiti government on the World Bank's Consultative Groups for Egypt, Morocco, Sudan and Tunisia.

Table 6.21
Sectoral Distribution of Loans Signed by KFAED, 1983/84 — 85/86 (percentages)

Sector	1983/84	1984/85	1985/86
Agriculture & primary sector	22	7	44
Energy	44	51.5	31
Transport & communications	45	35	28
Industry	18	3	7
Water & sewerage	7.5	3.5	—

Source: KFAED, 1985, 1986

During the year 1985/86 (to 30 July 1986), KFAED signed loans for 15 projects in 12 countries, for a total value of KD 88 million. This represents a considerable rise in volume, from KD 68 million in the previous year. But at the same time the geographical spread was much reduced (figures for 1984/85 in brackets): the aid went to 6 Arab countries (4) with 65.8 per cent of the value (31.8); 2 African countries (7), with 5.2 per cent of the value (27.3); 4 Asian countries (4), with 29 per cent of the value (29.7); in 1984/85 another 3 countries had received 11.1 per cent of the value of loans signed in that year [KFAED, 1985, 1986]. The sectoral distribution of KFAED's loans in the years from 1983/84 to 1985/86 is given in Table 6.21. The most striking feature is the huge rise in the share of the agriculture and primary sector, to 44 per cent in 1985/86. For the Fund's cumulative financing operations up to the end of 1986, the geographical distribution (covering 65 countries) was as follows: 49.7 per cent went to Arab countries; 18.7 per cent to African countries; 30.4 per cent to Asian countries; and 1.2 per cent to others. As to the sectoral distribution over this period, the largest share has gone to transport and communications (30.2 per cent), followed by electricity, oil and gas (27.7 per cent), agriculture and livestock (21.1 per cent), industry and mining (16.1 per cent), and water and sewerage (4.1 per cent) [AFESD, 1987b].

Kuwait's ODA has traditionally not been tied to domestic commercial interests. Pressure from the business community had, up to the beginning of 1986, not changed this and all aid officials interviewed by this author were adamant that it would not change. But in March 1986 KFAED and GBSAG made it known that Kuwaiti firms should henceforth be favoured for projects financed by them. It is not clear if or how the move has been implemented [*MEED* Special Report Kuwait, April 1986: 12]. Thus far, Kuwaiti firms had always been given full and timely information about projects, but tendering was strictly competitive. Moreover, two political elements have recently begun to play a bigger role. In September 1985 the Foreign Minister declared that all aid — including that from KFAED — would in future be dependent upon the potential recipient's stance on Arab questions. In practice this means: (a) no loans to countries that establish or re-establish diplomatic relations with Israel; (b) no more aid to Nicaragua which is deemed too pro-Iranian and which voted against the GCC resolution in the Security Council on free shipping in the Gulf. For several years the Kuwaiti National Assembly was urging cuts in, or suspension of, aid to Syria, because of that country's support for Iran in the Gulf War. Since 1984 this aid has indeed been reduced; it is also no longer listed in the budget. The Foreign Minister declared in September 1985, however, that Kuwait would still give KD 53 million to Syria, as well as KD 47 million to the other 'frontline states' — Jordan and the PLO. Moreover, aid can now be disbursed at the government's discretion [*EIU QER, Kuwait,* 1985, no.4]. The suspension of the National Assembly in 1986 has also removed all formal outside control on the government.

Saudi Arabia

Saudi Arabia has been an important donor since the late 1960s, when it began providing mainly politically-motivated aid to Arab countries after the 1967 Khartoum summit. The commitment then made was reinforced in 1974 (Rabat) and particularly at the Baghdad summit of 1978. Non-frontline states also benefited from this Saudi contribution to Arab solidarity. From 1970 the Yemen Arab Republic has received large annual subventions — motivated directly by security and ideological concerns (see section on aid to Yemen in Chapter 6) — while Bahrain and later Oman also received special attention. But in the course of the 1970s countries farther afield also began to receive Saudi aid. By the end of 1984, about US\$ 46 billion worth of assistance had been disbursed to some 70 countries [SFD, 1985]. This means that the Kingdom since 1974 has been the second largest donor in the world, behind the USA, providing more than half of total OPEC aid. In 1982 the Kingdom ceded second place to France, and in 1983 third place to Japan [OPEC, 1985: 10]. In 1984/85 Saudi Arabia still provided 7.9 per cent of world ODA [OECD, 1986: 49]. According to the official figures, some 47 per cent of Saudi aid was in grant form, the rest being mainly highly concessional loans. It should be noted that Saudi authorities have always been reticent to divulge details of their aid flows. Less than half the official Saudi ODA since 1978 is formally accounted for, and several observers feel that real flows may be even higher. By far the greatest part of Saudi aid, then, consisted of general support assistance grants, the majority of which went to Arab countries.

The Ministry of Finance and National Economy was always the country's most important channel, at least for overt ODA. In Figure 6.3 the Saudi aid–dispensing administration is depicted. The King and Royal Family have an absolute right to grant aid themselves (given internal consensus where important amounts are concerned), which the Ministry may or may not handle. Apart from their personal fortunes, senior members of the Royal Family can dip into the massive reserves presided over by the Saudi Arabian Monetary Agency (SAMA). With the growing importance of project aid during the 1970s, the need was felt to set up the Saudi Fund for Development, which started operations in 1975. The Fund works on the lines of KFAED, but draws to a large extent on outside expertise. The Fund has been responsible for only a small part of Saudi ODA. Its share rose to over 10 per cent in 1981 and 1982, but even though overall aid flows are dropping again (to c. US\$ 2.6 billion in 1985 — or 2.9 per cent of GNP), SFD's share has since been reduced, reaching only 3.9 per cent of Saudi ODA in 1985 [OECD, 1986]. Though magnificently housed, SFD is still small and young, which is reflected in its as yet comparatively inexperienced but able staff. The Fund in 1986 employed 250 people, including some 200 professionals. By the end of fiscal year 1984–85, SFD's ODA commitments had amounted to SR 20.7 billion (US\$ 5.8 billion), spread over 266 projects, of which 51 per cent went to 18 Asian countries and 46 per cent to 37 African countries. Arab countries (included in the previous figures) re-

Figure 6.3 Saudi Arabia: the Administration of Aid

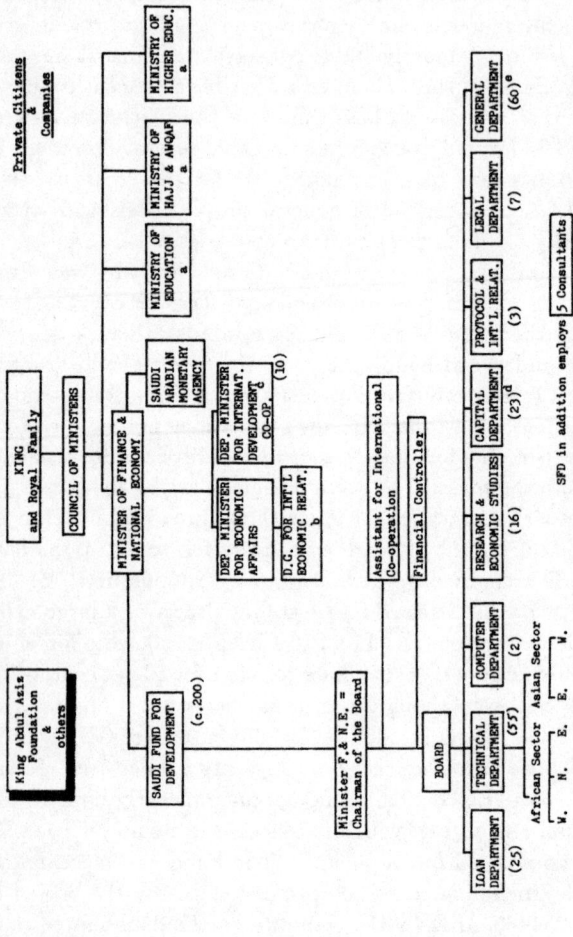

a. Autonomous for scholarships and technical assistance.
b. Multilaterals, IMF, IBRD.
c. A recent addition to the structure; responsible for contributions to OPEC/Arab institutions, Balance of Payments Support administration, Relief Aid, in addition to some project-oriented assistance.
d. Acts as the 'bank'.
e. Employees affairs, financial affairs, public relations.

ceived c. 36 per cent. Some 55 per cent of the allocations went to Low Income Countries — about half of which were 'Least Developed' [SFD, 1985]. Although infrastructure has attracted a major part of SFD assistance, it is clear that the SFD-administered part of Saudi ODA has been oriented towards a broad developmental approach. Projects for social development received particular attention from the Fund.

In addition to the Royal Family, the Cabinet, the Ministry of Finance and National Economy and the SFD, the Ministries of Education and Higher Education can autonomously give scholarships or forms of technical assistance. The Ministry of Hajj and Awqaf is yet another official channel, and the Ministry of Petroleum has been ordered on several occasions to provide other countries with large amounts of free oil. One such case was King Fahd's decision in March 1986 to provide Sudan with four months' oil supply free of charge [*IHT*, 24-3-86]. But there are other, not directly government-related donors, such as the King Abdul Aziz Foundation, as well as wealthy private Saudis and companies. Often this kind of aid is related to educational or Islamic causes.

Leaving private donors aside, the main motivations for Saudi generosity seem to have been ideological concerns linked to security concerns. Commitment to Third World development and long-term economic motives should not, however, be discounted. Aid has been used as an important instrument in the strategy of trying to create a stable, non-threatening environment in the Middle East and the world beyond [see Porter, 1986: 59-66, and Hunter, 1984: 124 — 144].

The United Arab Emirates

The UAE in 1975 doubled its concessional assistance to around US$ 1 billion — an annual level that was roughly maintained until 1981. This represented an extraordinarily high percentage of GNP (11.6 per cent in 1975). By 1985 the UAE's ODA had dropped to less than $ 60 million, representing a mere 0.24 per cent of GNP — the second year that the UN-inspired 0.70 per cent was not reached. With the passing of time and with a drastically reduced oil income, aid lost its status as a vital instrument for a newly- independent, vulnerable state to carve out its niche in the regional and international system, and had to make way for other priorities. This is precisely what happened in the even smaller state of Qatar (which in 1985 became a net recipient).

UAE aid has been provided almost exclusively by the Emirate of Abu Dhabi. It has remained very much in the domain of Arab politics and of the ruling elite's policies. Most of the aid took the form of bilateral grants from the Federal and Abu Dhabi Governments (both headed by Sheikh Zayid), a large part going to the frontline states. Outside of this 'Arab Summit' aid, general support assistance and aid for infrastructure (such as that for the Marib Dam in Yemen) have taken precedence over socio–culturally oriented projects.

The Abu Dhabi Fund for Arab Economic Development (ADFAED) was created in 1971 and signed its first loan agreements in 1974. Its part in total ODA was always small — although proportionately larger than that of the SFD in Saudi Arabia — but its importance has extended beyond its own loans (the larger proportion from 1983–4 arises only because of the dramatic drop in total ODA). Up to the end of 1986 total operations administered by the Fund amounted to some $ 2.1 billion. ADFAED loans accounted for c. 52 per cent of this. The rest was made up by equity participation and technical assistance (from the Fund as well as from the government): 5 %; Abu Dhabi Government loans: 24 %; Abu Dhabi Government grants: 9 %; and projects and activities within the UAE, administered by the Fund: 11 %. Whereas the policy of equity participation (staunchly propagated by the Adviser–General Dr Hassan Selim) sets the Fund apart from mainstream Arab aid policies, the equally distinctive function of administering projects within the UAE reflects the confederal nature of the state, several of whose members were exceedingly poor when the UAE was formed in 1971. Most of these intra–UAE projects have been in Fujairah, an oil–poor Emirate only recently brought out of its isolation on the Gulf of Oman [see ADFAED, 1987]. Another characteristic distinguishing ADFAED from other Arab Funds is that its terms are much harder and the level of concessionality of its loans lower. Some of its loans have, indeed, been non–concessional (although commercial banks would probably have had doubts about signing them). Otherwise criteria and rules of procurement and follow–up are similar to those of KFAED and SFD. The Fund has, however, allocated 75 per cent of its loans to Arab countries. A disproportionate share has gone to less needy but important neighbours: Oman (the largest recipient) has gained 21 per cent of the total, while tiny Bahrain was the 6th largest recipient (at end 1986) [ADFAED, 1987].

In addition to administering non–ADFAED operations for al-

Figure 6.4 United Arab Emirates: the Administration of Aid

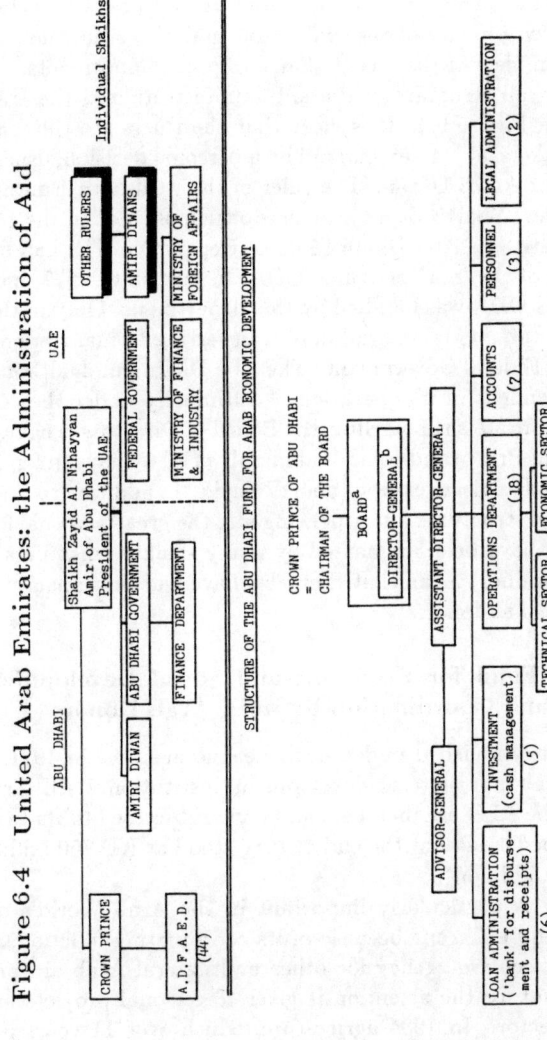

ABU DHABI

```
                    ABU DHABI                        UAE
CROWN PRINCE   Shaikh Zayid Al Nihayyan              OTHER RULERS   Individual Shaikhs
               Amir of Abu Dhabi
A.D.F.A.E.D.   President of the UAE
   (44)
               AMIRI DIWAN   ABU DHABI GOVERNMENT   FEDERAL GOVERNMENT   AMIRI DIWANS

                             FINANCE DEPARTMENT     MINISTRY OF FINANCE   MINISTRY OF
                                                    & INDUSTRY           FOREIGN AFFAIRS
```

STRUCTURE OF THE ABU DHABI FUND FOR ARAB ECONOMIC DEVELOPMENT

```
CROWN PRINCE OF ABU DHABI
          =
CHAIRMAN OF THE BOARD

                    BOARD[a]
                    DIRECTOR-GENERAL[b]

                    ASSISTANT DIRECTOR-GENERAL

ADVISOR-GENERAL

INVESTMENT          OPERATIONS DEPARTMENT   ACCOUNTS   PERSONNEL   LEGAL ADMINISTRATION
(cash management)        (18)                 (7)        (3)              (2)
     (5)
                    TECHNICAL SECTOR

LOAN ADMINISTRATION   ECONOMIC SECTOR
('bank' for disburse-
ment and receipts)    Arab Countries Asian C.   African C.
     (6)
```

Notes: a. includes Presidential Adviser, Chairman of Abu Dhabi Nat. Oil Co., Chairman of Finance Dep't,
Minister of Foreign Aff.,
b. has the status of Minister (at time of writing, the D.G. is also federal Under-secr. of Finance
& Industry.

most as much again as the amount of its own loans, the Fund also
represents the UAE government in international fora on development co–operation as well as on the Consultative Groups of the
World Bank and the African Development Fund. Given these
tasks, it has a strikingly small and indeed shrinking staff of less
than 45 professionals (see Figure 6.4). There are complaints about
work overload, but top officials insist it merely indicates increased
efficiency. The shrinkage is in fact more likely to be a reflection
of the reduced priority of the aid sector, and also seems not un-
reasonable in view of the recent sharp drop in commitments.

The overall structure of the aid administration in the UAE
is charted in Figure 6.4. It is clear that the rulers are the main
decision–makers, able to extend aid by a personal decision, usually
through their Amiri Diwan. The ruler of the wealthiest Emirate,
UAE President Shaikh Zayid, can thus offer most aid. In the case
of his Emirate, the Abu Dhabi Finance Department has handled
a large part of the 'non–personal' ODA. In fact, until 1977, most
of the UAE's ODA was handled by this department. Only in that
year was a start made on gradually transferring formal responsibility to the Federal Government. The Abu Dhabi Fund, although
fairly independent in its operation, is ultimately under the control of the Emirate's ruling elite: the Board of Directors is chaired
by the Crown Prince and composed mainly of Al–Nihayyan family
members, and advisers close to Shaikh Zayid. In addition to these
governmental structures for dispensing aid, the great personal fortunes which have been ammassed by many shaikhs (members of
the ruling families) mean that they also have had the capacity to
act as occasional donors.

The Arab Fund for Economic and Social Development (AFESD) and Coordination between Arab Donors

AFESD was established under Arab League auspices in 1971 as
the first Arab multilateral development institution. All Arab
states and the PLO are members and have subscribed to its capital (subscribed capital at the end of 1986 stood at KD 750 million
(over US$ 2.5 billion).

AFESD is particularly important in the Arab World's development and aid scene because of its coordinating function, its
role as an executive agency for other multilateral Arab aid programmes, and for the attention it gives to regional projects and
the social sector. In 1984 agriculture, which over 11 years had
received a share of 21 per cent of AFESD's allocations, saw its

share increase to 51 per cent for that year. By the end of 1986, during which year 52 per cent went to agriculture, it had become the largest sector in AFESD's total assistance, accounting for 31 per cent of cumulative operations [AFESD, 1985c; 1987b].

AFESD is concerned with the development of the Arab world, rather than the Third World as a whole. Starting operations in 1974, by the end of 1986 the Fund had committed loans to seventeen Arab states; the share of the 'Least Developed Country' category was 40.5 per cent. For the year 1986, their share was 57.2 per cent of the total AFESD commitments of KD 66.9 million. The Fund's cumulative signed loans up to the end of 1986, which amounted to the equivalent of $ 2,696 million, made it, if one excludes the Islamic Development Bank, the third largest Arab development institution in terms of operations — after SFD and KFAED (see Table 6.16).

In addition to providing finance for development projects, the Fund's brief includes attracting public or private investment to where it contributes to the development of the Arab economy, and providing technical assistance. Moreover, AFESD has administered other multilateral Arab development projects, it has undertaken studies on potential intra-regional projects (until 1981 jointly with UNDP, then taken over by the Research and Studies Department), it has administered IFAD operations in the Arab world since 1980, and acts as the technical secretariat of AG-FUND, the Arab Gulf Fund for United Nations Development. Further, the Fund has co-operated closely with Arab League agencies, the Arab Monetary Fund, OAPEC and the Inter-Arab Investment Guarantee Corporation. Thus, for example, the annual *Unified Arab Economic Report* is produced jointly with the AMF and the Arab League Secretariat. AFESD is also responsible for administering the Programme of the First Arab Development Decade, since 1980.

The Fund's central position in the Arab development effort is further enhanced by its provision since 1975 of a home for the Coordination Secretariat of Arab National and Regional Development Institutions. Thus, coordination between all these institutions (including the OPEC Fund and the Islamic Development Bank, as well as the Government of Qatar) has received an administrative focus. The Secretariat collects all data on the institutions' commitments and disbursements — including also those to non-Arab countries — and publishes these in quarterly and annual reports. Twice a year, technical staff from the funds meet

Table 6.22   AFESD: Sectoral and Country Distribution of Loans during 1974-1984

(KD millions)

	Percentage	TOTAL	Sudan	Morocco	Yemen Arab Republic	Egypt (to April 1979)	Syria	Jordan	PDRY	Algeria	Tunisia	Mauritania	Somalia	Iraq	Oman	Djibouti	Bahrain	Lebanon	Palestine
Transport	20.1	158.6	33.6	-	11.5	12.0	15.0	14.6	18.6	18.0	3.8	8.5	16.5	-	-	1.5	-	5.0	-
Telecommunications	8.3	65.8	7.7	4.0	1.4	-	4.7	6.0	2.5	7.8	4.7	6.1	2.9	5.0	3.0	4.0	6.0	-	-
Energy (Electr.,oil)	17.4	137.7	-	-	25.9	12.0	19.0	16.9	11.4	-	6.0	10.7	6.8	-	15.0	3.0	5.0	6.0	-
Water & Sewerage	11.1	87.4	4.3	1.3	17.7	18.0	20.0	2.8	10.0	-	7.9	0.4	5.0	-	-	-	-	-	-
Agriculture	30.2	238.2	24.5	71.5	14.1	-	3.7	15.0	15.9	23.3	28.5	6.6	8.3	18.9	3.0	1.9	-	-	3.0
Industry & Mining	10.2	80.6	16.9	9.0	-	25.9	4.1	5.0	-	-	7.0	12.0	-	-	-	0.7	-	-	-
Services	2.7	21.0	-	0.6	1.8	-	0.6	0.4	2.3	9.7	0.6	4.5	-	0.5	-	-	-	-	-
TOTAL	100.0	789.3*	87.0	86.4	72.4	67.9	67.1	60.7	60.7	58.8	58.5	48.8	39.5	24.4	21.0	11.1	11.0	11.0	3.0
Percentage	100.0	100.0	11.0	10.9	9.2	8.6	8.5	7.7	7.7	7.4	7.4	6.2	5.0	3.1	2.7	1.4	1.4	1.4	0.4

Note: (*) Loans for a value of 6,619 million KD were not used and were cancelled

Source: AFESD, 1987a.

Figure 6.5 Arab Fund for Economic and Social Development (AFESD)

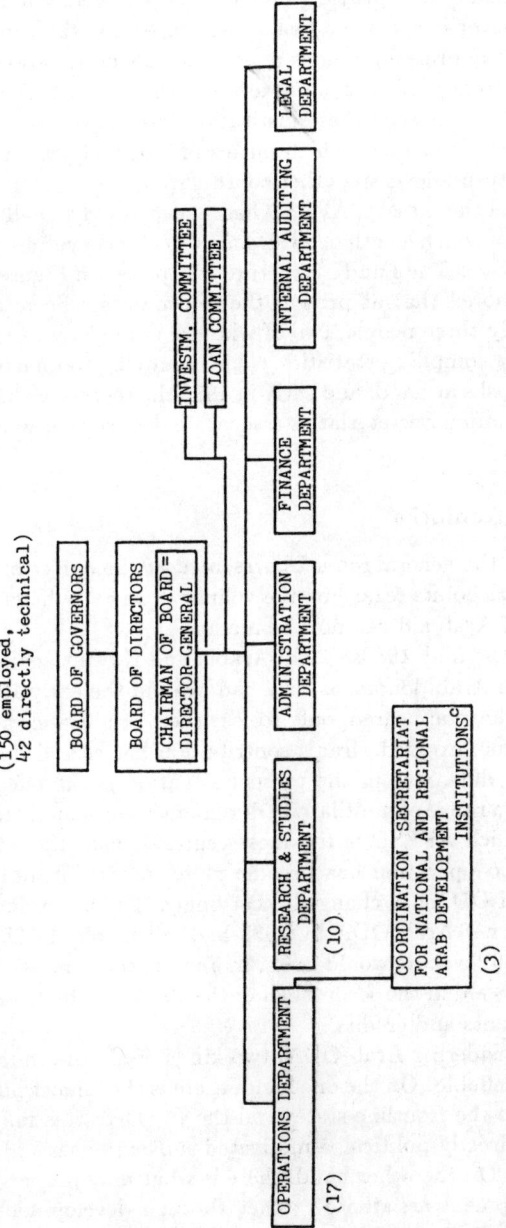

(150 employed,
42 directly technical)

BOARD OF GOVERNORS

BOARD OF DIRECTORS
CHAIRMAN OF BOARD =
DIRECTOR-GENERAL

INVESTM. COMMITTEE
LOAN COMMITTEE

OPERATIONS DEPARTMENT
(17)

RESEARCH & STUDIES
DEPARTMENT
(10)

COORDINATION SECRETARIAT
FOR NATIONAL AND REGIONAL
ARAB DEVELOPMENT
INSTITUTIONS[c]
(3)

ADMINISTRATION
DEPARTMENT

FINANCE
DEPARTMENT

INTERNAL AUDITING
DEPARTMENT

LEGAL
DEPARTMENT

Notes: a. Each member state appoints one governor and one alternate governor for a 5-year term. Meets once a year and
when requested by at least 3 members having 1/4 of total voting power, or by Board of Directors.
       b. Six members, elected for renewable 2-year term by Board of Governors.
       c. 1986: thoughts of setting it up as a separate department.

at the level of director of operations to review and preview past, on–going and planned projects, looking at their financing and the gaps to be filled. Often projects are then co–financed, while the major contributor is given the task of administering the project. At times, joint appraisal missions may be sent. Coordination between the different institutions has also occurred on other levels. One result is that most of these institutions now have very similar procurement guidelines, which makes life for recipients much easier and in turn allows smoother coordination.

Despite all these tasks, AFESD has a surprisingly small staff of about 150, of which less than a third are directly concerned with technical matters. The Fund's structure is depicted in Figure 6.5. It should be noted that at present the Coordination Secretariat consists of only three people, two of who are administrative staff responsible for compiling statistics. This is proving too narrow a basis for the tasks at hand, and early in 1986 the re–establishment of the Coordination Secretariat as a separate department was under discussion.

Concluding Remarks

Expanding on the general remarks presented at the outset of this chapter, several points regarding the volume, nature, policies and motivations of Arab aid can now be made.

Towards the mid–1980s, Saudi Arabia and Kuwait again became the main Arab donors, as they had been in the early 1970s. Other donors have appeared, only to lose their significance again when oil income dropped. Iraq's contribution has ceased due to the war. One difference in the present situation is the effective functioning of a range of multilateral development–oriented organisations, of which AFESD is the most central. Institutionalised development co–operation has become more important and the composition of ODA has changed accordingly. The fact remains, however, that net Arab ODA by 1985 had fallen to only 38 per cent of its 1980 level. It would seem, moreover, that one striking feature of Arab aid in the second half of the 1980s will be the shift towards oil grants and credits.

When considering Arab ODA, two kinds of aid are immediately distinguishable. On the one hand, there is the almost purely political aid to the frontline states and the PLO. To this may be added other directly politically–motivated subventions mainly by Saudi Arabia. On the other hand, there is what may properly be called 'development assistance', either through development institutions or otherwise. This latter kind of assistance has been fairly evenly distributed geographically, although Latin America has been largely excluded. The distribution is comparable to that of other donors, *mutatis mutandis*. When making generalisations about Arab aid, it is necessary to keep in mind the distinction between these two kinds of assistance.

As to the national development institutions, they have all been modelled to some extent on the World Bank, receiving an initial government capital injection from which investments can be made both to fulfil their functions and to expand that capital. The governments provide further grants when that is deemed appropriate. Although their Boards of Directors are nominated by the government, the national development institutions have on the whole considerably more autonomy than their Western counterparts — but of course they handle only a very limited part of their countries' ODA. The Kuwaiti Fund, in particular, has a reputation for allocating its aid on merit in terms of the viability and developmental impact of projects, rather than on political grounds. The SFD and ADFAED follow in a similar mould, but 'the Iraqi Fund [is] more obviously the agent of the Iraq Government' [Porter, 1986: 52]. On the whole, aid channelled through the national — or, for that matter, the regional — Arab development institutions, has a clear developmental purpose. The share of these institutions in overall ODA has risen; moreover, their functions have been expanded to include administration of some governmental ODA as well as representation in international fora.

Starting with the establishment of a Coordination Secretariat in 1975, a high degree of coordination has been achieved. Funds' procedures are fairly uniform, and co–financing and joint or delegated administration of projects has become common. Co–financing has also become a characteristic feature of Arab Institutions' aid outside the Arab donor community. Often a comparatively small commitment to a project has attracted other donors or investors, either bilateral or multilateral. This has become a conscious policy and has allowed Arab aid to be spread widely over the last decade.

Equity financing in certain projects with a developmental impact is an option which so far only the Abu Dhabi Fund has taken up in any significant way (in addition to the multilateral Arab Agency for Agricultural Investment and Development, AAAID). Direct government participation (for instance Kuwait in the Sudan) has in some cases been important. At present a consensus seems to be emerging about the need to make the link with private capital.

Finally, some observations are in order on the objectives of Arab aid. The evidence indicates that they can be grouped around four interrelated motivations:

(1)   Security
(2)   Ideological concerns
(3)   Economic concerns
(4)   Third World Development.

These four are present to varying degrees for all Arab donors. The first motivation is particularly important for the major donors – the Gulf states. Their environment is one which is characterised by vulnerability, potential instability and envy on the part of the 'poor relations'. It has been imperative, therefore, to direct all efforts — including aid — towards acquiring domestic and international legitimacy. A concern for the Third World which is shown to be real fits in well with this strategy. The same is true for another aspect of the pursuit of security, viz. the efforts to create a more stable environment. If aid can help achieve economic well-being in a recipient country, there is every chance that stability in that country will be enhanced. A major destabilising factor in Middle Eastern politics is the Palestinian question, which continues to feed radical tendencies in all Arab countries, including the Gulf. It is not surprising, then, that the settlement of that question is one of the main concerns of the Gulf Arab donors. Aid has been used as a means of influencing Third World countries' attitudes towards Israel. The Arab protagonists in the Palestinian question have been bolstered, which at the same time has had a legitimacy–generating function. This is not to say that there has not been a genuine commitment to the Palestinian cause. The Palestine issue aside, it is clear that massive amounts of (often unspecified) aid have gone into shoring up friendly regimes or buying off potential critics.

Ideological concerns partly fit into the above, but also have salience on their own. They are of three kinds: the 'radical' – 'conservative' contest; Islam; and the Arab cause. Saudi Arabia (with Algeria and Libya on the other side of the fence) has been particularly active on the first scene. It has also used aid in 'furthering the cause of Islam' by giving grants in the fields of Islamic education and helping regimes seen to be favouring an Islamic system. In the overall picture of Arab aid, however, it is erroneous to view Islam as a major determining factor: the geographical spread does contain a large proportion of Islamic recipients, but that can largely be explained by (a) the bias towards *Arab* countries, (b) the bias towards other regional neighbours and (c) the plain fact that a large number of developing countries are Muslim. It is of course important to realise that the matter of Jerusalem and Palestine has a powerful Islamic rationale. The Arab concern has a twofold focus: Arab economic and political solidarity, and the Palestinian question. It also has a place in any strategy for generating domestic and international legitimacy.

Thirdly, there are economic motives, although these have not generally carried the same weight as in the case of the DAC donors. It has been more important for the more developed (export-oriented) economy of Iran, prior to the revolution, than for the Arab donors, but Hunter [1984: 75] finds that the economic factor has also been salient in the cases of Libya and Iraq:

> In the case of Libya ... the desire to have access to manpower and technological bases played an important role, although investment – related considerations have not been insignificant. However, in the case of Iraq, the traditional motive of securing export markets seems to have played a role. Iraq has shown a desire to establish long-term oil–sale relationships, thus ensuring safe markets for its oil. This motive could account for the large share of credits for oil purchases in total Iraqi aid.

Concern for future markets has been of some importance for the other donors, too, but has never been a main concern. It seems useful to insert at this point Hunter's classification of OPEC donors according to the relative importance of the three previously discussed motives in their aid programmes (Table 6.23). Hunter's dismissal of true developmental considerations as a motive in OPEC aid, however, is unjustified. Even though such concern, again, does fit in with that of security, it also, again, does have its own salience. There is, first, the concern with the overall development of the Arab region, of which the Arab donors form part and which is important not only for reasons of 'Arab solidarity' but also for the donors' own long–term economic survival. More directly, there is the example of the Breadbasket strategy for the Sudan — even though that appears to have failed. In 1980 the First Arab Development Decade was inaugurated. Although the initial programme prepared by Arab development economists was slashed by the politicians to a fraction of what had been intended (and was in fact largely 'highjacked' by President Saddam Hussein of Iraq as a political public relations excercise for Iraq and the Gulf states), what was left was still a programme of US$ 5 billion over 10 years, aimed at the Least Developed Arab countries (both Yemens, Sudan, Somalia, Mauritania, Djibouti), administered by AFESD.

Table 6.23
Motives for OPEC Aid and their Relative Importance

	Security	Political/Ideological	Economic
Algeria	L	H	L
Iran	H	M	H
Iraq	L	H	M
Kuwait	H	M	L
Libya	L	H	M
Qatar	H	M	L
Saudi Arabia	H	H	L
UAE	H	M	L

L: low; M: medium; H: high

Source: Hunter, 1984: 97

Secondly, there are the activities of the national development funds — particularly the Kuwait Fund with its growing share in Kuwaiti ODA. Added to these there are the multilateral institutions whose ethos is indisputably developmental — a perfect example being AFESD. Significant is the comparative degree of autonomy of many of these national and regional organisations, to the extent that even in the multilaterals it has been possible for imaginative individuals with a genuine commitment to development to make a strong impact.

When considering OPEC's commitment to Third World development one should also not overlook the creation of the International Fund for Agricultural Development (IFAD) in 1978. OPEC countries agreed to provide 52 per cent of the latter's finances. This has certainly boosted Third World interests, even though there is now uncertainty over future sharing of the burden. The Gulf War has caused the effective demise of a wider OPEC initiative with implications for the Third World, viz. its original 'Long Term Strategy' that was to have included OPEC contributions to a world fund for energy and development. OPEC's contributions were to be linked to oil price rises, DAC's to increases in their export prices. In conclusion, although Third World solidarity has obviously not been the main motivation behind Arab aid, and although several initiatives which did go in that direction have withered away, it is indisputable that developmental objectives have indeed been salient in the Arab aid effort as a whole, though varying in strength from country to country.

7   SUMMARY AND CONCLUSION

The Middle East today is characterised by the divisions between oil–rich and oil–poor countries, and (largely parallel) that between thinly and more heavily populated ones. The capital–surplus oil–exporters can be described as rent–economies, dependent as they are on the sell–off of their oil reserves. This prevalence of rent–economy and oil–dependence has to an important degree spread to the non–oil countries. The latter have become dependent on the direct inflow of funds either as assistance or as investment, and on the labour markets of, and flow of remittances from, the wealthier states. This dependence on unpredictable factors, coupled to the perceived need for an open economy in order to attract remittances and investment, has led to a certain loss of control by governments over their national economies. This trend has been reinforced by a conscious opting for *infitah* — as a natural result of the above factors, as well as of the on–going integration of the Middle East into the world economy, and of political imperatives for (or predilections of) ruling groups.

Varying backgrounds notwithstanding, the State throughout the region has acquired similar functions and undergone similar expansions in its power and its executive apparatus — the bureaucracy. Colonisation, as well as established tradition (particularly in Egypt) played a role in this, but equally important, especially for the oil monarchies of the Gulf, were the intervention of foreign powers and the wealth bestowed upon the regimes by the advent of the oil age. Imitation, without and within the region, also helps the explain the similarities. In the Marxian vein, it can be argued that the integration of the Middle East into the world economic system implied certain functions and characteristics for the state in the countries concerned. On a less theoretical level (and reflecting a widespread perception among people in the Third World), it is clear that, once a Third World society (or elite) has adopted the value system of 'modern development', only the state is in a position to oversee all the components of the process supposedly leading towards that goal. At least initially only the state can acquire/accumulate the resources to go into that process. In the Middle East this is accentuated by the spreading of the rentier–economy.

In addition to the above factors, the region's 'political under-development' — resulting from the colonial and pre-colonial situation — has played a large role in determining the shape and functions of the region's state forms and bureaucracies. In looking for ideological frameworks, the newly independent countries had to start almost 'from scratch'. The resultant lack of legitimacy helps explain why regimes have had to rely on force and control to remain in power and why widespread participation has not become the norm. Direct, physical control is ideally complemented by popular acquiescence, which will result from (a) the creation of popular dependence on the regime; (b) pacification and co–optation; (c) genuinely legitimising acts and ideology. Finally, there is the important consideration of external support for such regimes — a consideration which will again to some extent determine shape, functions and actions of the state bureaucracy. Genuine development is not, however, always incompatible with these concerns; it will indeed at times be an indispensible part of such a strategy. It is worth mentioning, finally, the concept of the 'charity economy', which implies that the economy and bureaucracy of a highly dependent recipient of aid and external financial flows are often shaped more by that external factor than with reference to domestic structures. Such bureaucracies, therefore, tend to be organically linked to, and oriented towards, the outside world rather than the indigenous aspects of development.

The characteristics and problems of Middle Eastern development administration, then, as derived from the above in addition to considerations of political power and socio–cultural traditions, can be classified into four categories: (1) those related to the international environment; (2) those stemming from domestic politics; (3) those caused by the general underdevelopment; and (4) those related to cultural/behavioural causes. They overlap and interrelate.

Under the first category comes the fact that long–term planning often proves a futile excercise due to the dependence on unpredictable factors such as the state of the oil market (or the markets for other raw materials), foreign assistance, and the labour markets in the oil–rich countries. In addition, there are the problems associated with the charity–economy phenomenon. One of the main factors in the second category is the control–function of the bureaucracy, which helps explain its rigid, monolithic nature and the concentration of decision–making at the top. Among the most detrimental results are slowness; fear of taking decisions on the part of lower–ranking civil servants; decision–making by non–experts; and a wide scope for personal preferences and interests of the top, as well as for corruption by domestic and foreign groups. It was explained, also, how the structure of power allows for frequent changes of staffing and structures, for political expediency as well as for the elite to preserve control. Two main results of this are inexperience among staff, and discontinuity in policies. In addition, it was found that the potential for intra–bureaucratic conflict is often built in on purpose, again to reinforce the power–position of the leadership. On the whole, political realities often necessitate the withdrawal of political support for a technically-elaborated long–term development policy. Finally, the political implications of tribal organisation remain significant in most of the Middle East. In countries such as the Yemens and Djibouti, central government can not simply impose its will on the tribal groups. In order to have an impact and not see its chances for survival destroyed, the central government must on the one hand respect the tribal balance of power, and on the other try to use that balance for its own purposes.

The general underdevelopment of the region (the third category) was found to have four major consequences with implications for the shape and functioning of development administration: (1) an underdeveloped human resource base; (2) a lack of resources, leading, among other things, to low wages which in turn result in a lack of commitment among civil servants, and in corruption; (3) the lack of reliable data, which can cripple planning efforts from the start; and (4) the fact that the lack of resources and experience reinforces dependence on the donors in formulating priorities and policies.

As to the final category, it was argued that although the non–achievement of an industrialised society in the Middle East cannot be blamed on the religion of Islam, some other elements of the dominant culture of the region have had a negative impact on the kind of development administration one has tried to develop. This often happened in conjunction with, or because of, the factors mentioned previously. Two concrete points are the nature of education (still to a large extent based on memorising rather than on independent thinking), and the strongly paternalistic family traditions, which conceivably inhibit enthusiasm for independent decision–making. A crucial cultural factor, however, was felt to be the very difference between the Western–originated bureaucratic idea, and local culture. The idea of a Weberian administration was introduced from abroad and had little connection with local traditions, customs and values. It is this gap which is largely responsible for most of the 'behavioural' problems with which Middle Eastern administrations are beset. It was almost inevitable that people who came in contact with this foreign system of organisation and decision–making, both inside it and outside it, would apply their own standards and values in interpreting it. The form could be assimilated, but it was perceived differently, and was attributed different functions.

As a result of all this, the basic framework for successful planning and for an effective 'modern' development administration, is absent. Development plans therefore often come to serve essentially as window–dressing excercises, for the benefit both of potential donors, and of the domestic audience as a way to generate legitimacy.

Drawing on the observations of chapter 3, as summarised above, and on the case studies of eleven countries, it was concluded that these characteristics (with their practical effects of inconsistency; the predominance of the legitimacy/ survival imperative; a growing trend towards *infitah*; and generally the ineffectiveness of development administrations) arise from both international and domestic causes. The international factors comprise (a) dependence on the developed economies and (for the oil–poor countries) on the capital–surplus oil–exporting countries; and (b) the inherent outward rather than inward orientation of administrations in a 'charity–economy' context. The domestic factors are (a) political underdevelopment; and (b) the fact that the physical and socio–economic framework is not 'ready', either for the technical tasks at hand, or for the socio–political implications of consistently–planned change.

Accepting that 'modern development' values are, it appears, here to stay, it was argued that the 'ecological–contingency' approach to administrative development offers the best prospects of helping to create a better–adapted administration. The approach advocates learning from such successes as have been reached, and building on these within the given social, political and cultural context — rather than merely focussing on obstacles to a Western, Weberian system.

Foreign assistance is a prominent facet in the international

context of the issues of development and development administration. At the same time, many of the background factors listed
previously also have helped determine the way in which aid has
been administered and allocated. These questions featured already in Chapters 1 — 3, and were expanded upon in Chapter 4,
which focussed on aid to Middle Eastern countries.

The presumed positive effects of aid are obvious (economic
growth; bridging vital technological or financial gaps; disaster relief, etc.). From several perspectives, however, strong cases have
been argued against aid — or at least against the forms it has
taken so far. Some of the major criticisms which have been
rightly made, are that massive foreign assistance has tended to
skew the economic and administrative structure and orientation
of the recipient (the 'charity–economy' concept is one formulation
of this critique); that alien values have been brought in; that in
many cases a situation of dependency has been created (with aid–
reliance figures reaching 20 per cent of GNP in some cases); that
the debt situation has been exacerbated; that much of this aid,
under donor–influence, has been inappropriately allocated; and
that both resources and local administrators' energy have been
deflected from genuine domestic development concerns. It was
argued, however, that (1) aid is not inherently detrimental; (2)
a positive or negative verdict on the impact of aid must depend
on empirical observation of each individual case; (3) many of the
negative effects of aid on development and development administration have been the result of specific policies, modalities and
conditions asociated with aid. Even conceding that foreign assistance will continue to have at least *some* negative effects in
some cases, there is still in most cases no alternative for the fore-
seeable future, if one takes the recipients' present situation as a
given. With the modern development values which the countries
of the region have adopted, and the predicament which they find
themselves in, both financial and technical assistance will remain
an essential requirement for a long time to come. If the balance
of the aid effort is to be clearly positive, however, it is crucial
to proceed from the caveats referred to, always bearing in mind
the specific conditions prevailing in the recipient country. Concrete requirements for an 'ideal' ODA profile were suggested as
(1) the absence of political or commercial ties; (2) a high proportion of grants and highly concessional loans; (3) the integration
into an overall development strategy; (4) close consultation with,
and large autonomy for, the recipient; and (5) attention for rural

development and small–scale projects, in addition to those sectors which already receive more than their due.

Admittedly, the self–interestedness of most donors makes it unlikely that this ideal will ever be approached. Yet the picture is not uniform. The record of the Arab donors in some respects has been better than average, particularly as regards quantity, and in terms of the aid–tying criterion. Arab aid flows have been an important element of regional, 'south–south' co–operation. A striking feature of Arab aid has been the rise and fall of secondary donors such as Qatar, the UAE and Libya (parallel with the rise and fall of oil income), leading to a return of the situation prevailing in the early 1970s, when Saudi Arabia and Kuwait were the two significant Arab donors. In the meantime, however, a range of national and multilateral development funds and institutions have emerged, the most central of which is AFESD. Coordination among the various institutions has reached an exemplary level. It is clear that concerns of security and ideology have been the main motivations behind Arab aid. The issue of Third World development, however, has also been both a genuine motivating force and, often, a real beneficiary.

AAAID	Arab Authority for Agricultural Investment and Development
ABEDA	see BADEA
ADFAED	Abu Dhabi Fund for Arab Economic Development
AFESD	Arab Fund for Economic and Social Development
AFTAAC	Arab Fund for Technical Assistance to African and Arab Countries
AGFUND	Arab Gulf Fund for the United Nations Development Organisations
AMF	Arab Monetary Fund
AOAS	Arab Organisation for Administrative Sciences
BADEA	Arab Bank for Economic Development in Africa
CAPMAS	Central Agency for Public Mobilisation and Statistics (in Egypt)
CYDA	Council of Yemeni Development Associations
CMEA	Council for Mutual Economic Assistance
CPO	Central Planning Organisation
CSO	Central Statistical Organisation
DAC	Development Assistance Committee (OECD)
GCC	Gulf Cooperation Council
GDP	Gross Domestic Product
GNP	Gross National Product
ECWA	Economic Commission for Western Asia
EIU, QER	Economist Intelligence Unit: *Quarterly Economic Report*
FT	*Financial Times*
FY	Financial Year
IBRD	International Bank for Reconstruction and Development
IDA	International Development Association
IFAD	International Fund for Agricultural Development
IJMES	*International Journal of Middle Eastern Studies*
IMF	International Monetary Fund
IsDB	Islamic Development Bank

JD	Jordanian Dinar
JOCE	*Journal Officiel des Communautés Européennes*
KD	Kuwaiti Dinar
KFAED	Kuwait Fund for Arab Economic Development
LDA	Local Development Association
LDC	Less Developed Country
LLDC	Least Developed Country
MEED	*Middle East Economic Digest*
MEJ	*Middle East Journal*
MENA	*The Middle East and North Africa*
MERIP	Middle East Research and Information Project Reports
NGO	Non–governmental Organisation
ODA	Official Development Assistance
OECD	Organisation for Economic Co–operation and Development
OAPEC	Organisation of Arab Petroleum Exporting Countries
OFID	OPEC Fund for International Development
ONCCP	Office of the National Committee for Central Planning (Ethiopia)
OPEC	Organisation of Petroleum Exporting Countries
PDRY	People's Democratic Republic of Yemen
PQLI	Physical Quality of Life Index
RCC	Revolutionary Command Council
SFD	Saudi Fund for Development
SR	Saudi Riyal
UAE	United Arab Emirates
UNCTAD	United Nations Conference on Trade and Development
USAID	US Agency for International Development
WPE	Workers' Party of Ethiopia
YAR	Yemen Arab Republic

In addition to the journals and periodicals quoted in the text, the following books, articles and documents were consulted:

Abdel–Khalek, Gouda (1984) 'Egypt's Recent Aid Experience 1974–1983'Paper presented at the fourth EADI General Conference, Madrid 3–7 September 1984

Abdel–Mu'ti Muhammad 'Asaf (1983) *at–tanzim al–idari fi–l–mamlaka al–'arabia as– sa'udiya*, Amman: Dar al–'ulum lit–taba'a wan–nashr (for AOAS)

Abu–Laban, B. & Abu–Laban, S. McIrvin (1986) *The Arab World: Dynamics of Development*, Leiden: Brill (= *International Studies in Sociology and Social Anthropology*, XLV)

Abu–Lughod, Janet (1984) 'Culture, Modes of Production and the Changing Nature of Cities in the Arab World', in: Agnew, Mercer & Sopher (eds.), *The City in Cultural Context*, London: Allen & Unwin, pp. 94–119

Abu Sheikha, N.A. & Abdel–Mu'ti Muhammad 'Asaf (1985) *Al–idara al–'aamma fi–l–mamlaka al–urduniya al–hashimiya'* Amman: AOAS

Abu Sheikha, N.A. (1986) 'Hawla al–banya at–tanzimiya li–l–idara al–'aamma fi ad–duwal al–'arabiya' in: Saigh, 1986: 75–149

Achilli, M. & Khaldi, M. (eds.) (1984) *The Role of the Arab Development Funds in the World Economy*, London: Croom Helm

ADFAED (1985) *Annual Report, 1983 & 1984*, Abu Dhabi: AD-FAED

— (1987) *Annual Report, 1986*, Abu Dhabi: ADFAED

AFESD (1982) *The Unified Arab Economic Report*, Kuwait: AFESD

AFESD Coordination Secretariat (1983) *Arab National and Regional Development Institutions: Statement of Financing Operations- 31 December 1982*, Kuwait: AFESD

—   (1985a) *Summary — Financing Operations — Arab National and Regional Development Institutions — December 31, 1984*, Kuwait: AFESD

—   (1985b) *Financing Operations — Arab National and Regional Development Institutions — Summary of Sectors — December 31, 1984*, Kuwait: AFESD

AFESD (1985c) *Arab Fund for Economic and Social Development — Annual Report 1984*, Kuwait: AFESD

—   - Coordination Secretariat (1986) *Summary — Financing Operations — Arab National and Regional Development Institutions — December 31, 1985*, Kuwait: AFESD

AFESD (1987a) *Arab Fund for Economic and Social Development — Annual Report 1986*, Kuwait: AFESD

—   Coordination Secretariat (1987b) *Summary — Financing Operations — Arab National and Regional Development Institutions — December 31, 1986*, Kuwait: AFESD

Agarwal, R. (1983) *Planning in Developing Countries, lessons of experiences* (= World Bank, Staff Working Paper no. 576), Washington: World Bank

'Akash, Fawzi Abdallah al-, (1983) *Al-hukm al-mahalli wal-idara l-mahalliya. Al-usus wal-tatbiqat*, Al Ain: Al Ain University

Alavi, H. (1972) 'The State in post–colonial societies — Pakistan and Bangladesh', in *New Left Review*, no. 74: 59–81

Al-Buraey, M.A. (1986) *Administrative Development: An Islamic Perspective*, London: KPI

Allan, J.A. (ed.)(1987) *Politics and the Economy in Syria*, London: Centre for Near & Middle Eastern Studies, SOAS

Alnasrawi, A.(ed.) (1984) *The Impact of Money: Dynamics of Power and Dependency in the Arab World*, (= *Arab Studies Quarterly*, Vol. 6, nos. 1–2)

—   (1986) 'Dependency Status and Economic Development of Arab States', in Abu–Laban & Abu–Laban, 1986: 17–31

American Embassy Cairo (1985) 'Economic Trends Report: Egypt'

Amin, S. 'Development and Structural Change', in Ward *et al.* 1971: 312–333

Amin, S. (1978) *The Arab Nation,* London: Zed Press

Asam, Mukhtar al- (1986) 'Tajarib mutamayyiza fi–l–islah al–idari fi–l–hukm al–mahalli fi–l–watan al–'arabi: masr was–sudan, dirasa tahliliya muqarina', in: Saigh, 1986: 897–953

'Ashur, Ahmad Saqr (1986) 'Nazara mustaqbaliya li–stratijiyat al–islah al–idari fi–l–watan al–'arabi', in: Saigh, 1986: 1113–1142 (English version in Saigh, 1986b: 44–85: 'Administrative Reform in Arab Countries: A Search for Strategy'

Awad, Mohamed Hashim (1983) 'Why is the Breadbasket empty?' (= DSRC Seminar No. 40) Khartoum: University of Khartoum, DSRC

Ayubi, Nazih N.M. (1980) *Bureaucracy and Politics in Contemporary Egypt,* London: Ithaca Press

— (1982a) 'Organisation for Development: the politico–administrative framework of economic activity in Egypt under Sadat', in: *Public Administration and Development,* Vol. 2, pp. 279–294

— (1982b) 'Implementation Capability and Political Feasibility of the Open Door Economic Policy in Egypt' in: Kerr, M. & Yassin, El–Sayid, *Rich and Poor States in the Middle East,* Boulder: Westview Press, pp. 349–413

— (1984) 'Local Government and Rural Development in Egypt in the 1970s', in: *Cahiers Africains d'Administration Publique / African Administrative Sciences,* no. 23, pp. 61–74

— (1985) 'Arab Bureaucracies: Expanding Size, Changing Roles'. Paper delivered at the International Conference on State, Nation and Integration in the Arab World, Corfu, 1–6 September 1984. Revised version January 1985

— (1986a) 'Bureaucratization as Development: administrative development and development administration in the Arab world' in: *International Review of Administrative Sciences,* Vol. 52, pp. 201–222

— (1986b) 'Anmat wa–tawajjuhat al–idara al–'aamma fi–l–watan al–'arabi', in: Saigh, 1986: 43–59

— (1986c) 'Al–halaqat al–mansiya wa–l–manatiq al–makhtura fi– al–islah al–idari al–'arabi', in: Saigh, 1986: 839–860

Azizi, Muhammad al- (1979) *At-tanmiya al-iqtisadiya wal-idariya fi-l-jumhuriya al-'arabiya al-yemeniya,* Cairo: Dar gharib lit-taba'a (for AOAS)

Azzam, H.T. (1981) *Development Planning Models in the Arab World: Problems and Prospects,* Beirut: ILO, 1981

Baster, N.(ed.) (1972) *Measuring Development: The Role and Adequacy of Development Indicators,* London: Frank Cass & Co.

Bauer, P.T. (1970), 'Unctad and Africa', in Meier, 1970

—   (1976) *Dissent on Development,* London: Weidenfeld & Nicholson

—   & Yamey, B. (1982) 'The Political Economy of Foreign Aid', in: *Lloyds Bank Review,* January

Bernard, D.M. (1985) 'Mobilisation and legitimisation: the political ambience of plan implementation', in *Public Administration and Development,* 5, no. 3: 251–263

Birks, J.S. & Sinclair, C.A. (1980a) *Arab Manpower: The Crisis of Development,* New York: St Martin's Press

—   (1980b)*International Migration and Development in the Arab Region,* Geneva: ILO

Bishai, A. (1984) 'Egypt and the Helping Hand', in Sullivan, 1984: 68–73

Blair, H.W., 'Review Article: Reorienting Development Administration', in: *Journal of Development Studies,* 21, no. 3: 449–457

Bonnenfant, P. (dir.) (1982) *La Péninsule Arabique d'Aujourd'hui,* 2 Vols. Paris: CNRS

Bornshier, Chase Dunn, & Robinson (1978) 'Cross–national evidence of the effects of foreign investment and aid on economic growth and inequality', in *American Journal of Sociology,* 84, no. 3

Bowen–Jones, H. (1982) 'Development Planning in Oman', in: *The Arab Gulf Journal,* 2, no. 1: 73–79

Brandt, W. (Chairman)(1980) *North–South: A Programme for Survival,* London: Pan

—   (1983) *Common Crisis, North–South: Co-operation for World Recovery,* London: Pan

Brown, R. (1985) 'A background note on the final round of economic austerity measures imposed by the Nimeiry regime: June 1984 to March 1985' (= DSRC and ISS Working Paper) Khartoum: Khartoum Universtity (DSRC)

Butter, D. (1987) 'Debt and Egypt's financial policies'. Paper presented at the Conference on Politics and the Economy in Egypt under Mubarak, School of Oriental and African Studies, London, 18 May 1987

Calhoun, Drummond & Whittington (1986) 'The Machine in the Desert: Lessons from the Design and Inplementation of a computer system for the Sudanese Ministry of Finance and Economic Planning'. Paper presented at the BRISMES Annual Conference at SOAS, London, July 1986

Central Bank of Jordan (1985) *Twenty First Annual Report 1984*, Amman: C.B.J.

Chatelus, M. (1982) 'De la rente pétrolière au développement économique: perspectives et contradictions de l'évolution économique dans la péninsule', in Bonnenfant, 1982, I: 75–154

—— & Schemeil, Y. (1984) 'Towards a new Political Economy of State Industrialisation in the Arab Middle East', in: *IJMES*, 16: 251–265

Chenery, H. & Strout, A. (1966) 'Foreign Assistance and Economic Development', in *The American Economic review*, September

Claus, B. & Hofmann, M. (1984) *The Importance of the Oil-Producing Countries of the Gulf for the Development of the Yemen Arab Republic and the Hashemite Kingdom of Jordan*, Berlin: German Development Institute

Clements, F.A. (1980) *Oman, the Reborn Land*, London: Longman

Cooper, M. N. (1979) 'Egyptian State Capitalism in crisis', in: *IJMES*, 10: 481–516

—— (1982) *The Transformation of Egypt*, London: Croom Helm

Corbridge, S. (1986) *Capitalist World Development: a critique of radical development geography*, London: Macmillan

Development in Yemen (YAR); bibliography and informative abstracts of selected research, 1970–1982, Berkeley: Development Research Services, 1983

Dickinson, J.M. (1983) 'State and Economy in the Arab Middle East', in: *ASQ*, 5, no. 1: 22–50

Drysdale, A. & Blake, G. H. (1985) *The Middle East and North Africa. A Political Geography,* Oxford: Oxford University Press

ECWA (1979) *Evolution of Economic Cooperation and Integration in Western Asia,* Beirut: ECWA

—   – (1981–1985) *Survey of Economic and Social Developments in the ECWA Region, 1980(–1984)* (annual), Beirut — Baghdad(from 1983)

—   – (1982) *International Migration in the Arab World. Proceedings of an ECWA Population Conference, Nicosia, Cyprus, 11–16 May 1981*   Beirut: ECWA

Escher, H.A. (1982) 'Considérations sur l'infrastructure du Yémen' in: Bonnenfant, 1982, II: 47–71

Fathaly, Omar el-, & Chackerian, R. 'Administration: the forgotten issue in Arab Development' in: Ibrahim, 1983: 193–209

Fei, J. & Paauw, D. (1965) 'Foreign Assistance and Economic Development: A Reappraisal of Development Finance', in: *The Review of Economics and Statistics,* August

Garcia–Zamor, J. Cl. (1973) 'Micro–bureaucracies and Development Administration' in: *International Review of Administrative Sciences,* 39, no. 4: 417–423

Gellner, E. (1981) *Muslim Society,* Cambridge: Cambridge University Press

—   & Ionescu, G. (eds.) (1970) *Populism, its Meaning and National Characteristics,* London: Weidenfeld & Nicholson

Goulet, D. & Hudson, M. (1971) *The Myth of Aid: the Hidden Agenda of the Development Reports,* New York: International Documentation North America

Griffin, K. & Enos, J. (1970) 'Foreign Assistance: Objectives and Consequences', in: *Economic Development and Cultural Change,* April: 313–327

Halliday, F. (1984) 'Labor migration in the Arab World', in: *MERIP Reports,* May 1984: 3–11,30

Halpern, M. (1963) *The Politics of Social Change in the Middle East and North Africa,* Princeton: Princeton University Press

Hammad, K. (1981) 'Foreign Aid and Economic Development: the Case of Jordan: 1959–1979'. Unpublished Ph.D thesis, University of Southern Illinois at Carbondale

Handoussa, H. (1984) 'Conflicting Objectives in the Egyptian–American aid relationship', in: Sullivan, 1984: 84–94

Hayter, T. (1971) *Aid as Imperialism,* Harmondsworth: Penguin

— (1981) *The Creation of World Poverty,* London: Pluto

Hinnebusch, R. A. (1982) 'Syria under the Ba'th: state formation in a fragmented society', in: *Arab Studies Quarterly,* 4, no. 3: 177–199

Hofmann, M. (1984) *Development Potential and Policies in the South Arabian Countries,* Berlin: German Development Institute

Holden, D. & Johns, R. (1982) *The House of Saud,* London: Pan Books

Hope, R. K. (1984) *The Dynamics of Development and Development Administration,* Westport/London: Greenwood Press

Hopkins, N. S. (1982) 'Development and Center–building in the Middle East' in: Cantori, L. & Harik, I. (eds.), *Local Politics and Development in the Middle East,* Boulder: Westview Press, pp. 88–131

Hunter, Sh. (1984) *OPEC and the Third World. The Politics of Aid,* London: Croom Helm

Ibrahim, I.(ed.) (1983) *Arab Resources. The Transformation of a Society,* London: Croom Helm

Imady, M. (1984) 'Patterns of Arab Economic Aid to Third World Countries', in: Alnasrawi, 1984: 70–123

Ismael, T.Y. & Ismael, J.S (1986) *PDR Yemen: Politics, Economics and Society,* London: Frances Pinter

Jacquemot, P. (1984) 'Crise et Renouveau de la Planification du Développement', in: *Revue Tiers Monde,* 25, no. 98: 245–266

Jad, Nasif Abdul–Khaliq (1986) 'Tajarib al–islah al–idari fi–duwal majlis at–ta'awun al–khaliji: dirasa tahliliya muqarina', in: Saigh, 1986: 861–896

Jordan, National Planning Council *Five Year Plan for Economic and Social Development 1981–1985,* Amman

KFAED (1985) *At-taqrir as-sanawi ath-thalith wal-'ishrun 1984–1985,* Kuwait: KFAED

—   (1986) *At–taqrir as–sanawi ar–rabiʿwal–ʿishrun 1985– 1986,* Kuwait: KFAED

Khafaji, Al– (1984) *Ad–dawla wat–tatawwur ar–ra'smali fi– l– ʿiraq,* Cairo

Khatib, F. (1987) 'Foreign Aid and Economic Development in Jordan: an empirical investigation'. Paper presented at the Conference on Politics and the Economy in Jordan, at the School of Oriental and African Studies (London), 19 May 1987

Koenig, K. & Bolay, F. (1982) 'The evaluation of an administrative cooperation project in North Yemen and its significance for German aid policy', in: *Public Administration and Development,* 2, no.3: 225–237

Kubursi, A. (1984) *Oil, Industrialization and Development in the Arab Gulf States,* London: Croom Helm

Lackner, H. (1985) *P.D.R. Yemen: Outpost of Socialist Development in Arabia,* London: Ithaca Press

Lappé, Collins & Kinley (1980) *Aid as Obstacle,* San Fransisco: IFDP

Le Cour Grandmaison, B. (1982) 'L'économie Omanaise: 1970– 1981', in Bonnenfant, 1982, II: 319–370

Mahmud, Ibrahim Muhammad (1986) 'Ajhiza wa muʾassassat at–tanmiya al–idariya fi–l– watan al–ʿarabi', in Saigh, 1986: 150–196

Mallakh, R. El (1986) *The Economic Development of the Yemen Arab Republic,* London: Croom Helm

Mathias, G. & Salama, P. (1983) *L'état surdéveloppé,* Paris: La découverte/Maspéro

McLachlan, K. (1980) 'Natural Resources and Development in the Gulf States', in: Niblock, 1980: 80–94

Meier, G. (ed.) (1970) *Leading Issues in Economic Development: Studies in International Poverty,* 2nd edn, New York: Oxford University Press

Meyer, G. (1987) 'Economic Development in Syria since 1970', in: Allan, 1987: 39–62

(The)Middle East and North Africa, 1984–85 idem. *1986* (Both published in London: Europa Publications, resp. 1984 and 1985)

Morris, M. D. (1979) *Measuring the Condition of the World's Poor: The Physical Quality of Life Index*, New York: Pergamon Press

Mulat, T. (1985) 'Planning in Ethiopia', in: Ndegwa,Mureithi & Green (eds.), *Development Options for Africa in the 1980s and Beyond*, Nairobi: Oxford University Press (East & Central Africa), pp. 85–100

Niblock, T. (ed.) (1980) *Social and Economic Development in the Arab Gulf*, London: Croom Helm

—   (1982) *Iraq: the Contemporary State*, London: Croom Helm

—   (1985) 'Sudan's Economic Nightmare', in: *MERIP Reports*, September 1985, pp. 15–32

Nijim, B. K. (1985) 'Spatial Aspects of Demographic Change in the Arab World', in Hajjar, S.G. (ed.), *The Middle East. From Transition to Development*, Leiden: Brill, pp. 30–53

Nonneman, G. (1986) *Iraq, the Gulf States and the War*, London: Ithaca Press

Nowais, N. al– (1984) 'The Experience of the Abu Dhabi Fund in the Aid Process', in: *The Arab Gulf Journal*, April 1984, pp. 7–17

Nugent, J. (1981) 'Towards a feasible path to economic co-operation and integration in Western Asia', in: ECWA, *Studies on Development Problems in Countries of Western Asia*, s.l. (Beirut): ECWA, pp. 7–146

Nurallah, K. (1978) 'at–tanmiya al–iqtisadiya wal–ijtimaʿiya wat–tanmiya al–idariya fi–l–watan al–ʿarabi', in: *Al–Mustaqbal al–ʿarabi*, 1, no. 4

OECD (1983) *Aid from OPEC Countries*, Paris: OECD

—   DAC (1985) *1985 Report. Twenty–Five Years of Development Co–operation*, Paris: OECD (= *Development Co–operation*, 1985)

—   (1986) *1986 Report. Development Co–operation*, Paris: OECD

Oesterdiekhoff,P. & Wohlmuth, K. (eds.) (1983) *The Development Perspectives of the Democratic Republic of Sudan*, München/London: WeltforumVerlag

Oman, Sultanate of–, Development Board *The Five–Year Development Plan 1976–1980*, Muscat

—   (1979) *The Second Five-Year Development Plan 1981–1985*, Muscat

Oman, Sultanate of–, Development Board (1985) *Oman. Facts and Figures 1985*, Muscat: Development Council Technical Secretariat

OPEC Fund for International Development (1985) OPEC Aid and OPEC Aid Institutions — A Profile Vienna: OPEC

Osama, Abdul Rahman (1987) *The Dilemma of Development in the Arabian Peninsula,* London: Croom Helm

Oweiss, I. (1983) 'The Arab Development Funds and Arab Foreign Aid', in: Ibrahim, 1983: 115–124

Owen, R. (1983a) 'Arab Nationalism, Unity and Solidarity', in: Asad, T. & Owen (eds.), *Sociology of "Developing Societies". The Middle East,* London: The Macmillan Press, pp.16–22

—   – (1983b) 'The Political Environment for Development', in: Ibrahim, 1983: 139–146

Palmer, M. & Nakib, Kh. (1981) 'La fonction publique et le développement dans le monde Arabe', in: Khader, B. (ed.), *Monde Arabe et Développement Economique,* Paris; le Sycomore, pp. 63–85

Papanek, G.F. (1972) 'The Effect of Aid and Other Resource Transfers on Savings and Growth in Less Developed Countries', in: *Economic Journal,* 82, September

Paul, S. (1982) *Managing Development Programs: The Lessons of Success,* Boulder: Westview Press

Payer, Ch. (1974) *The Debt Trap: The IMF and the Third World,* London: Monthly Review

—   (1982) *The World Bank: A Critical Analysis,* London: Monthly Review

Peterson, J. E. (1982) *Yemen: the Search for a Modern State,* London: Croom Helm

Porter, R.S. (1986) 'Arab Economic Aid', in: *Development Policy Review,* 4: 44–68

Poulson, B. & Wallace, M. (1979) 'Regional Integration in the Middle East: the evidence for trade and capital flows', in: *MEJ,* 33: 466–478

Quah, Jon S.T. (1979) 'Regressive Administration: some second thoughts on the concept of Development Administration', in: *Administrative Change,* 7, no. 1: 25–36

Rahman, M. (1968) 'Foreign Capital and Domestic Savings', in: *The Review of Economics and Statistics*, 50

Rawi Abu Taha, Muhammad Fakhri al- (1986) 'Nazara fi-l-ba'd as-siyasi li-t-tajriba al-idariya fi-l-watan al-'arabi', in: Saigh, 1986: 60–74

Richards, A. (1982) *Egypt's Agricultural Development, 1800–1980*, Boulder: Westview Press

Riggs, F. (1971) *Frontiers of Development Administration*, Durham: Duke University Press

Robertson, A.F. (1984) *People and the State: An Anthropology of Planned Development*, Cambridge: Cambridge University Press

Rodinson, M. (1966) *Islam et Capitalisme*, Paris (Published in English in 1978 in Austin: University of Texas Press)

Rondinelli, D. (1983) *Development Projects as Policy Experiments*, London: Methuen.

Rosenstein–Rodan, P.N. (1961) 'International Aid for Underdeveloped Countries', in: *Review of Economics and Statistics*, 2

Roy, D. A. (1975) 'Development Administration in the Arab Middle East', in: *International Review of Administrative Sciences*, 41, no. 2

Sadik, Ali Tawfik (1984) 'Managing the Petrodollar Bonanza: Avenues and Implications of recycling Arab Capital', in: Al-nasrawi, 1984: 13–38

Sa'igh, Nasir Muhammad al- (ed.) (1986) *Al-idara al-'aamma wal-islah al-idari fi-l-watan al-'arabi*, Amman: AOAS

—   (1986b) *Administrative Reform in the Arab World: Readings*, Amman: AOAS

Sayigh, Y. A. (1983) 'A new Framework for Complementarity among the Arab Economies', in Ibrahim, 1983: 147–167

Selim, Hassan M. (1983) *Development Assistance Policies and the Performance of Aid Agencies*, London: Macmillan

—   - (1985) 'The performance of Arab/OPEC development funds', in: *Arab Banking and Finance 1985*

Serageldin, Socknat, Birks, Li & Sinclair, (1983) *Manpower and International Labor Migration in the Middle East and North Africa*, Washington: Oxford U.P. for the World Bank

SFD (1985) *Annual Report 1404-05 AH (1984-85)*, Riyadh: SFD

Shaw, R. P. (1984) 'The Political Economy of Inequality in the Arab World', in: Alnasrawi, 1984: 124–154

Shihata, Ibrahim F.I. & Sherbiny, Naiem A. (1986) 'A Review of OPEC Aid Efforts', in: *Finance and Development*, March 1986, pp. 17–20

Smith, A. D. (1983) *State and Nation in the Third World*, Brighton: Wheatsheaf Books Ltd.

Sobhan, R. (1979) 'The Politics of Food and Famine in Bangladesh' in: *Economic and Political Weekly*, 14: 1973–79

— (1983) *The Crisis of External Dependence: The Political Economy of Foreign Aid to Bangladesh*, London: Zed Press

Spero, J.E. (1985) *The Politics of International Economic Relations*, 3rd edn, London: George Allen & Unwin

Springborg, R. (1985) 'Infitah, Agrarian Transformation, and Elite Consolidation in Contemporary Iraq'. Paper presented to the International Political Studies Association's Annual Conference, Paris 15–20 July, 1985

Stone, M. (1984) 'The U.S. Agency for International Development in Egypt', in: Sullivan, 1984: 26–36

Stookey, R. W. (1982) *South Yemen: A Marxist Republic in Arabia*, London: Croom Helm

Sullivan, E. D. (ed.) (1984) *Impact of Development Assistance on Egypt*, Cairo: American University in Cairo (= Cairo Papers in Social Science, Vol. 7, Monograph 3)

Swanson, J. (1979) *Emigration and Economic Development: the case of the YAR*, Boulder: Westview Press

— – (1982) 'Histoire et conséquences de l'émigration hors de la République Arabe du Yémen', in: Bonnenfant, 1982 II 107–134

— – (1985) 'Emigrant Remittances and Local Development: Co–operatives in the Yemen Arab Republic', in: Pridham, B. (ed.), *Economy, Society and Culture in Contemporary Yemen*, London: Croom Helm, pp. 132–146

Syria — Prime Minister's Office (Ri'asat al–wuzara') (1980) *Ad-dalil at-tanzimi lid-dawla*, Damascus: Prime Minister's office

Syria, sd (1981) *Fifth Five Year Economic and Social Development Plan of the Syrian Arab Republic 1981-1985*, Damascus: Arab Office for Press and Documentation

Taylor, C.L. (ed.)(1980) *Indicator Systems for Political, Economic and Social Analysis,* Cambridge, Mass.: Oelgeschlager, Gunn & Hain

Todaro, M.P. (1977) *Economics for a Developing World,* London: Longman

Townsend, J. (1977) *Oman, the Making of a Modern State,* London: Croom Helm

—   – (1982) 'Industrial Development and the decision–making process [in Iraq]', in: Niblock, 1982: 256–277

—   – (1984) 'Philosophy of State Development Planning', in: Azhari, M.S. el– (ed.), *The Impact of Oil Revenues on Arab Gulf Development,* London: Croom Helm, pp. 35–53

Turner, B. S. (1974) *Weber and Islam,* London: Routledge and Kegan Paul

—   (1984) *Capitalism and Class in the Middle East,* London: Heinemann

UNCTAD Secretariat (1985) *Financial Solidarity for Development. Development Assistance from OPEC members and institutions to other developing countries, 1977–1983,* New York: U.N.

UNDP (1982) *Proceedings of the Development Policy Seminar for senior UNDP Executives. 15-26 November 1982,* The Hague: ISS Advisory Service

UNDP Damascus (1985a) 'Report on Development Co–operation: 1984 Syrian Arab Republic'
Damascus: UNDP (mimeographed)

UNDP Djibouti (1985b) 'Report on Development Assistance to Djibouti in 1984', Djibouti: UNDP (mimeographed)

UNDP Sanaa (1985c) *Development Co-operation Report for the year 1984 — Yemen Arab Republic,* Sanaa: UNDP

United Nations — Dep't of Technical Co–operation for Development (1981) *Priority areas for action in public administration and finance in the 1980s,* New York: U.N. (doc. ST/ESA/SER.E/26)

—   – (1982) *Changes and Trends in Public Administration and Finance for Development. Second Survey 1977–79,* New York: U.N. (doc. ST/ESA/SER.E/27)

USAID (Cairo) (s.d.) *Ten Years of Progress. USAID in Egypt 1974–1983,* Cairo: USAID

Ward, d'Anjou & Runnalls (eds.) (1971) *The Widening Gap: Development in the 1970s*, New York: Columbia University Press

Ward, M. (1980) 'Composite Measures of Development' in: Taylor, 1980: 25–37

Waterbury, J. (1984) *The Egypt of Nasser and Sadat. The Political Economy of two Regimes*, Princeton: Princeton University Press

Weinbaum, M. G. (1982) *Food, Development and Politics in the Middle East*, Boulder: Westview Press

Weisskopf, T. (1972) 'The Impact of Foreign Capital Inflows in Underdeveloped Countries', in: *Journal of International Economics, 2*

Whelan, J. (1985) 'Oman's Development Strategy'. Paper presented at the Symposium 'Aspects of Oman' at the University of Exeter, June 1985

Wilson, R. (1977) *Trade and Investment in the Middle East*, London: Macmillan

— – (1983) *Development Planning in the Middle East: the Impact of Foreign Influence,* (= *Conflict Studies*, 156)

Wittfogel, K.A. (1957) *Oriental Despotism*, New Haven: Yale University Press

Wohlers–Scharf, T (1982) 'Les fonds nationaux arabes de développement', in: Bonnenfant, 1982 I: 307–342

Wohlmuth, K. (1983) 'The Kenana Sugar Project: a model of successful trilateral Co-operation?', in: Oesterdiekhoff & Wohlmuth, 1983: 195–236

World Bank (1979a) *People's Democratic Republic of Yemen. A Review of Economic and Social Development*, Washington: the World Bank

— (1979b) *Yemen Arab Republic. Development of a Traditional Economy*, Washington: World Bank

— (1983) *World Tables. Vol. II, Social Data*, Baltimore: Johns Hopkins University Press

— (1985) *Sudan and the World Bank*, Washington: World Bank

Wriggins, W. H. (1969) *The Ruler's Imperative: Strategies for Political Survival in Asia and Africa*, New York: Columbia University Press

Ziwar–Daftari, M. (ed.) (1980) *Issues in Development: The Arab Gulf States,* London: MD Research & Services Ltd.

Zubir, M.K. el– (1983) 'Foreign Aid and Economic Development: The Experience of the Sudan 1960–1980'. Unpublished Ph.D thesis, University of Bangor (UK)

—   —   —

In addition, use was made of World Bank Reports of restricted access, Central Bank reports of the various countries, and unpublished material and documents provided by governmental and non–governmental aid–institutions, ministries in the countries concerned, and UNDP field offices.